Praise

The Practical Visionary

"*The Practical Visionary* is a highly engaging synthesis of the ageless wisdom and practical tools for changing the world—by spiritual activists whose hearts are on fire for humanity. They give you keys to the new world within you—and to the new world of social innovators all around you. They reveal the higher evolutionary plan unfolding today, and inspire us to find our part in co-creating a more radiant future."—Deepak Chopra, author of *Reinventing the Body, Resurrecting the Soul* and *The Ultimate Happiness Prescription*

"No one has been more faithful to the pursuit and practice of spiritually based activism than Corinne McLaughlin and Gordon Davidson. *The Practical Visionary* resounds with their wisdom. They summon us to trust both our own gifts and this unrepeatable moment of history as we co-create a New World."—Joanna Macy author of *World as Lover, World as Self*

"Although they can be terrifying, the challenges and stresses of our current world present us with unparalleled opportunities for growth and understanding—if we can acquire the skills required to see in new ways. *The Practical Visionary* can assist anyone in this journey. It provides wise guidance in seeing the patterns that connect. If you are interested in standing firmly in the storm, and experiencing fulfillment in the process, this is a book for you."—Larry Dossey, M.D., author of *The Power of Premonitions* and *The Extraordinary Healing Power of Ordinary Things*

"Read this amazing story of practical visionaries who've been in the trenches of social change—and soared to the heights in spiritual practice. Corinne and Gordon share what they've learned, from starting an ecological community in Massachusetts, to working with a Presidential Council in Washington D.C. They provide a unique and exciting overview of the New World today, with numerous examples of heroic pioneers and social enterprises. And most important, they give you the practical tools to make your own vision a reality and attract the financial resources you need."—Lynn Twist, author of *The Soul of Money*

"Corinne McLaughlin has lived this book through 30 years as a spiritual activist, with heart open and feet planted firmly in both soul and pragmatism. She has followed her inner light, not the latest issue or trend. She has never relinquished her knowledge that out of paradox, held dispassionately, come wisdom and solutions that work. She now brings us the fruits of her life in this readable, encouraging and far-ranging book (In these times of collective stress, it's not easy to convince anyone that this turbulence is actually our passage into a greater collective maturity—but she does just that) with great grace and good cheer, and gives us a new road map for spiritual activism."—Vicki Robbin, author of *Your Money or Your Life*

"What a jolt of remembrance that as world citizens, each of us has a calling to be a Practical Visionary and thereby contribute to the creation of an enlightened society. The principles and practices provided in this book confirm that we are by nature fully equipped to answer that call. Corinne and Gordon strip away the notion that visionaries are only news headliners of past or present who play on the world stage. No! They live right next door, in our household, in our own community. 'They' are our very own self."—Michael Bernard Beckwith, author of *Spiritual Liberation: Fulfilling Your Soul's Potential*

"*The Practical Visionary* is nothing less than a blueprint and a plan of how we might create a new world closer to the desires of our hearts. It will challenge you and help you find your soul work and service to the world."—Sam Keen, Ph.D., author of *Fire in the Belly* and *Faces of the Enemy*

"One look at today's news media makes you pessimistic. But never mind, underneath it all there is an evolutionary movement of consciousness going on that few people can see. Corinne McLaughlin is one of those few seers. Read her book; it will make you optimistic, nay, downright enthusiastic about our future, your future—so much so that you may consider playing an active role in it. Why not? Corinne gives you many good ideas for how you can participate." —Amit Goswami, Ph.D., author of *God is Not Dead*, *Creative Evolution* and *The Self-Aware Universe*

"At a time when we are subjected to so many grim predictions of our future, we need the hope of inspired visions and positive, practical actions to implement them. Corinne more than meets this need. With graceful writing, she gives us a clear look at the positive possibilities before us and our power to bring them into reality. Without question, this is a handbook for a new world, and I recommend it unreservedly. It is the right book at the right time to make a difference in our future."—David Spangler, author of *The Call, Subtle Worlds,* and *Facing the Future*

"Corinne has created a superb study guide for like-minded spiritual students to facilitate global transformation from home. She is a profound global thinker, distilling truth that transcends time and any sense of duality, so we can experience the unification that comes from dismantling perceived opposites. As we live from the awareness and application of a higher synthesis we facilitate global peace."—Rev. Richard Mantei, former chair of the Association of Unity Churches International and member of Unity's Board of Directors

"This book is full of positive insights into the evolving role of morality and spirituality in the economic market, which the authors considered to be a powerful transformative force in modern society. It contains a wealth of wisdom acquired through personal experiences that span the gamut from sobering to inspirational, to downright humorous on some occasions. It is a worthwhile read for anyone interested in becoming an agent for societal change, as well as for those who simply need well-founded encouragement to persevere in this direction."—Ambassador John McDonald, chairman and CEO of the Institute for Multi-Track Diplomacy

The Practical Visionary

A New World Guide for Spiritual Growth
and Social Change

Corinne McLaughlin

With Gordon Asher Davidson

The Practical Visionary

Cover design: Ginger Young

Interior design: The Covington Group, Kansas City, MO

Library of Congress Control Number: 2009941656

ISBN: 978-0-9835691-4-5

Golden Firebird Press
369B 3rd Street #563
San Rafael, CA 94901

Dedication

This book is dedicated to M, DK, and R

And the new group of world

    servers— especially the next

    generation— with great love and

    appreciation.

CONTENTS

Contents

Foreword

I welcome *The Practical Visionary* for many reasons. Most important is the fact that our planet is now our programmed learning environment—and is teaching us directly. Our global economy is going through many wrenching crises and transitions—due largely to limited human understanding of the natural systems of our wondrous planet. Myopic economic theories mistook money for the real wealth of nations: enlightened, healthy people and healthy ecosystems.

Today all of our crises are based on faulty human perception: global financial debacles rooted in tsunamis of printed money, easy credit and blind computer models trading illusory assets and peddling erroneous risk management. Commodity prices will continue to be wildly volatile until we understand that the planet cannot meet the soaring expectations of fossil-fueled industrialism and growth of money-based GDP.

In this programmed learning environment, our planet is teaching us lessons involving peak oil, peak water, peak food, peak fertilizer and other peaks in production of cement, copper and many other minerals that undergird the unsustainable production processes and overconsumption of so-called developed countries.

The good news is that we humans are not terminally stupid. In fact, the new awareness of our situation is spawning the rapid growth of human consciousness and the growing ranks of "planetary citizens." I was fortunate some years ago to discuss all of these issues with Dr. Jonas Salk over breakfast—at a meeting of the Independent Commission on Population and Quality of Life chaired by the late Prime Minister of Portugal, Maria Pinto-Silgo, a member of the spiritual order of The Grail. The report of this 1996 commission, Caring for the Future, is still worth reading. Dr.

Salk, inventor of the Salk polio vaccine, told me that he was carefully monitoring the rise of global citizenship worldwide and firmly believed that humans were learning from all of the evidence around them—that their values must change.

In this book, Corinne McLaughlin and Gordon Davidson update the evidence that Dr. Salk believed to be so important. This book relates the inner yearnings and strivings for personal growth and deeper understanding to the changes taking place in our institutions as they adapt to expanding human consciousness.

My life's journey has intersected with Corinne's and Gordon's from times spent at Scotland's Findhorn Community, to partnership in their Center for Visionary Leadership, to Corinne's invitation to me to present at President Clinton's Council on Sustainable Development and my membership in the Social Investment Forum, of which Gordon was an early director. I remember Gordon's brainstorm in a phone conversation of the idea that later became the Ceres Principles of Environmentally Responsible Economies. Today, the Ceres group's member companies represent over $3 trillion of assets managed in this more responsible manner.

I have been observing these inner and outer transitions for 30 years, tracking similar evidence. Corinne and Gordon have been pioneers, thinkers, doers, experimenters, activists and inspired authors of *Builders of the Dawn*, *Spiritual Politics* and this newest road map to understanding our opportunities for personal development and cultural, economic and social renewal. They deeply understand that spiritual striving is incomplete without some expression in social action as practical visionaries.

This book is valuable on many levels, distilling the experience of two world-class agents of positive social change. Corinne and

Gordon are the kind of role models needed today, particularly as citizens of maturing industrial countries living through the transition from the age of fossil-fueled industrialism to the now rapidly-dawning solar age. Corinne McLaughlin documents this new world of practical visionaries with clarity, wit and deep understanding to help us all move forward.

Hazel Henderson
Ethical Markets Media, LLC
St. Augustine, Florida

Introduction

AWAKE!

The breeze at dawn has secrets to tell you.

Don't go back to sleep.

You must ask for what you really want.

Don't go back to sleep.

People are going back and forth across the doorsill

Where the two worlds touch.

The door is round and open.

Don't go back to sleep.

— Rumi[1]

P ractical visionaries are awake: their eyes are on the horizon, their feet are on the ground, and their hearts are on fire. They're thinking like a world community, creating a new soundtrack for Earth, with the rhythm of a universal heartbeat and a chorus of a million voices worldwide.

The New World is the collaborative expression of practical visionaries in every country. Rather than fanatical idealism, they are creating a new rhythm of practical spirituality. Synthesis is their keynote—transcending dualities such as inner and outer, reflection and action, and personal and political—and finding higher common ground amidst conflict.

We can navigate through the escalating crises and confusion of the present if we become more visionary and invoke the magic of our souls. As we do, we'll perceive astounding evidence of a New World, filled with innovative solutions to our toughest problems and providing genuine hope for our future. It's growing right through the cracks and crevices of our current world—if you know where, and most important, *how* to look.

The Practical Visionary will help you see the New World—both within you and all around you—more clearly. You'll be surprised by the many examples of the New World in every field, and you'll learn about the people, organizations and resources. This book will help you find the unique contribution you can make. It will help you network and co-create with other visionaries in this hyperlinked New World.

Visionary doesn't have to mean unrealistic or illusionary. Starry-eyed dreamers and romantic idealists who can't relate to the real needs of the present aren't enough today. We need *practical* visionaries to help us through the current crises. Now is the time to become more sensible and skillful, to make our visions become reality, and to meet urgent human needs.

While vision essentially comes from the spiritual dimension within you, being practical is focusing on what's needed, appropriate and timely when applying your vision. It is knowing realistically what you're up against in the old, dying world that's resistant to change. It is being strategic in your approach—and also doing the detailed follow-up that's needed.

[handwritten margin note: what's the need?]

This book is like a year's worth of weekly seminars I've given, illustrating a more hopeful yet realistic vision of our future, despite current crises. I offer deeper perspectives on themes such as the soul and synthesis not widely available today. Both pragmatic and imaginative approaches are provided. With so many good individuals and groups unable to manifest their visions, I've learned by co-creating an ecological village that the practical dimension is just as sacred as the visionary. Getting the details right can be just as important as getting the big picture right, as one small, wrong detail can wreak havoc. And, common sense and good relationship skills need to be more common among visionaries if we really want to help the world.

Visionary leadership has been a major theme in my life— developing my inner, spiritual vision and learning to be more effective in manifesting it. My passion is communicating achievable visions for a world in desperate need of new road maps for our future and sharing what I've learned. I'm continually learning myself—especially from the younger generation and their power of using social media tools for change.

I began my journey as a practical visionary in the early 1970s after graduating from the University of California, Berkeley, and attending graduate school at UCLA. While at Berkeley, and later while working at Harvard, I was a political activist, catalyzed by the Vietnam War, the destruction of the environment and the inequalities I was experiencing as a woman. But I had trouble integrating my political activism with my spirituality.

Although I was raised as a traditional Christian and went to church regularly, I often felt closer to God when I was in a beautiful, peaceful place in nature. After college, I began exploring many different spiritual paths and attending talks by numerous teachers and gurus, who seemed to be everywhere in California in those days. No one moved me very deeply until one day I heard a talk by a young spiritual teacher that went straight to my heart. I was attending a conference on "Unity in Diversity" in Los Angeles in 1974 that featured many gifted teachers from various spiritual traditions. I was sitting in a hotel auditorium on a warm afternoon listening to David Spangler, a gifted young philosopher who was becoming very popular.

Suddenly he said something with such profound truth that it made the proverbial bells ring in my head. He said, "Find the face of God that is your own face." Although I'd heard about these bells, I'd always thought of it as a poetic reference rather than an actual internal experience. This was the first time in my life that I actually experienced these mysterious inner bells, so it really got my attention! I've since learned that dramatic experiences of inner sounds in my ears or chills up my spine can be cosmic punctuation—a truth my soul wants me to pay attention to.

I'd never before considered that God or Spirit might be within me as an inner source of wisdom, an aspect of God expressing in a unique way through me. He (or She) always seemed so distant and beyond human knowing. I'd grown up in a traditional religious way and only knew about God Transcendent, the Father/Creator. I'd neither experienced the bliss of God Immanent, the inner divinity, nor had I ever been taught anything about its true nature.

Right then, I knew that my life direction had changed. I felt that I had come home, and I was bursting with an immense sense of joy. I began to explore this inner divine presence, the experience of my soul, through a daily practice of meditation. This has been the source of my vision of the New World and my confidence about a positive future for humanity. It also accelerated my development, helping me more fully embody my values and vision in daily life in a practical way.

As I experienced more of my indwelling soul in my daily meditations, I began to also recognize what many spiritual traditions call the Divine Mother, who holds all matter, all form of life on Earth in her loving embrace. This helped me appreciate the sacredness of physical matter and why we need to take good care of our bodies, the earth, and all life. It encouraged me to include the practical side in my development as a visionary, and it helped me realize why being in nature was such a profound spiritual experience for me.

A couple of years after my first startling experience of the inner light, I had another profound experience that led to an important insight about my life purpose and work as a practical visionary. I knew that when you sincerely ask for spiritual help in a crisis, you receive it. I had just broken up with my boyfriend on Christmas Eve, and I was meditating and praying in the sanctuary at the spiritual community I had recently joined. Everyone had just left the evening ceremony, and I was still there alone in the stillness after midnight, praying for help. It was cold that night, and the lights were turned down low. Tears ran down my face as I reflected on all of the difficulties I had had in relationships with men over the years. "Why does this keep happening?" I demanded. "Why do I keep attracting relationships that have to end so painfully? Why don't I attract men that I like—and who also like me? What's wrong with me?" I asked, feeling very miserable and sorry for myself.

Just then my soul seemed to whisper to me, "You didn't come to Earth to find the perfect relationship. You came here to serve humanity in some way."

the vision

Wow! I realized that I was facing a significant fork in the road and had a major choice to make. I needed to release my attachment to finding meaning in my life solely through a romantic relationship in which I'd walk off into the sunset with my partner and live happily ever after. On a spiritual level, I needed to align with my higher purpose and prioritize what was most important—serving a higher evolutionary plan.

Fortunately, I made the right decision: a commitment to service. I suddenly experienced an amazing inflow of light circulating throughout my whole body. It felt like a light bulb was turning on in my head each time I took a breath. The light seemed to come in from above and also from below me, and circulated through my whole body. The next day I knew that something very powerful had happened, but I wasn't quite sure what it was. My vision had expanded, and I realized that my heart felt more open to humanity as a whole. I was more concerned about the suffering in the world. In the days that followed, I began to feel a truer sense of inner peace and a clearer sense of purpose for the first time in my life. I was happy to become more deeply immersed in my work and service, instead of always looking for a romantic relationship to fulfill me.

The inner commitment to service that I made was the key that opened more doors to the New World within me. I began noticing many hopeful signs, like the amazingly creative projects started by practical visionaries everywhere that were solving human problems.   The New World all around me suddenly seemed to light up. I hadn't noticed it before.

Luckily, I didn't have to give up relationships forever! I soon attracted a wonderful partner to my life, my co-author, Gordon Asher Davidson, whom I married and have been with for more than 33 years. His ideas, edits and loving support have contributed greatly to this book, and we share the same work and life purpose as practical visionaries. Although I'm writing in the first person as the main author, Gordon's inspirations have been key. Together we've authored two other books and started a successful spiritual/ecological community in Massachusetts, a nonprofit leadership institute in Washington D.C., and an international meditation network. I know that I wouldn't have attracted such a wonderful life partner as Gordon to my life if I hadn't first made a deep commitment to service.

"Before we met," Gordon said, "I had experienced periods of a monk-ish existence, immersing myself in spiritual studies, interspersed with a series of relationships that were incomplete and unfulfilling because they didn't include all levels — physical, emotional, mental and spiritual. I was coming to an end of this unsatisfying way of life and was ready for a committed, multidimensional, deeply loving relationship."

Many years after my first mystical experience of the bells in a lecture using Christian terminology, I had another profound experience, this time in a Buddhist context while meditating with the Dalai Lama at his residence in Dharamsala, India. I was invited to join the Synthesis dialogues with a group of innovative leaders from many fields, organized by the Association for Global New Thought. Some of our dialogues were later captured in the remarkable film *Dalai Lama Renaissance*, narrated by Harrison Ford.

After an exhausting 14-hour flight and a harrowing 18-hour bus ride up narrow mountain roads in the monsoon rains, it seemed only our prayers helped us make it safely to Dharamsala. Compared to the surrounding area, the Dalai Lama's compound (a re-creation of his summer palace in Tibet) was an oasis of beauty and peace where Tibetan arts, like tanka painting, were being preserved.

After five days of dialogues with the Dalai Lama, he invited us to meditate with him and, if we wanted, to recite the ancient Buddhist prayer of refuge, the vow of the Bodhisattva. The prayer was about renewing our commitment of service and helping relieve suffering "as long as space remains, as long as sentient beings remain." Although I'd never heard this prayer before, it seemed surprisingly familiar, like I'd said it many times before. It took me into a deep inner space that shook me to the roots of my being.

Although this profound experience was in a Buddhist context, I wasn't a practicing Buddhist. I've come to understand that all true spiritual paths lead to the same place — compassion and service to humanity and all life. The inner world is connected to the outer world: spirituality and social activism can go hand in hand, and each helps inform and refine the other. The visionary and the practical can mutually reinforce each other in a new synthesis, and the Dalai Lama's teachings affirmed this.

Although I hadn't found all of the answers I needed from my traditional Christian upbringing, I didn't want to throw it all out and replace it with another religion. Like many people, I want to take the best from it and expand on it, incorporating teachings from other spiritual traditions. I discovered that all religions have some version of the Golden Rule, "Do unto to others as you would have them do unto you." Most have similar teachings on peace, compassion and finding the inner light within you.

There is a "golden thread" that connects the deeper, inner teachings at the heart of the world's religions, East and West, and is often referred to as the "perennial philosophy" or "the ageless wisdom." This wisdom dates back thousands of years to ancient texts, such as the Upanishads, the Yoga Sutras of Patanjali, the Zohar, and the Bible, and to teachers such as Hermes, Moses, Buddha, Pythagoras, Plato, Jesus and Mohammed. More recent teachers of the ageless wisdom whose teachings I've explored include Ramakrishna, Helena Blavatsky, Alice Bailey, Rudolf Steiner, Helena Roerich, Dion Fortune, Charles and Myrtle Fillmore, Ernest Holmes, The Dalai Lama, Sogyul Rinpoche, Dzongsar Khyentse, Lucille Cedercrans, Teilhard de Chardin, Alan Watts, Houston Smith, Manly P. Hall, Torkom Saraydarian, David Spangler, Deepak Chopra, Eckhart Tolle, Ken Wilber and many others.

Although many of these teachings may appear contradictory on the surface, when their inner mysteries and deeper truths are studied in depth, a remarkable harmony and correlation can be seen, and this is what drew me to study the ageless wisdom. The teachings are transmitters of the same fundamental truths under the veil of local symbols, appropriate to the time and culture.

As you examine the microcosm (your human nature), you begin to understand the macrocosm (the cosmos) and vice versa. "As above, so below; as below, so above," Hermes said thousands of years ago. Over the entrance to the temple of Delphi in ancient Greece were the words "Man, know thyself and thou will know the universe and the Gods." Our task is to more fully understand ourselves so that we can understand the larger mysteries of our world today.

9

I found that you can apply the truths from any spiritual tradition in your daily life and test them for their truth. In fact, only those truths applied in your own life become real for you and bear fruit. Being a practical visionary is about *applying* and *embodying* truth in daily life.

The real test is to apply these truths to the many collective problems we face today. If recent crises—economic, political, environmental and epidemic—have been a stressful wake-up call, you can reframe crises, both personal and collective, as spiritual awakeners. Crises offer lessons, as well as new opportunities, for spiritual growth and social change. You can look for the deeper meaning to everything now occurring, as there is a greater purpose for human life than most people recognize.

As you connect more deeply with the inner light within you, it will reveal the light in the world around you. A powerful global shift to a New World is under way everywhere today. As you discover the bigger evolutionary picture of what is occurring, it will inspire you with hope for our future. Instead of being overwhelmed by crises, you can develop the spiritual strength and practical resiliency to deal creatively with challenges that arise.

How can you find the New World and participate in it? Do you have to travel to a new territory, like the colonists who discovered the new world of America? No, you don't have to travel anywhere outwardly, but you do have to travel inwardly, taking an intuitive, spiritual journey to explore your soul, the New World within you.

Some find the New World within through dedicated spiritual searching, some through intensive practices such as meditation, prayer, yoga, chanting or support groups. Some experience it spontaneously while they're running or engaged in sports and suddenly enter "the zone" where time slows down and everything becomes clear and effortless. Some find it when they're in a quiet, reflective space and are deeply moved by the beauty of nature. Some discover it when a major crisis shakes them out of their usual routines and creates a deep re-evaluation of their lives and values. Some even discover it through an inwardly guided Internet search.

The New World is actually already here within each of us. It merely needs to be discovered, invoked and deepened. When you invoke your soul, or higher self, and align with your higher purpose, your inner life gets a powerful upgrade. Your intention is the key.

This book will help you strengthen the New World within you so that it expands beyond a fleeting experience and becomes a steady and sustained anchor amidst whatever storms may arise in your life. It will help you move from experiencing temporary states of blissful consciousness to more permanent stages of awakened soul consciousness.

This book illuminates the mysterious connection between the New World within you and the New World all around you, between inner, spiritual change and outer, social change. It offers insights and techniques to help you deepen your spiritual life and become a practical visionary. As you explore the inner and outer, individual and collective dimensions simultaneously, you will begin to notice how the seeming duality of inner and outer, practical and visionary, dissolves and how they become one, which is a goal of the path of enlightenment. Synthesis is one of the keys to the New World.

Practical visionaries work on changing the world and changing themselves at the same time, as the two are interdependent and mutually reinforcing. Both the inner and the outer dimensions are nurtured by each other and mutually supportive. What you learn in one area can help you in the other.

In the New World, spirituality is becoming more practical and embodied in everyday life, reflecting Gandhi's adage that "I must be the change I want to see in the world." Spiritual growth makes your service more effective, and in turn, your service in the world can give you an arena to embody your spirituality and enhance your growth. You can grow only so much by focusing solely on yourself. Offering some type of service to others is the secret to accelerating your own spiritual development.

This book will inspire you with the amazing service under way around the world by "strategic optimists" to create real solutions to our problems and build a future that works for everyone. Many students in the seminars that my husband and I have given over the years have asked that we put materials from our classes into book form. I was inspired to write *The Practical Visionary* because we've both seen so many good visionaries and spiritual people fail to effectively manifest their inspiring visions. Many good people don't seem to understand the larger spiritual context of what is unfolding today on our planet, so they become discouraged by negative stories in the media and give up on their visions. Often they are unwilling or unable to navigate the bureaucracies and do the practical administrative work needed to make their projects effective.

Many visionaries don't know how to shape their visions into clear strategies with achievable goals. Others seem hesitant to reach out to others in collaboration, or their egos get inflated and they get too enmeshed in conflicts with co-workers. Still others are uncomfortable with power—their own or others—or they are shy about raising money for their projects. This book addresses all of these issues and more.

12

In each chapter of this New World guide, I provide you with one of the eight keys to spiritual growth and social change: shifting from what is dying to what is being born, understanding the big picture and the evolutionary plan, making your livelihood a social change strategy, invoking the magic of your soul, turning within to find a source of spiritual strength, clarifying your higher purpose and vision, seeing money as a spiritual asset, and transforming duality and conflict into a higher synthesis. Experiential exercises, meditative techniques and tools to apply in your own life are included at the end of each chapter.

It is my heartfelt wish that this book will help you see the New World growing all around you, find your higher purpose and develop the skills to be an effective, practical visionary. I invite you to read this book with an open mind, letting any new or challenging ideas simply percolate in your consciousness as you reflect on them. Accept only those ideas that ring true in your own experience and intuition, and disregard the rest, as I make no dogmatic claim of authority. Regard as truth only that which you can comprehend with your own heart and mind, and trust your own inner wisdom.

Corinne McLaughlin
San Rafael, California

The Practical Visionary

Key #1

Shift From What Is Dying to What Is Being Born

Discover the New World of Practical Visionaries

Arise and listen:

Cast off your tatters of consciousness,

And know the new that seeks birth within you.

Take comfort from this and feel not alone.

The world moves into a new cycle.

Come forth, you builders,

And build the new heaven and the new earth.

— David Spangler[1]

Practical Approaches to Social Change in Unusual Places

Bob Dylan said it best, "He not busy being born is busy dying." We need to continually renew ourselves, being born anew each day so that we can see the world with fresh eyes.

The first key to being a practical visionary is shifting your attention from what's dying—what's dysfunctional or running out of energy—to what's being born—the new and positive within you and in the world around you.

Did you know that there's concrete evidence of a vibrant New World of practical visionaries growing everywhere today right in the middle of the old world?

How can you help co-create the New World? When you shift your perception, you find this New World growing in all kinds of amazing places where you'd least expect it, such as big corporations and the federal government, as well as rural spiritual communities. The good work of thousands of practical visionaries worldwide can inspire you with solutions they've created to all of our problems today. Their examples may spark some creative ideas for how you might get engaged and contribute your gifts.

I'd like to share some of my own journey as a practical visionary—from growing organic gardens in alternative communities to teaching meditation classes in the federal government (Yes, you read that correctly!)

After practicing meditation for many years, I was inwardly guided to start the Government Employees Meditation Service in Washington D.C. with a colleague. I taught meditation at the U.S. Environmental Protection Agency, the U.S. Department of Housing, the Administrative Offices of the U.S. Courts, and even the Pentagon. Did you know that there's been a meditation room for prayer and reflection in the Pentagon for more than 30 years? Discovering this certainly shook up my reality when I first moved to Washington.

In the early days of the Clinton administration, I worked on the Health Care Task Force. Nearly all of us on the task force were volunteers, including doctors and policy specialists with years of experience. It was thrilling to work in the White House, or more precisely, in the ornate and prestigious Old Executive Office Building next to the White House where most policies are made.

I was interested in helping include preventive and holistic health initiatives in the policies recommended by the task force, but I was also interested in environmental policy as I had co-founded an environmental community in Massachusetts many years previously and wanted to inform White House policy on grassroots initiatives on sustainability.

Like hundreds of other environmentalists in Washington D.C., I'd been trying to meet Katie McGinty, newly appointed by Vice President Gore to head the White House Office on Environmental Policy, a key office for innovative policies in the new administration. Katie's schedule was packed since her office just opened and hardly anyone was getting in to see her. But one day as I was heading to work at the Health Care Task Force office, I suddenly felt an inner intuition to walk down the hall toward Katie's office and check in with her scheduler. While I was talking to her assistant, Katie walked out of her office and heard me asking about an appointment. She said, "Well, I happen to have a few minutes before my next appointment, so why don't you come in?" She asked me about whether the Health Care Task Force was considering the effects of the environment and pollution on health care, and I told her about the practical side of sustainability and local demonstration centers around the country. I suggested that these centers could host citizen dialogues on White House environmental initiatives.

Later, I was invited to her office for brown bag staff lunches with environmental luminaries, such as Wendell Berry and Lester Brown, and other visionaries such as Sam Keene. Her office was a magnet for New World leaders and ideas—right there at the upper levels of the federal government.

My colleagues were blown away when I told them about my experience of meeting Katie so soon. They couldn't believe that I was able to get some time with her so easily, as she was so busy. I know it was my soul that guided me to her with such perfect timing. It later guided me to land a prestigious job with President Clinton's Council on Sustainable Development in 1994, which related to my higher purpose of helping transform politics.

This presidential council was one of the places in the federal government where the New World was beginning to appear. Former adversaries in government, business and environmental groups met together to find common ground on the need to protect both jobs and the environment—instead of staying stuck and constantly fighting each other.

A key approach of the new transpartisan politics is creating a higher synthesis from adversarial positions to find practical solutions that benefit both sides. The council was composed of members of Clinton's cabinet, CEOs of major corporations and directors of national environmental organizations and social justice groups. The executive director of the council later confided to me that she had been an activist and former captain of a Greenpeace ship.

I coordinated a national Task Force on Sustainable Communities for the council, so I invited many of the experienced environmentalists who were also practical visionaries I knew from around the country to advise my task force. It was very empowering to provide an opportunity for them to affect national policy.

The council recommended policy incentives to protect our "green infrastructure," the environment, by creating tax incentives to promote "smart growth," to expand trade in cleaner technologies and to facilitate emissions trading.

Through the consensus process used by the council and its seven national task forces, environmentalists learned that they could be more effective if they didn't attack the business people on the council and make them the bad guys, but rather say to them, "Here's a problem, a creative challenge. How can we solve it together? How can we help you find ways to make a profit so that you'll want to solve it?"

The common ground process itself was transforming for many participants, as at least one member of Clinton's cabinet and one major corporate CEO admitted that getting to know their adversaries as human beings and finding mutually beneficial common ground had changed their lives. They had witnessed the successful outcomes of this new political process. Working for this council was probably the most interesting job I ever had.

A few years after my experience with the council, I was deeply involved with another New World initiative in the nonprofit sector of Washington, D.C., when Gordon and I founded the Center for Visionary Leadership in 1996. Its mission is to provide people with the inner spiritual resources needed to be effective leaders. We focused on practical tools for spiritual development, meditation, leadership training, conflict resolution and synthesis in many arenas. We brought together black people and white people for Racial Healing Dialogues, Democrats and Republicans for

Transpartisan Dialogues, and Christians and Jews, Muslims and Hindus for Interfaith Dialogues.

We organized major national conferences on Spirit and business with CEOs of companies and on Spirit and politics with presidential candidates, congresspeople, other government officials and political activists. These conferences were hailed as cutting-edge initiatives and received major media attention, including stories in *The Washington Post* and *The New York Times*.

Most participants in our programs were professionals in government, business or the nonprofit community who were relieved to find an oasis of like-minded people and a network of support in the heart of Washington, D.C. We also launched a regular online newsletter called *Soul Light* with spiritual practices, innovative solutions to social problems and commentary on current events.

Today our Center has offices in the San Francisco area, and we offer seminars on spirituality and leadership around the United States and Europe, as well as teleseminars by phone and national meditation conference calls. We also offer personal coaching to help people become practical visionaries, find their higher purpose, strengthen their spiritual lives, resolve major issues and thrive in challenging times. In difficult times like these, when so much of the world is in crisis, people are looking for inspiration as well as practical tools to use in their own lives.

Civilizational Chronic Fatigue

Look at how fast old, dysfunctional forms are breaking down today. We could say that our institutions and the mental paradigms that support them are suffering from "civilizational chronic fatigue." So many major institutions based on greed, deception and divisiveness are becoming increasingly dysfunctional and morally bankrupt. New scandals revealing corruption in high places headline our papers daily. Although many old patterns no longer work and create more harm, countless people continue them, despite feeling exhausted and stressed out. They do not see any other way to live.

As the moldering garbage pile of old, limiting beliefs heats like a compost pile, you can smell the old world odor of decay. The current upheaval is composting the old forms to nurture the growth of new forms carrying new light and vision.

The breakdown of physical and mental forms often seems to precede breakthroughs in consciousness. Solutions to our crises don't lie within the current consciousness and patterns of divisiveness and greed. As Einstein so wisely remarked, we can't solve our current problems with the same consciousness that created them. We have to expand our consciousness to new levels of awareness and think more systemically and holistically.

We must also remember that evolution ever continues. The new forms and institutions being created today will also one day become worn out and limiting and need to be replaced by more appropriate ones.

The Cosmic Tipping Point

Here's the good news that you don't often see on TV: Despite the crises, more people are seeing a higher purpose behind what's unfolding in the world today. Have you noticed how it's much harder to hide corruption and deceit lately—in government, business and elsewhere? So much is now coming to light and being transformed. The deeper causes of world events are being revealed daily on the nightly news. The karma created by our collective negative thoughts and actions is showing up regularly in our media, and people are demanding change.

Thank God our karma is interwoven with golden threads of grace and higher purpose in the unfolding tapestry of life. As we watch major crises unfold, we are learning collective lessons that give us opportunities to make changes.

We are at a cosmic tipping point—the threshold of dramatic change. There is a clear path ahead and illumined steps that you and I can take to contribute to the New World that is now unfolding.

Yes, this is a time of evolutionary stresses—great upheavals and purification as native peoples around the world and mystics in all religions have prophesized. Some call these "the End Times." Others fear that the end of the world or major transformation will occur as foretold by prophets. Many old, dysfunctional ways of doing things are clearly not working any longer and are collapsing all around us. It's important to not be in denial about this.

Here's a wonderful secret: these are also "the Beginning Times"! Today we are experiencing the winding down of the worst of the old world, making room for the blossoming of a new and brighter one amidst the old.

God gave us two eyes for a reason: so that we can see both things at once—endings and beginnings, darkness and light— and go beyond this duality. We want to savor and keep the best of the old while embracing the best of the new. We want to be aware of the darkness while focusing on the light and what's positive.

So many people are longing for a ray of hope, some sense of goodness, beauty and truth. But guess what? We need only to change our consciousness—the lens through which we look at the world—to see the beauty in the New World that is now emerging all around us. What we each see is a direct result of who we are.

Space is no longer "the final frontier" as *Star Trek* proclaimed. Consciousness is the final frontier. Our minds are entangled, as scientists such as Dean Radin have discovered, and our thoughts are affecting others despite separation by vast distances. This entanglement, or "nonlocal" effect, travels 10,000 times faster than the speed of light. Human consciousness is boundless, infinite and omnipresent. In fact, all matter in the universe is connected on the subatomic level through a constant dance of quantum energy exchange. As Einstein famously noted, separation is an optical illusion.

The veils are being lifted, and we all have the potential to see reality more clearly now—if we choose to look. Each dysfunctional political leader and each problem or crisis we face can be reframed as a spiritual awakener, asking us to pay closer attention and learn the spiritual lessons being offered, as well as to respond to the practical opportunities suddenly available.

With the economic crisis, for example, many laid-off workers are discovering a new creativity and entrepreneurial spirit by starting small businesses. Others with free time suddenly available are experiencing the satisfaction of volunteering or are spending more time with their families. Many are needing to cut expenses and so are simplifying their lives and reducing wasteful consumption and pollution. Others are learning the virtues of saving, rather than spending everything and going into debt. We each have a tremendous opportunity today to transform both our consciousness and the world we collectively experience.

Which Path Will We Take?

Each and every member of the human family is facing a great soul choice: which path will we take in the coming years of upheaval and change? The choice is between holding on to old separative, greedy patterns of thought, feeling and living that are clearly not working for much of humanity, or choosing to open to the New World, new ideas, possibilities and compassionate ways of thinking and living. Each of us is creating our personal future as well as our collective future, right now, in each choice, each small decision we make moment by moment.

One set of choices leads to increasing crises and chaos—learning the hard way through suffering and a series of cascading collective crises caused by selfish, short-sighted actions. The other set of choices leads to community and oneness with all life, offering the opportunity to speed up our evolution and create a New World based on compassion, long-term thinking and the good of the whole. As we each learn the spiritual lessons of our own personal crises, we become wiser and more compassionate and can help mitigate the need for more intense collective crises.

Here's something to ponder: in the ageless wisdom teachings of the East, it's said that time and karma are synonymous. The length of time it will take us to make real change depends on how much of our collective negative karma we as humanity are willing to face and transform.

The evolutionary tide is turning. More and more people are waking up. We've been waiting for others to deliver us or show us the way, but we have the key buried deep within our own hearts.

The choices we make day to day are either helping birth a radiant New World or keeping us stuck in old patterns that are spiraling downward in spiritual poverty and lack of meaning and purpose. There is a higher reality beyond this duality of new and old worlds, but right now, at our human level, we must make choices and act.

Are you planting your feet firmly in the New World, taking a stand for humanity and all life on this planet, or are you still stuck in the worst of the old world that is running out of energy and dying?

The New World is not a spectator sport. All hands are needed on deck right now. We each have a soul-inspired part to play as practical visionaries building this New World.

The Planetary Initiation

Why is the awakening to a New World growing so rapidly today? One way to see it is that the planet itself is undergoing what might be called an initiation—a heightening of conscious-ness and awareness of a new purpose. It seems as if new energy is pouring into Earth, raising the frequency of all life. The speed of our spiritual growth and the rhythm of our daily lives seem to be increasing. Have you noticed how busy and speedy everyone is today? Have you noticed how quickly change occurs, both per-sonally and collectively on the world stage, like we've suddenly shifted into *Star Trek* warp speed? Scientific researchers are find-ing that the electromagnetic resonance of Earth, called the Schumann Resonance, has been increasing in recent years, but they are baffled at the cause.

Humanity is approaching the end of a long evolutionary cycle of matter and separateness, which was necessary for our growth as souls. We had to know ourselves as unique individuals and play out the devastating results of competing and fighting with people who are different from us.

Rather than seeing ourselves as exiles from the spiritual world who have fallen into the darkness of matter as a punishment, we should see that each of us as souls courageously volunteered to contribute to the evolution of this planet at this time. Clothing ourselves in the denseness of matter, we became part of the invo-lutionary cycle, entering physical bodies on Earth. We may feel like divers in heavy suits under thousands of pounds of pressure and forget for a time who we really are, but that is part of the process.

Although when born we identify ourselves as beings of flesh, emotions and thoughts, we all have a deeper sense that we are far more than this. The time has come in the involutionary/evolu-tionary cycle for us to awaken to our divine nature and the pro-found destiny that awaits us. We are inextricably one with the life flowing though the mineral, plant and animal kingdoms, and the life in the sea of stars and countless universes.

Metaphysical teachers say that a new ray of life, or flow of energy, is impacting our earth today, bringing a new rhythm and practical order into the material world. Spirit is radiating through matter, overcoming separation and differences. A new purpose is being realized, and a new note is being sounded: the note of syn-thesis. There is much fusing, blending and coming together in every arena.

Heaven is being brought down to earth, and the sacredness of the earth itself is being revealed. Everyday life is being seen as a spiritual teacher; life is constantly bringing us little lessons, if we're open to learning and growing. Spirituality is being freed from the confines of narrow dogmatism and becoming a practical guideline relevant for our lives. There is a growing awareness in millions of people across the world of the inner light or divinity, the soul within each of us. A new culture with a higher fre-quency of love, light and purpose is being born—ignited by the awakened hearts of visionary leaders in every nation, the "builders of the dawn" as Gordon and I called them in our first book in 1985.

You may say, "This sounds too positive. It's hard to accept. I want to live in a better world, but people with great political and financial power are abusing it and taking us rapidly toward disaster. So many things seem to be getting worse day by day!"

To this, I say: Abuse of power, war, poverty, environmental destruction and obsessive consumerism are simply the darkness before the dawn. They are magnified by the media's focus on them and its neglect of positive stories about the New World emerging all around us. Everything unfolds in cycles, and none of this will stand for long. As Gandhi said, "Whenever I despair, I remember that the way to truth and love has always won. There may be tyrants and murderers, and for a time, they may seem invincible, but in the end, they always fail. Think of it—always."[2]

Being a Fulcrum for Change

What we see in the world today is the result of karma created by our past collective thoughts and actions—from years ago, days ago, or even minutes ago. We are constantly creating the reality we see in the world. Yes, some groups and individuals have been very self-centered and cruel and have some hard lessons to learn. Many people have sold their souls for things of no enduring value. But there is a massive rebalancing of the scales of justice and fairness under way.

New spiritual energies are impacting the mass consciousness, creating a condition of fluidity and instability. Because of this condition, there is more receptivity to change and new approaches. We are at the beginning of a cycle of purification and decision, foretold by the ancient prophets, that is needed to strengthen and deepen our inner lives. Those of us who are more spiritually awake are faced with a tremendous challenge and responsibility at this time. We must educate, guide and inspire humanity so that the choices confronting us can be clearly seen and a higher path can be chosen.

The key is to detach from what is dying, and from images of destruction so that you don't feel overwhelmed and hopeless. It may not be your soul's purpose to fight the darkness in the old system, but it is the special mission of certain souls who are political activists and whistle-blowers. They know who they are and what they must do. We appreciate those courageous souls who are shining light on long-hidden corruption and injustice. They are confronting the powerful, who have a vested interest in maintaining control and are causing great harm and suffering to people and the earth.

A natural process of change—death and rebirth—is unfolding on our planet today. We must help preserve the best of the old civilization during this process. There is so much that is good and beautiful in the world that humanity has created over the centuries, not to mention the comforts of modern life. Let's make sure that the baby is not thrown out with the bathwater.

Remember the widespread fear that the modern world would collapse on January 1 of the new millennium because of the Y2K computer problem? Instead of disaster striking at midnight, we experienced incredible inspiration and awe when our media captured the beautiful ceremonies and spiritual rituals of so many cultures around the world as midnight struck in one time zone after another. This was the soul of humanity celebrating the future, with positive energy and hope for a better world as the new millennium began.

Y2K was the first time when humanity was able to course-correct on such a major scale, having the foresight to see impending disaster and then acting to fix the problem. But even those countries who didn't fully fix the computer problem   also avoided disaster. This was an example of grace and a true blessing for the world, and it holds a key for us today as we face the immense problems of financial upheaval, global warming and other disasters. In truth, we can each be a fulcrum for positive change in the world, through both spiritual prayers and practical action. Most encouraging is that, according to recent research, the next and largest generation (the Millennials) is the first truly globally aware generation and the most optimistic generation, already embodying many New World values. They are more embracing of diversity, and are postpartisan, politically pragmatic and are concerned about protecting the environment.

They are also more sensitive to higher-frequency vibrations and are more community oriented, appreciating open-source collaboration, participatory democracy and civic volunteerism. They are already transforming our society through their activism and social media networks and will have even greater impact in the future.

This "wired" generation grew up with new technologies, such as online social interaction Web sites, and is more upbeat about change than Gen X and Boomers. They are rapidly getting engaged politically, as witnessed in the recent elections. Giving back to society, the "gift economy" and "paying it forward" are all part of their psyche.

Don't you think that it's time for all of us to tune more fully into the New World and put it on our mental playlist, just like we put our favorite tunes on our iPods?

The Portal Into the New World

Today thousands of dedicated servers and reformers who are lit from within are active in all fields of life and in all nations. Most have spiritual practices that help them apply a vision of the

New World in their daily lives. Called the "new group of world servers" in the ageless wisdom, they are working tirelessly to better the human condition.

This new group of servers is working in every field—from politics and business to health and science. They are the new social entrepreneurs, creating tools for alleviating problems from war and terrorism to poverty and environmental destruction. They are creating socially responsible businesses, sustainable agriculture, preventive health care, renewable sources of energy, and many other innovations.

There is no global, formal organization that includes them all. And although reports of these new visionaries and their breakthrough solutions can be found here and there in the mainstream media, few people are connecting them to show the bigger picture of the change now occurring.

Do you know people who may be a part of this New World, even though they themselves may not be aware of it? How about you? Are you a part of this group, or would you like to be?

We each have a unique part to play in this New World and the higher evolutionary plan. Each of us is needed to help co-create it now.

Why We Need More Practical Visionaries Today

We need members of all generations to become practical visionaries. While visionaries may dream grand dreams of a distant future, *practical* visionaries find effective ways to solve problems today and make their dreams useful to people with real life challenges. Practical visionaries are both idealistic and professional. They create realistic and achievable strategies for expressing their visions, and they focus on what works.

A practical visionary is someone with inner wisdom who has dissolved the dichotomy between being visionary and being practical. Essentially it's about transcending duality and bringing together opposites. A practical visionary may be someone like you, someone who has an intuitive vision and a passion to make a contribution that is relevant and effective.

Practical visionaries see a bigger, long-term vision of a positive future and develop the skills needed to turn that vision into reality. They stand on solid ground and focus on the next step they need to take, responding creatively to what is right in front of them. Conscious, thoughtful steps lead to the full manifestation of the vision.

Practical visionaries find a way to make a personal contribution to a better world, despite the demands of everyday life and family responsibilities. In fact, responsibilities help them become more disciplined, focused and practical. They're also practical about time and take on only what they can realistically accomplish.

In metaphysical terms, being a practical visionary is about externalizing—bringing yourself and your vision more fully out in the world, so that you're both visible and accountable.

Essentially, it's all about the embodiment of your values and vision in daily life. It's about coherence between what you say you believe, what you embody and what you do. Your vision can be about something major for the whole world, or it can be about something major for your own life that helps others as well.

Synthesis is a keynote of practical visionaries. They transcend many dualities and bring all separated parts together in a higher fusion, like a full orchestra sounding greater than its individual instruments. Most significantly, practical visionaries overcome the duality between their spiritual ideals and how they live their daily lives. They work on embodying their values and bring Spirit into matter.

Connecting the Inner and Outer Worlds

While you may have read about some aspect of a postmodern New World here or there, you have to connect the dots to see the big picture unfolding everywhere. You have to see with an integral perspective that unites the inner and outer, the personal and collective dimensions. Then you can begin to observe a magnificent, evolutionary plan unfolding before your eyes. You will realize that there is a meaning to everything and that everyone has a higher purpose. You will notice thousands of compassionate, courageous practical visionaries who are in touch with their souls and are creating solutions to the problems we face as humanity by addressing the deeper causes.

How do the subjective experience of the New World within you and the actual manifestation of the New World around you intersect? How do you connect them?

Experiencing the New World subjectively (in your own soul) helps rewire your brain and awakens you to the New World unfolding in the outer society. If you discover any aspect of the New World around you and begin to explore it in depth, this can catalyze a process of inner growth that helps you get in touch with more of the New World within you. The good news is that inner and outer change are mutually reinforcing and transforming.

When you begin to see with the eyes of your soul, you perceive things differently in society. You see more beauty and harmony in the world. It's as if blinders of isolation and fear are lifted and you notice different things.

You suddenly discover new stories and new ideas in your newspaper. You meet compassionate new people. You notice new books, magazines, organizations, Web sites, blogs and networks with holistic, sustainable values. You're drawn to new events, conferences and activities. Under the law of resonance, you attract to your life whatever is vibrating within you.

The new books, magazines, Web sites and activities you find in the New World around you in turn support your inner growth. They create a supportive learning environment. They teach you spiritual practices that help you experience the New World within yourself more fully.

You might learn techniques for yoga or meditation to still your mind, for example. Or you might discover how to become healthier with holistic techniques and organic foods, which then makes it easier to meditate and experience your soul. You might learn about socially responsible business approaches and apply these in your workplace, which brings you a greater sense of fulfillment and inner peace. You might learn about science and how quantum physics proves the truth of many spiritual teachings, which deepens your inner life. You might learn about ways to protect the environment, which draws you to spend more time in nature and enriches your inner life.

You also begin to create sustaining relationships with the practical visionaries you meet in the New World around you who share similar values. They become a support network for you as together you explore your inner and outer worlds and co-create new possibilities with one another. You build a sense of community, collaboration and shared spiritual practice that enhances your inner growth and leads to more creativity in the outer world. Recent scientific research has found that social forces in our environment have a major effect on our personal development.

At the same time, your inner spiritual experience of the New World may guide you to new work in the outer New World. Your inner transformation may also enable you to participate more effectively in these outer activities, since you may be more creative and harmonious, getting along better with people and contributing more. You may receive honest feedback from people about how well you embody your spiritual values and where changes are needed, and this in turn accelerates your inner growth. You may stop projecting your own problems and negativity on other people, and the world will begin to look much more positive and inviting.

The inner and outer worlds are nurtured by each other. People who focus on only personal, spiritual growth and don't respond to invitations to connect with the New World around them tend to limit their growth. And those who dabble only in the outer activities of the New World tend to stay on the surface and never benefit fully from the inner resources that are available. To be whole, we need a deep synthesis of the inner and outer dimensions.

New World Values

What are some of the values on which the New World is based? The following values are visionary and inspirational, but also practical because they make your work more effective:

❦ Spirit—honoring the deeper ethical and spiritual dimensions within humanity and all kingdoms of life.

❦ Community—nurturing a collaborative spirit through participatory, inclusive practices.

❦ Synthesis—transcending dualities and bringing together the best from all sides into a new fusion.

❦ Whole Systems, Integral Thinking—seeing a larger context, and taking into account how each part affects the whole and how each issue is interconnected with all others.

❦ The Good of the Whole—working for the well-being of the greatest number, rather than only a privileged few.

❦ Multiculturalism and Diversity—honoring the innate value of all people and encouraging the contributions of diverse races, religions, ethnic groups and genders.

❦ Long-Term Sustainability—honoring the sacredness of the earth as a living organism and protecting the natural environment and ecological diversity for future generations.

❦ Intuition and Inner Guidance—encouraging inner wisdom, rather than relying on outer authorities, whether religious, scientific or political.

❦ Self-Reliance—supporting citizens in taking responsibility for their own well-being by self-organizing themselves, rather than depending on government or big institutions for everything.

❦ Compassion, Justice and Fairness—developing more loving relationships and helping those who have been neglected.

❦ Balancing Rights With Responsibilities—encouraging a sense of personal responsibility through giving back to society.

❦ Finding Common Ground to Address Conflicts—using dialogue to appreciate differences, find mutually beneficial solutions, and act on commonalities.

❦ Prevention—developing proactive strategies in the present to prevent problems in the future.

❦ Transparency and Accountability—encouraging honesty and authenticity and ensuring access to information and decisions that affect people's lives.

Let me be clear about one point: There have been enlightened souls who embodied New World values through the ages, even though their societies did not widely reflect those values at the time. But today, millions of people and thousands of institutions around the world are honoring these values and working to embody them.

Exploring the New World Around You

How do you begin your exploration of the New World in the culture around you? You might begin, for example, by calling a health care practitioner, such as a chiropractor, osteopath, acupuncturist or homeopath, about a particular health concern you have. From there, you might discover a whole New World of mind/body practices such as yoga and biofeedback. The practitioner's office might have an environment with Zen-like, calming music, water flowing softly in a fountain, fragrant candles and inspirational art.

In this holistic office, you can learn more about how your mind affects your body and vice versa, and you may be introduced to a healthier diet, herbs, organic foods and energy medicine. New friends you meet there may tell you about a nearby health food market and an independent bookstore where you can find books and magazines about many New World ideas. Around the corner, you might find a community center with information on electronic barter networks and local currencies.

When you start exploring this New World, you suddenly notice other things right in front of you that you somehow missed before. As you walk down the street, you may suddenly notice a new "green" office building with an environmentally sustainable design, sleek solar panels, recycled rainwater and edible plants growing on the roof.

This experience may lead you to an environmental demonstration center, such as the Solar Living Institute started by John Schaeffer in Hopland, California. At the institute, practical visionaries teach you how to install a solar panel on your home and reduce your energy bills. You can participate in hands-on demonstrations of permaculture gardening methods, composting and biodiesel fuel. You can learn about wind energy and plant-based waste management systems.

If you attend the annual Bioneers Conference in San Rafael, California, started by Kenny Ausubel and Nina Simons, you'll meet cutting-edge environmentalists such as green builder David Johnston, green jobs advocate Van Jones, and activist Julia Butterfly Hill. You might then get inspired to take spiritual activist training from Julia or a yoga class from teacher Seane Corn, who together founded the Engage Network and Off the Mat Into the World.

If you need a new carpet, you'll discover that there's a company that rents carpets and recycles the components of old carpets to make new ones. Interface, started by the late Ray Anderson, is one of the most successful sustainable businesses worldwide and has already reduced environmental waste by more than 50 percent in only a few years. Anderson estimated that his carpet company has saved $393 million on waste reduction efforts alone over the past 13 years by eliciting ideas from teams on the company floor. Sales are up 66 percent due to the good PR from going green. Eighty- two new products have been designed on bio-mimicry principles, solving problems by imitating how nature does it.

Learning about green businesses such as Interface may inspire you to invest in companies that are more socially responsible in how they treat the environment and their employees. The Social Investment Forum, a professional association of social investment advisors, is a great resource. Its partner, Green America, directed by Alisa Gravitz, promotes environmental sustainability and social justice through its *Green Money* newsletter, Green Living Expos and the Green Business Network. Visit *www.greenamerica.org* and *www.wiserearth.org* for information on thousands of New World organizations.

On your next vacation, you could enjoy a week at a meditation center, such as Spirit Rock in Woodacre, California, or a holistic education center, such as SpiritPath in Unity Village, Missouri; Esalen in Big Sur, California; Kripalu Center for Yoga and Health in Stockbridge, Massachusetts; The Crossings in Austin, Texas; or Findhorn Foundation in Forres, Scotland. At Omega Institute in Rhinebeck, New York, started by Stephan Rechtschaffer, M.D., and Elizabeth Lesser, you can immerse yourself in the New World on a beautiful 195-acre campus, attending conferences about the most innovative ideas in New World fields such as sound healing, conscious relationships and mindfulness training. You'll have a wonderful experience and meet some like-minded new friends.

You could also check out accredited universities teaching New World topics, such as John F. Kennedy University, California Institute of Integral Studies, Fielding Institute, New College, Bainbridge Graduate Institute, Presidio School of Management, Saybrook College, and many others.

You can also explore the extensive online resources available from the Integral Institute and Integral Life in Louisville, Colorado. Leading thinkers in psychology, business, politics and medicine, inspired by the breakthrough work of philosopher Ken

Wilber, provide research, training, coaching and online seminars in an integral, whole systems worldview.

There is an exhilarating, celebratory spirit present wherever practical visionaries creating the New World come together. They gather at national conferences such as Bioneers, The Greens Festival, The Institute for Noetic Sciences, Association for Global New Thought, Agape, Pachamama Alliance, The Social Venture Network, Alliance for a New Humanity, Integral Theory, Power Shift, Lifestyles of Health and Sustainability (LOHAS), and Technology, Entertainment, Design (TED). Practical visionaries also meet at international conferences of nonprofit organizations at the United Nations and the World Social Forum, in thousands of worldwide chat rooms and social networking sites on the Internet, and in living rooms across the world where neighbors meet together to solve problems and create healthier communities.

You might be lucky to catch philosopher Eckhart Tolle on *The Oprah Winfrey Show*, teaching millions of people how to meditate and live more fully in the present moment. This might lead you to study his books and learn meditation. Then you might go on to study at a meditation center such as Naropa Institute in Boulder, Colorado, or Rigpa in Berkeley, California.

However, with the exception of programs on *The Oprah Winfrey Network*, *Ethical Marketplace* on the Public Broadcasting Service (PBS), *Global Spirit* on Link TV and fundraising segments featuring teachers like Deepak Chopra and Wayne Dyer on PBS, you won't see many programs about the New World on television. You'll see only a few stories and examples. But you will find much of the philosophical basis of the New World in television reruns of *Star Trek: The Next Generation!*

You can find many stories about the visionaries creating this New World if you know where to look. Check out magazines such as *Yes, Utne, Kosmos, Positive News, Good, Spirituality & Health, Common Ground, Whole Life Times, Tikkun, Business Ethics* and *Green Money Journal.* Visit online Web sites such as *integralinstitute.org, wiserearth.org, worldchanging.com, global-mindshift.org, radicalmiddle.com,* and *ethicalmarkets.com* for stories about these visionaries. You can also find the New World increasingly on social networking sites, like Facebook, and microblog sites such as Twitter. You can see the outlines of this larger movement, this great shift or turning, in books that have a more-expanded overview of spiritual and social change, such as *Global Shift* by Edmund Bourne, *The Shift Report* by the Institute of Noetic Sciences, *Ethical Marketplace* by Hazel Henderson, *Blessed Unrest* by Paul Hawken, *Worldchanging* edited by Alex Steffen, *The Great Turning* by David Korten, *The Great Awakening* by Jim Wallis, *The Hope* by Andrew Harvey, *The Translucent Revolution* by Arjuna Ardagh, *The Flip* by Jared Rosen and David Rippe and *Soulutions* by William Bloom.

You can also find many inspiring video clips with New World values and information on sites such as *YouTube.com.* You can hear the vibrations of the New World in music by sound-healing pioneers such as Dean Evenson and Steve Halpern and in joyful songs by popular artists like Celine Dion's *A New Day Has Come* or U2's *It's a Beautiful Day.* You can also hear the New World in "world fusion" music, which blends diverse musical traditions from around the world— Western jazz, Eastern sitar, Latin rhythms, etc.—such as Putumayo's *One World, Many Cultures* CD, with lively collaborations between leading musicians from diverse countries. Synthesis is one of the keynotes of the New World.

More and more people are beginning to discover the New World and are wanting to get engaged. The Lifestyles of Health and Sustainability (LOHAS) e-newsletter reported that there is more than a $228 billion U.S. marketplace for goods and services focused on New World values such as holistic health, environmental protection, social justice, personal development and sustainable living. Significant financial flows are being redirected into these areas.

Sociologist Dr. Paul Ray found that more than 30 percent of the adults in the United States, or 50 million people, are currently consumers of these goods and services and make conscientious purchasing and investing decisions based on their social and cultural values. They are the future of business and of progressive social, environmental and economic change in the United States and elsewhere. According to a 2007 values study by Dr. Ray and TNS, the largest commercial research company, 34.6 percent of Americans feel that a new culture is growing out of the cracks in the old one and 49.6 percent say it is very important to have their work make a contribution to society.

Examples of New World Solutions

What are some successful New World solutions to problems we face? Solutions are beginning to emerge everywhere from the creative hearts and minds of people who recognize that there are alternatives to planetary crises. They are the builders of a New World, turning the tide of history.

"Best practices" are being pioneered by various groups worldwide—nonprofit organizations (the social profit sector) and new businesses (the for-profit sector). A best practice can be defined as a project, product, service or organization that presents an innovative approach with proven effectiveness, visible, measurable results, that is accessible to the public and can be replicated by others. Solving problems on a larger scale requires only the expansion and spread of initiatives like the following:

War, violence and terrorism are being addressed by medi-ated dialogues and win-win approaches to bring all parties to the negotiating table, where everyone's grievances can be heard and mutually beneficial solutions can be discovered. Groups like Search for Common Ground and Institute for Multi-Track Diplomacy mediate between adversaries with deep-seated ethnic conflicts in places like Palestine, Burundi and Somali. (See Chapter 8 for more information.)

Poverty is being reduced by microcredit systems, such as The Grameen Bank in Bangladesh (and now also in the UnitedStates) and FINCA (Foundation for International Community Assistance) and ACCION. Rather than giving handouts, they "teach a man to fish," as the Bible recommends, by giving small groups of the poor very small loans to start businesses and by relying on peer relations to pay them back, with 99 percent payback rates.

High unemployment and lack of cash are being overcome by computerized labor trading systems (also called *service credits* or *time banking*) that help people trade what they have for what they need. Systems such as LETS (Local Exchange Trading Systems), the Time Dollar Institute, and Time Banks USA keep resources in the community and renew cash flows in the local economy. Participants sign up with a computerized data bank, listing their skills and services. All services have an equal worth in terms of time or dollars, regardless of their market value. Craigslist, Freecycle and other Internet trading systems also informally match needs and resources and help local markets starved of credit. Local currencies, such as Ithaca Hours in Ithaca, New York, and BerkShares in Massachusetts, enable people to buy from local businesses when they're low on regular cash.

Crime is being reduced by more than 1,000 victim-offender reconciliation programs worldwide, such as Restorative Justice in Virginia, which brings together victims and offenders for professionally mediated dialogues. The process of restorative rather than retributive justice helps foster empathy in offenders when they see the consequences of their actions in the suffering of the victims. It helps victims address their emotional needs by confronting the offenders. Penitence on the part of the offender and forgiveness on the part of the victim are encouraged, and the offender has the responsibility of restitution—financial or otherwise. Program participants are seldom repeat offenders and often make major changes in their lives as a result. The process is a very effective way to reduce skyrocketing costs for courts and of incarceration.

Environmental pollution is being reduced by bioremediation and green business methods. Fungi Perfecti, started by Paul Stamets, uses natural organisms, such as mycelial networks (especially oyster mushrooms), to totally consume toxic lead and oil in the soil and decontaminate radioactivity.

Green business approaches, like those pioneered by McDonough Baungart Design Chemistry in Virginia, create a "cradle to cradle" approach for the life of a product, rather than "cradle to grave." Instead of waste that pollutes, discards are food for future products (e.g. fabrics that are totally recycled or "upcycled" into food), and toxic water that is made safe for drinking.

GreenFuel Technologies Corporation removes most of the carbon dioxide from power plant exhaust by using greenhouses and algae in a process of photosynthesis, with ethanol or biodiesel as lucrative by-products. Solix Energy, started by the Southern Utne Indians in Colorado, transforms carbon dioxide from natural gas to grow algae for food.

An inexpensive LifeStraw, developed by Mikkel Vestergaard Frandsen with the Carter Center, filters up to 700 liters of water to block bacteria, viruses and parasites. It is currently saving thousands of lives across the developing world.

Declining farm prices and food quality are being remedied by more than 1,200 community-supported agriculture farms (CSAs), such as Brookfield Farm in Hatfield, Massachusetts. A CSA is a partnerships of mutual commitment between farmers and a community of supporters. Members of the CSA cover the farm's yearly operating budget by purchasing a share of the season's harvest in advance at below-retail prices, assuming the risks along with the farmer and sharing in a healthy supply of seasonal fresh produce throughout the growing season. In return, farmers and growers are guaranteed a reliable market for a diverse selection of crops.

Global warming, oil and resource depletion are being addressed by carbon footprint reduction, energy efficiency and renewable energy initiatives. PowerLight in Muhlhausen, Germany, provides green electricity for 9,000 homes, and Verdant is harnessing the tides flowing in and out through the East River for power in New York. Stirling Energy Systems is building giant solar thermal plants in the California desert that use mirrors to concentrate sunlight for energy.

Profit at the expense of human values and nature is being brought into balance by social entrepreneurship and natural capitalism. Social entrepreneurs—the so-called "Fourth Sector" (beyond the three sectors of business, government and nonprofits) are "common good companies" or "social benefit companies" whose main mission is to help solve socioeconomic or environmental problems, such as the $1 billion *google.org* and the consulting firm Ashoka. The Natural Capitalism Institute, the Investors' Circle and the Slow Money Institutes promote sustainable business practices to protect the earth for future generations. "Social banks" and "green banks," such as Triodos in the Netherlands, and RSF Social Finance and the New Resource Bank in the United States, invest in organic farms, sustainable energy and agriculture.

Separative, fanatical fundamentalism is being addressed by interfaith programs such as those offered by United Religions Initiative, Parliament of the World's Religions and the Interfaith Conference.

School dropouts and gang violence are being reduced by programs in character education, self-help and mindfulness, such as Character Counts, Challenge Day, Soul Shoppe, InnerKids, Impact Foundation and Teach for America.

Drug and alcohol addiction and psychological problems are being helped by 12-step programs, family systems therapy and psychological counseling, such as that offered by Delancy Street, Psychosynthesis and Education Trust, HeartMath, Process Oriented Psychology and Voice Dialogue.

Political manipulation and voting fraud are being addressed by transparency, multistakeholder dialogues, text-messaging activism and voter self-verification in projects such as Community Visioning, AmericaSpeaks, Instant Run-off Voting, Clean Money, Clean Campaigns and the Velvet Revolution.

Increasing media control and centralization is being offset by the new "webocracy" and interactive television and viewer-created content. Internet activism, blogging, open-source technology, social networking, hyperlinked networking and video pods are found at sites such as *Wiserearth.org, Worldchanging.com, Global-mindshift.org, MoveOn.org, DailyKos.com, Digg.com, Wikipedia.org, YouTube.com, Facebook.com and Twitter.com.* Current TV is a viewer-created television network. Mainstream Media Project, Be the Media and Reclaim the Media empower people with the tools to transform the media.

Pesticides and chemicals in foods are being eliminated by <u>organic and biodynamic farming, permaculture design and health food markets,</u> such as The Occidental Arts and Ecology Center, Spring Valley Farm, Organic Valley Co-op, the Permaculture Institute, Whole Foods Market and the Edible Schoolyard.

Rising health costs and declining health care quality are being addressed by <u>holistic, preventive health care , integrated medicine and energy medicine</u> at The Center for Mind-Body Medicine, the Arizona Center for Integrative Medicine, the Chopra Center for Wellbeing, Beth-Israel Department of Integrated Medicine, the Center for Integrated Medicine and Kripalu Center for Yoga and Health.

All of these initiatives are seeds of a New World, based on values that deeply honor human life and the natural world.

On a larger scale, the United Nations' Millennium Development Goals, based on commitments of member nations to reduce poverty, pollution, terrorism and disease, is a significant first step in developing on an international level the political will to create a better world. It wisely links the causes of security, development and human rights, as each depend on one another. When I co-led seminars on the new civilization with sociologist Dr. Paul Ray, co-author of *The Cultural Creatives,* we invited people to participate in a deep reflective process and respond to the statement "Tell me about a world your heart yearns for." Amazingly, people everywhere in all walks of life describe a similar world of peace, love, cooperation and creativity. This is really exciting to me!

Coming Soon to a Neighborhood Near You: The New World

There is light at the end of the dark tunnel we find ourselves in today. If you are living in a cloud of foreboding and fear, shift your awareness from what is breaking down to the dynamic new life that is growing all around you. Change the frequency of your vibration from the fear and self-protection of the ego to the expansion and optimism of your soul or higher self. Focus on the breakthroughs in consciousness, the new ideas and creative projects that are being developed at the same time that the old forms break down. See what you can do to help and you'll immediately feel a sense of upliftment.

We are all needed now to build the new culture and civilization, to show what inspired human creativity can do, and to give hope to those who are despairing that a better world is possible.

Do not scorn the forms of the past or mourn their loss, but detach yourself from them while honoring the positive idea or truth at their heart. Create a higher synthesis of the best of the old with the new that is emerging. Live the future today.

When you speak about and live the values of the New World, you call it forth more fully into being. The task for each of us is to bring a vision of heaven down to the earth and lift earth toward heaven. No situation or crisis, however dire, is left without the possibility of spiritual help to create transformation—but we need to ask for it.

As former Vice President Gore said in his acceptance speech for the Nobel Prize, "When we unite for a moral purpose that is manifestly good and true, the spiritual energy unleashed can transform us."

SPIRITUAL PRACTICES

Frequency Adjustment Meditation

Begin by finding a quiet place to sit. Take a few deep breaths, and exhale deeply to relax. Bring your attention more fully to the present moment. Notice the quality of the sound inside your head.

Imagine that you are sitting at a control panel like one for a sound system. In front of you, you see a dial that looks like a volume control for sound, but instead it controls the frequency and harmony of vibrations.

Turn the dial to the lowest position. Notice the vibrational frequency, the resonance, that you experience at this level. You may experience frequency as sound, light, sensation, etc. Does the frequency seem dense, heavy and slow, or dissonant and chaotic?

With each breath you inhale, turn the dial higher and see what you experience. Notice how the frequency rises and becomes more resonant and harmonic, like a wall of sound surrounding you. Feel all of the cells in your body vibrating in resonance. Feel the light radiating from within you.

As your frequency keeps rising, feel it vibrating your chakras, or energy centers, especially the crown center at the top of your head.

Turn the dial to its highest point until all sound and frequency seem to disappear into a deep silence and radiant light ... lose all sense of self ... and expand into infinity ... the benevolent heart of the universe ... Stay in this place for as long as feels appropriate.

48

Then, listen for a faint sound becoming closer and closer, a quiet heart-beat ... It's your heart pulsing in resonance with the universe.

When you're ready to bring your meditation to a close, reset the knob to the position where it feels most comfortable to go about your daily life. Then, open your eyes and take a few deep breaths.

Meditation to Heal a World Crisis

Begin by stilling your body, emotions and mind and aligning with your higher self or soul.

Recognize a higher purpose outworking in the world, serving human evolution in some way.

Hear the invocative cry of humanity to God or Spirit, and see this invocation connecting with the source of light, love and will that flow down to Earth.

Hold open your heart in love to the human suffering in the world, and send healing energy to the victims of the crisis.

See the emotional level becoming calm and stabilized, with light, love and peace shining through it so that fear and anger may be transformed.

Examine the inner, spiritual forces at work behind the scenes: Observe the spiritual lessons being learned through the crisis, seek to understand the deeper meaning of the crisis by identifying with the participants, and reflect on the deeper causes and karmic cycles that have created the crisis.

Hold world leaders involved in the crisis in the light, asking that they align with their highest selves to make decisions for the greatest good of humanity.

Visualize a flow of loving wisdom awakening humanity, as people around the world learn the deeper lessons presented by the crisis.

Close with a blessing for humanity, using a prayer such as the Great Invocation.

Meditation on the Harmonics of the New World

Begin by taking a few deep, relaxing breaths … going more deeply within. Let go of awareness of your body as a temporary expression of who you are … Let go of your feelings as temporary   expressions … Let go of your thoughts as temporary expressions…

Feel yourself becoming lighter and lighter, more expanded and free.

Raise your vibrational frequency to resonate with your soul, invoking the presence of God or Spirit. Imagine yourself journeying into the future, a few years from now, and becoming your future self. From this vantage point, look back at today's world.

Observe the dysfunction and destruction of the old world as if from a detached distance. Notice the dissonant sound the old world creates. Notice what spiritual lessons are being learned from the breaking down of the old world.

Raise your frequency higher, so that you can resonate with aspects of the higher evolutionary plan, the big picture. Notice the plan's beauty and harmony, its all-encompassing synthesis of life. Hear a new note being sounded, the note of heaven being brought down to Earth, Spirit into matter, and experience its harmonic frequency.

See the seeds of new life growing everywhere, positive solutions to prob-lems being created by people around the earth, like radiant points of light building a new culture, a new world. Visualize these seeds of a new culture very specifically to help energize them.

See these new seeds being enlivened by Spirit and nurtured with love, supporting the courageous pioneers who have planted them. Visualize these seeds growing in strength and maturity. See them linking with other radiant seeds around the earth, forming a lattice-work of light and new life.

Experience the beauty and the joy of this New World in your heart. Recognize your contribution to this new culture. See this positive future as a magnet, drawing you forward. Ask yourself what you can do to help—in your thoughts and in your actions.

Slowly return to the present, committing yourself to doing your part to help create this New World, taking the next step you need to take.

Slowly, as you're ready, open your eyes, and write down any insights you had from this meditation as a way to remember the experience and ground it in your daily life.

In the next day or two, as you take a walk or read the paper, focus on something of beauty, something positive that reflects the New World growing all around you.

KEY INSIGHTS TO REFLECT ON

◆ A New World is growing everywhere and you can find it, if you know where and how to look.

◆ This is our planetary wake-up call: not the End Times, but the Beginning Times.

◆ Our planet is undergoing an initiation of synthesis where everything is fusing and blending.

◆ Our state of consciousness affects the type of world we each perceive and experience.

◆ Each of us has a unique contribution and part to play in this New World.

◆ There are creative New World solutions already under way for every problem we face.

Key #2

Understand the Big Picture and the Evolutionary Plan

Find Your Part and Get Engaged

All things by immortal power,

Near or far

Hiddenly to each other linked are;

Thou canst not stir a flower

Without troubling of a star.

> — Francis Thompson, "The Mistress of Vision"[1]

Living the Future Now

It is important to understand the big picture today, because everything is changing so rapidly and there's so much confusion. When you grasp the outline of the higher evolutionary plan that is now unfolding, you can make a wiser assessment of how to fit your contribution into the larger context. You can find the right time to be most effective.

Thirty years ago, after totally burning out on political activism as the only way to change the world, I had my first experience of the New World and the bigger evolutionary picture. I read the book *The Magic of Findhorn*, which is about a pioneering ecological/spiritual community of practical visionaries who grow huge vegetables in sandy soil in cold, northern Scotland. More amazingly, the community grows conscious, compassionate people, without dogma or gurus, and pioneers a sustainable ecological village. It drew me like a magnet.

As an aspiring practical visionary, I found that experiencing Findhorn was like living the future in the present—a powerful, transforming experience of living a sustainable, spiritual lifestyle. At Findhorn there was a new rhythm and vibration and an amazing sense of group consciousness and connection with all life. Totally immersing myself in this pioneering expression of the New World—living, working, playing and transforming problems—left a deep imprint on the DNA of my cells. It gave me a solid and realistic sense of hope for humanity and the unfolding of a higher evolutionary plan behind the scenes.

At Findhorn, I found hundreds of practical visionaries—from young American hippies to elderly European aristocrats—living in harmony with one another and with the earth. The British Soil Association investigated their miracle of growing an unusual variety of large vegetables and roses in the snow in a harsh, northern climate. They called it "Factor X," which turned out to be ordinary people communicating with the spiritual side of nature and working co-creatively with the forces of nature in the organic gardens.

Work at Findhorn is called "love in action," and experiencing this lifestyle showed me the secret of how to make everyday life joyful—a new experience for me. The first day I visited the community, I was struck by how many people sing aloud as they worked.

The emphasis at Findhorn was on finding God or Spirit within your heart through meditation, rather than relying on any outer teachers or gurus. I arrived at Findhorn at the time of a crucial shift when authority was being transferred from the original founders, Peter and Eileen Caddy, to a group, and I was asked to be a part of the governing group during this transition. Decisions were made through meditation and group consensus, and this was a new and exciting experience for me.

Findhorn has now grown into a world-renowned ecovillage and demonstration center for sustainability and holistic education. More than 100,000 visitors from around the world have taken courses there or joined as residents. It's also become a mecca for innovative art and culture in the region. The community offers a wonderful blend of spirituality and practical, conscious living—solar and wind energy, organic gardens and a community-based currency for buying goods and services. It's now officially a nongovernmental organization (NGO) consulting at the United Nations.

At Findhorn, I experienced a new and practical vision for humanity. I knew that it was possible because I was living it every day.

Then I had a jarring experience. In 1978 I returned to the United States with my husband after three years at Findhorn and felt like I had stepped out of the future, back into the present. I remember walking into a store in my husband's hometown, in Plymouth, Massachusetts, and being amazed that most things were still the same as when I had left years before. Small things were different, like the titles of currently popular books and technology products. Everyone seemed to be living and working just to buy and consume more stuff. How could life still be going on in the same old boring way? I now knew that it was possible to live in a more harmonious, conscious way and that there was a higher purpose to life. I sensed intuitively that the United States was ripe for major transformation.

Gordon and I traveled around the United States for a year after we left Findhorn, offering a seminar that we called *Individual and Planetary Transformation*. We found many other spiritual communities and innovative educational centers that were also seeds of a New World like Findhorn. They pioneered some of the first experiments in holistic health, renewable energy (wind, solar, ethanol), organic farming, green building, conflict resolution, sexual equality and leadership roles for women.

We called them "research and development centers for society" and in 1978 in Massachusetts, we started one we called Sirius (after the star), which I'll describe later. Although none of these centers are exemplary in all aspects, they are the early signs of a new culture and a New World.

Most of these early R & D experiments have been successfully integrated into the mainstream culture. Holistic health care is now a billion-dollar industry; organic foods have reached $14 billion in sales; energy-efficient green building is all the rage; wind, solar and renewable energy are some of the fastest growing businesses; and women are assuming leadership positions in every profession.

My personal experience of seeing the seeds of this new culture mature since the 1970s has given me optimism about the future and provided me with an understanding of the big picture and how the higher evolutionary plan is unfolding.

The Evolutionary Design

Today the New World is exploding everywhere, and it's important to understand why. There is a higher purpose for human evolution, and help is available from the spiritual realms to fulfill this purpose when we ask for it. A higher evolutionary plan is unfolding in perfect timing and can be seen in the many expressions of the New World all around us.

This evolutionary plan is subtle and intelligent, yet infinitely just and compassionate. The Taoists, for example, understand this plan as the Tao, "the way." Jewish people see it embodied in the Kabbalah, the tree of life. Christians see it as the Divine Plan. And scientists study it as the story of life itself.

This higher plan is encoded within all life. In the macrocosm (the larger world), it is the emerging pattern lying behind events in the outer, visible world. In the microcosm (the smaller world within each of us), it is the pattern of spiritual development encoded in the DNA of our souls, which we can choose to follow or not. It's the inner compass for our evolutionary journeys.

Evolution is moving in a clear direction, and there is a brighter, more-enlightened future ahead for all of us. The purpose of our evolutionary journey is to learn how to love and how to be conscious co-creators with God, experiencing how everything in the universe is connected and part of a larger whole, the One Life. As we expand our consciousness, we realize ever greater dimensions of ourselves. We are part of one cosmic family, and all life—mineral, plant, animal and human kingdoms—is sacred. The goal of the entire evolutionary process is to protect, nurture and finally reveal the hidden spiritual reality within all life.

Seeing a glimpse of the evolutionary design is like seeing all of the pieces of a puzzle fit together in perfect harmony. Awareness of this design brings a deep sense of joy and security, assuring us that our lives, and the life of this planet, are not just random series of events, going nowhere. There is a purpose to life.

The ageless wisdom refers to God as "the benevolent heart of the universe" and the "Cosmic Magnet," and scientists are discovering that the center of the Milky Way galaxy is a powerful source of magnetic energy through the action of magnetic filaments, which have a huge effect on planet Earth.

The evolutionary plan unfolds slowly, adapting to the needs of humanity and the kingdoms of nature. Since it is a living plan, we co-create it with God/Spirit/Universal Mind, working out the details after understanding the broad outline.

Most important, we can sense the higher plan when we become silent and go more deeply within ourselves. Life has encoded this design in every cell of our beings. It's what gives us each a sense of hope and joy despite outer circumstances. It's the dream that lives in the mind and soul of all humanity, written in the sacred fire of our hearts.

The best news is this: Each of us has a part to play in this evolutionary plan. Your main task is to discover your soul's unique purpose and function, and then to become really good at it, developing skill in action. When you do, you will feel much more fulfilled and purposeful, perhaps for the first time in your life. As more of us express our higher purposes, together we create a brighter future for humanity.

Finding Your Part in the Evolutionary Design

To find your part in the evolutionary design, you need to tune into the spiritual encoding within your soul. At first, you may grasp only an aspect of the higher plan abstractly, but you can work to give it concrete form, filling in the details and learning to embody it in yourself.

For example, you might recognize the need for creating greater understanding among people of different races as part of the evolutionary plan, so you decide to work on overcoming prejudice in yourself. Then you create a specific project to help achieve understanding, such as monthly public dialogues on racial healing.

The underlying objective of the higher plan is to synthesize all nations, races, and kingdoms of life into living as a mutually cooperative whole. Each aspect keeps its unique identity, but it expands its consciousness to realize its participation in the One Life. We are responsible for carrying out the ideas and guidance we intuitively receive—the fractions of the larger design related to our unique capabilities, gifts and life purpose.

Through the ages, in all cultures and religions, it has been said that humanity's highest purpose is to express the Good, the Beautiful and the True. As humanity, we are to redeem and transform matter—to bring forth light and love in the material world by understanding the higher purpose within ourselves and every form of life.

Doorways to the New World: How You Can Get Engaged

Within the higher evolutionary plan, there are many doorways to the New World. The first step is to change any old thoughts you have about spirituality. Let go of the idea that only transcendence of the world is spiritual. Spirituality removed from daily life is incomplete. Subjective abstraction in the inner worlds is not the only way to develop spiritually. In fact, it can be a way to avoid the work that is urgently needed to transform yourself. Spiritual truths have to be experienced, embodied and lived every day. It is essential to honor the material world because it holds surprising power for spiritual development.

By interacting in a conscious, loving way with the mineral, plant and animal kingdoms, you can be affected by the hidden power found within matter itself. Welcome this transforming experience. When you create, build, clean or organize something, you can practice drawing forth the light and beauty within the form. See this physical activity as an act of blessing.

To help co-create the New World, focus your energy in a field that you care passionately about, something that needs your light and your particular gifts.

Are you passionate about politics? Work for causes that overcome injustice and promote the greatest good for the greatest number. Avoid adversarial approaches, and work instead on finding higher common ground in any conflict—understanding the differences but acting on commonalities. Create multistakeholder dialogues for more-effective public policies. Promote transpartisan approaches to politics, transcending the usual liberal-conservative polarity. Bring a global, multicultural perspective to any issue. Support honesty and transparency in political campaigns and campaign finance and other reforms. Support political leaders who truly embody spiritual values.

Are you passionate about education or psychology? Help students discover their passions by teaching courses that engage their curiosity and creativity and encourage self-initiated learning. Include experiential learning and didactic learning, and teach emotional intelligence, such as good listening and communication skills. Create online, distance learning with information on New World ideas and projects. Organize adult education classes in new fields, such as permaculture and systems thinking. Study the latest breakthroughs in psychology, explore your inner psyche or work on your personal issues with a therapist or teacher.

Are you passionate about business or finance? Money is simply concretized energy. See it as a spiritual asset — a means to support good work in the world. Invest your money in socially responsible companies. Buy from companies with integrity and good values. Bring your spiritual values to your workplace. Help your company find ways to expand the bottom line beyond just profit. Corporations are amazingly efficient at producing and distributing everything we could possibly need or desire. All they need is to expand their missions to include higher values, such as the well-being of employees, giving back to the community, and reducing their impact on the environment. Engage in entrepreneurial philanthropy: invest in projects that serve the greater good. Be generous in your donations.

Are you passionate about art or music? Promote art as the universal beauty that can transcend borders and languages. Spontaneously explore your creativity by trying new mediums. Immerse yourself in color to enliven your emotional state. Create participatory art, in which people are no longer spectators but are involved in mutual creation. Infuse art and music with inspirational and spiritual content to uplift people, and share it widely. Support emerging artists who have transformative artistic messages.

Are you passionate about science or technology? Help people see that science and spirituality can complement each other. Test spiritual approaches to life, and prove their effectiveness. Examine the subtler realms of the mind and soul to understand how they affect the physical world. Research the scientific effects of meditation and prayer to prove that patients who have people praying or meditating for them heal much faster than patients in the control groups. Research and support new technologies that improve the quality of people's lives. Develop more open-source technology applications, where everyone contributes, creating greater value. Explore virtual reality games that help solve social problems. Share spiritual inspiration through social networking sites.

Are you passionate about spirituality or religion? Bring spirituality into all aspects of daily life, and make it more practical. Empower people by helping them discover their inner divinity, and teach simplified meditation techniques. Develop new participatory ceremonies and rituals, such as celebrating the summer solstice or honoring a young person's coming of age. Create rituals in nature, connecting people to the sacredness of the earth. Study different religions to broaden your perspective and develop greater tolerance. Focus on building group consciousness and community, rather than relying on charismatic individuals.

Are you passionate about the environment, food or health care? Research possible sources of pollution in your local water, earth and/or air quality. Educate your neighbors, and plan local action. Reduce your consumption and energy use. Support producers of natural, organic food and fair trade companies. Shop at local farmers' markets. Join a local CSA group (Community Supported Agriculture) in which subscribers support a local farmer and, in turn, receive all the fresh produce they can eat. Avoid prepackaged, preservative-laden and genetically modified food, and support legislation that requires food labels that alert consumers. Your body is sacred, a temple of Spirit. Bring greater health and vitality to your body through a holistic, preventive approach that uses natural remedies and energy healing, such as homeopathy, chiropractic, acupuncture and naturopathy.

There is so much work to be done to transform the world and so many areas of life that need greater light. Take some time for quiet meditation to reflect on what field of service calls you. Can you hear an inner message from your soul drawing you out into the world? As ancient Zen wisdom recommends, "Enter the marketplace with helping hands." Now is the time.

The Law of Cycles

It's important to understand the big picture and the evolutionary timing to see the larger context in which you make your contribution and service. There is a rhythmic order to evolution based on the Law of Cycles, which governs all life. Everything has a beginning or seed stage, a growing and maturing stage, a fruition or culminating stage and an ending with decline and seed bearing for the next cycle. For example, after crops have been harvested in the fall, the remaining seeds are turned back into the earth, where they are nurtured deep in the darkness of winter. In the spring, these seeds blossom forth as new life.

It is the same today in the cycle of cultures and civilizations. It's not a *Clash of Civilizations,* as Samuel P. Huntington claims in his book of that name, but rather human consciousness moving through different stages of awaking and realization within cycles of civilizations. When things are stuck or there's a regression, you need to realize this is just the resistance of human consciousness and a retreat to old patterns. Soon there will be a blossoming of new seeds that were nurtured in the darkness during the winter cycle.

When one country or culture that has experienced a long cycle of positive growth starts slipping backward in consciousness or values, you need to shift your perspective to see the bigger picture, the planetary picture. You can take heart from the new evolutionary energies bursting forth and impacting humanity's consciousness in many countries around the world. Evolution moves forward. Everything is impermanent and constantly changing, contributing to the further evolution of consciousness on our planet. The more you can detach from the negative and positive cycles of expression and observe without reaction, the more strategic and effective you can be in your work for humanity.

The Shift From Dogmatic Fanaticism to Practicality and Rhythmic Order

Understanding the immense changes we are in the midst of requires an understanding of the basic frequencies of energies that are sometimes called "rays" or "waves of energy" in the ageless wisdom teachings and in the works of more recent teachers such as Helena Blavatsky, Alice Bailey and Lucille Cedercrans The rays underlie everything we see. All life is an expression of different frequencies of energies or rays.

There are seven basic ray energies, like the seven colors of the rainbow or the seven notes on the musical scale. In their totality, the rays embody all aspects of God or Spirit. Various rays cycle in and out of influence on the planet over specific periods of time, providing different energetic impulses for the unfoldment of consciousness and the development of civilizations.

The rays are the first ray of will and power, the second ray of love and wisdom, the third ray of active intelligence, the fourth ray of harmony through conflict, the fifth ray of concrete science, the sixth ray of devotion and idealism and the seventh ray of rhythmic order and practical magic.

Long cycles of activity and whole civilizations are governed by incoming and outgoing rays, which affect all aspects of human life. As a ray cycles into expression on Earth, new ideas, impulses and life forces create changes in human life and society. As a ray leaves expression, the underlying energy that has supported the forms of a social order is withdrawn and structures begin their inevitable decline. This is the situation we face in the world today. Our planet is in the midst of a major shift from one energy frequency to another, which is why we're experiencing so much change and conflict.

The sixth ray of devotion and idealism has been a primary influence in human affairs for the past 2,000 years, but it is now passing out of expression as the seventh ray of rhythmic order and practical magic flows in, causing a clash between them. The shift is from an emphasis on fundamentalism, sacrifice and devotion to an emphasis on practical spirituality, community and rhythmic living.

The sixth ray has helped humanity develop the capacity to imagine and strive for higher ideals in religion, politics and all fields. It has helped people stay focused on and devoted in their aspirations to these ideals, whether religious, political or scientific, and it has created great ideologies and belief systems. It has created a worship of perfection but also an inability to attain it, except through immense suffering.

The sixth ray creates an obsession with public personalities, which we see in the adulation of movie, music and sports stars and even politicians and businesspeople. Many people become disillusioned when they see the huge gaps between the ideal aspired to and the reality, and they begin to tear down the formerly idealized personalities that they had put on pedestals.

This idealistic, devotional ray emphasizes aspiration toward a transcendent God, rather than God immanent within each of us, but often lacks application of ideals in daily life. The sixth ray has tendencies toward fanaticism and the desire to impose beliefs on others—tendencies that becomes more extreme when a ray reaches the end of its cycle of expression. Does this sound familiar?

The sixth ray of devotion and idealism is causing great conflict among adherents of rigid ideologies and religions. This ray is the deeper cause of the fanatical fundamentalism and religious wars we see in every religion and nation in the world today. People who are desperate, unheard, unloved and lacking hope for a better life cling to rigid religious orthodoxies as a life raft and lash out in violence and anger, committing terrible acts of terrorism, to "protect" their orthodoxies. Others, who hold extremely high ideals of perfection and see themselves as sinners or unworthy, are easily manipulated by unscrupulous religious leaders hungry for power. Have you observed this recently?

One of the major examples in recent years of the dangerous effects of the sixth ray has been the growth of fanatical, fundamentalist Islamic terrorism. But also dangerous to world stability is the fanatical response of fundamentalist Jews, Christians and Hindus. When people become blindly fanatical about   their religions or chauvinistic about their nations and trample on the rights of others, they are expressing the final stages of the sixth ray influence. This is seen in our newspapers daily.

The sixth ray of devotion and idealism isn't affecting just the religious world. You can also see this energy in chauvinistic patriotism, market fundamentalism and scientific dogmatism that refuses to admit new data or hypotheses from outside the current paradigm. Have you run up against this rigidity when trying to create change in the world?

The New Rhythm of Practicality

While the sixth ray is waning in influence, a new life wave of energy, the seventh ray of rhythmic order and practical magic, is growing. The practical visionary energies of the seventh ray are shattering crystallized and fanatical fundamentalism, whether religious, nationalistic, economic or scientific. Thank goodness!

While the sixth ray focused our attention on Spirit beyond the world and on transcendence of the material world, the seventh ray redirects our attention back into the world, to bring sixth ray ideals into a field of activity and practical application. This is Spirit in matter, directing intention and purpose into form.

The seventh ray connects the inner, spiritual dimensions with the outer, practical world in order to be more effective in serving human needs. Connecting the inner and outer dimensions is what magic is all about.

The gradually increasing seventh ray brings in an organizing energy. It organizes the relationship between Spirit and matter, with free circulation of energy in every direction. It invokes higher purpose into activity to produce rhythm and order in manifestation. It provides the energy to create innovative forms in business, politics, education, psychology, etc. It creates practical rhythms of daily living based on more inclusive forms of community, group consciousness and awareness of the whole, rather than individualistic or separative approaches to daily life.

The seventh ray sounds forth in time and space as a harmonic chord, bringing divine purpose into new forms. For example, it brings the creative fusion of new rhythms and musical styles from around the world, e.g. world beat and fusion music. It encourages new forms of participatory ritual, such as ceremonies to honor the earth in which everyone in the circle contributes in some way. New seventh ray organizations are beginning to incorporate light, sound, color and vibration in rhythmic expression and ritual.

The seventh ray helps us recognize the divine within ourselves and within all life. It brings together Spirit and matter so that Spirit irradiates physical forms. It provides the impetus for manifesting spiritual principles here on Earth in our daily lives. It helps us become practical visionaries. This emphasis is in contrast to the earlier sixth ray emphasis on an otherworldly spirituality — trying to reach a transcendent God beyond our sinful selves and a badly corrupted world.

The seventh ray sees all life — all peoples and species — as holy. The inflow of seventh ray energy is the inner, hidden cause of the growing environmental movement and the health and fitness movement. It emphasizes caring for the earth and for our bodies as temples of our indwelling Spirit. One of its keynotes is "there is a place for everything and everything in its place," recycling to reduce energy and protect the environment. Evidence of the seventh ray can also be seen in the growing popularity of products and services that help us be more organized — with our daily schedules, closets, finances, photos, etc. The widespread embrace of computers is another reflection of the seventh ray, as computer software is by nature an organizing influence, training us to create categories and files for our ideas and tasks and to think in an orderly manner.

Conflicts within and between nations are often based on clashes between people who want to conserve the past and people who want to promote progressive change. Many are working to "put things right" by working for equity in allocating global resources or protecting and restoring the natural environment. The way forward is to combine the best of traditional values, which have often been neglected in our materialistic culture, with the energy and impetus of the new progressive energies. Combining the old and new creates the higher synthesis of the New World that opens and expands consciousness while maintaining enough stability to allow us to adjust to the rapid changes.

The passing away of the influence of a ray occurs most smoothly when people integrate the best of its gifts into the new cycle of energy. Since each ray has a shadow as well, we need to be aware of the negative aspects of the incoming seventh ray: obsession with organization and the corresponding rigidity and bureaucracy.

Current Evolutionary Priorities

The higher evolutionary plan encoded within all life has a certain direction and timing. Different priorities are emphasized in different cycles of time. Since it's a living plan, we are co-creators with it, and we can work out the details better when we understand its broad outline and priorities. Following are six priorities of this living plan for our current cycle as I understand it.

Creating Synthesis, Unity and Fusion

A key evolutionary priority is transcending duality and polarization. The spirit of unity and synthesis is increasingly impacting our world. One of the top spiritual goals for our time is overcoming separateness.

Synthesis is a dynamic dance that transforms separateness and brings diverse parts into right relationships with one another and with the whole, resulting in something creative and enriching. It sounds a whole tone that tunes and harmonizes all other frequencies within its range of influence. Synthesis is both a value of the New World and a method or process for reconciling apparent diversity.

The light within you can help you transcend polarity and binary thinking, such as either/or and us vs. them (our Aristotelian two-valued system of logic), and focus instead on both/and thinking. The inner light helps you embrace a higher synthesis of seeming opposites, such mind and body, subject and object, form and emptiness, wave and particle, spirituality and science, rational and intuitive, Eastern and Western, traditional and innovative, personal and political, liberal and conservative, masculine and feminine, practical and visionary, and spirit and matter. The ageless wisdom, including the Bible, teaches about the importance of resolving duality: If your eye is single, all is light. You see how everything has a purpose and goodness to it. You walk "the razor's edge" between the two great lines of force.

Today many disparate things are blending, fusing and synthesizing. Nothing seems as separate as it did in past times—races, religions, cultures, nations, genders, styles. The walls between opposites are beginning to dissolve, and dualities are transforming into a higher synthesis.

The cutting edge in every field of the New World is fusion and synthesis: holistic, hybrid, integral, multiracial, multicultural, multinational, interfaith, transpartisan, creative "mash-ups." These reflect many aspects of the age of synthesis, described by scientists such as Dr. Carl W. Hall, that we're now entering.

Synthesis dictates the trend of all the evolutionary processes today. Everything is working toward larger unified blocs, toward amalgamations, international relationships, global planning, economic fusion, interdependence, interfaith movements and ideological concepts that deal with wholes rather than isolated parts. Now humanity is gradually building a synthesis in time and space through our modern, interconnected civilization and technology such as the Internet and jet travel.

An immensely popular holistic health industry, for example, unites mind and body. Hybrid cars blend gasoline and electric energy. Fusion music blends diverse styles and cultures. Social-benefit corporations fuse entrepreneurship and philanthropy. "Third way" politics synthesize the best of the left and right. New religions teach that Spirit and matter are no longer separate, as Spirit infuses matter. Spirituality is becoming more practical and applied to everyday life, which is attested by the new movements for Spirit in Business, Spirituality and Science, the Soul of Education and Spiritual Politics, that bring together seeming opposites. The signs are everywhere.

The ageless wisdom teaches that Spirit and matter aren't separate but are merely different frequencies along the same spectrum of energy. Spirit is matter at its highest frequency; matter is Spirit at its lowest frequency. You could say that matter is Spirit moving slowly enough to be seen.

Integral philosopher Ken Wilber notes that "Spirit is unfolding in this world and as this world." He goes on to note that in the nondual spiritual traditions, the absolute (Spirit) and the relative (form) are not two but one: "[I]n order to have a full realization of Spirit, you have to realize formlessness, this pure unmanifest presence, and you have to realize Spirit in action in the manifest world of form."[2] Spirit is present (immanent) everywhere in the world. It's about recognizing what already is present—seeing reality more clearly.

In the Spirit-matter polarity, many spiritual people like to only hang out in Spirit, but you need to move back and forth between Spirit and matter to grow and to generate energy, just as energy is generated in a battery or an electrical system.

True synthesis is a state of being that you can learn to recognize and identify with. The secret is aligning your personal will with the higher energy of divine purpose. Synthesis is an aspect of the divine will that holds all of manifestation in right relationship through all time and space.

Psychologist Roberto Assagioli noted that "Synthesis is brought about by a higher element or principle which transforms, sublimates and reabsorbs the two poles into a higher reality .... The method of synthesis, which is analogous in a certain sense to a chemical combination, includes and absorbs the two elements into higher unity endowed with qualities differing from those of either of them."[3]

There is a tremendous movement today toward fusion, convergence and synthesis in all fields. It's like individual musical instruments playing together to create the wonderful harmonies of a symphony—without a conductor to orchestrate it. It's similar to synchrony in nature, where the rhythmic interplay of parts unconsciously combine in patterns to make up a greater whole, e.g. the movement of schools of fish or the flashing patterns of fireflies.

On a practical level, how can you work on transforming duality and bringing this energy of synthesis into your daily life? You can begin exploring the larger pattern or whole that includes the opposites. For example, you can look for the grain of truth on each side of an argument to see how each contributes to the bigger picture. You can practice listening to someone who holds a different philosophical or political view from your own, and then look for points of agreement or common ground.

You can also work on walking in someone else's shoes and seeing the world from his or her perspective. This seems simple, but it is incredibly profound and revealing. You can psychologically role-play someone who is different from you to develop empathy. Seeking out different cultural, racial and religious experiences can expand your perspective as you learn to harmonize with them. Another good technique is reading the literature of people with opposing views and trying to keep an open mind, looking for the grain of truth.

We will have peace on the planet only after we have unity and justice, and we will experience abundance only when we have peace. Unity is first, then peace, then plenty—and significantly in that order. Trying to create peace when there is no unity among people is ineffective, because conflicts will soon re-emerge. Trying to create abundance or prosperity where there is no peace is impossible. For example, aid sent to developing countries at war (internally or externally) is usually pocketed by warlords and doesn't reach the people in need. War and conflict always draw off funds needed for economic development and discourage new business investment.

The first task is to create unity among people through ecumenical, interracial and international movements of understanding and goodwill. True unity is not conformity; it embraces diversity, both in form and in attitudes and values. Peace is not a stagnant condition, but rather a dynamic equilibrium between opposing forces, always evolving toward a higher realization and synthesis. Once there is greater unity with justice and sharing among people, there can be lasting peace.

Abundance for all can best be ensured by the generous circulation of goods and resources to those most in need so that they have no reason to initiate conflict or war. Developed nations need to understand this important lesson if they want to avoid creating more fertile ground for terrorists, who are often desperate because they have nothing.

The new integral approaches to life, in which both the inner and outer and the personal and collective aspects of every issue are addressed, are key methods for creating unity. The "integral revolution" spearheaded by author Ken Wilber is an important example. The *Spiral Dynamics* work by Don Beck and Chris Cowan is another, as they offer integrative maps of the different memes or developmental stages of consciousness of individuals and groups in society, and how to address their different needs. Each higher stage transcends yet includes the earlier stages.

Van Jones, a practical visionary and the former director of the Ella Baker Center for Human Rights, says today is the age of hybridity, when things are coming together in new ways. He says that the new generation doesn't want to be limited by binary thinking—either/or—that they want both/and. They want whole systems change—transforming the world at multiple levels simultaneously.

In this new age of synthesis, it's notable that the United States elected a president, Barack Obama, who embodies synthesis in his multiracial makeup, multicountry residences, multifocus career and transpartisan politics.

Disruptive, breakthrough innovations usually come about when you mash together different disciplines, says Salim Ismail, a former executive with Yahoo!, who directs the new Singularity University on the NASA Ames base in California. Their self-described mission is to solve the world's biggest problems by synthesizing academic disciplines.

The spirit of synthesis is emerging in every field today, as interdisciplinary approaches by practical visionaries become the leading edge in academia, government and business. Following are some examples.

In Politics

🖘 The creation of "third way" and transpartisan parties beyond left and right.

🖘 The resolving of polarizing conflicts through mediation techniques.the building of regional unions among nations.

🖘 The explosion of multisector partnerships—government, business, nonprofits.

🖘 The world café dialogues among diverse races, cultures, generations, etc.

🖘 The intergenerational collaborative movement among young and old.

🖘 The blending and intermarriage between races, cultures and sexes.

🖘 The fusion of hierarchy (leadership) and democracy (egalitarianism).

🖘 The melding of film with activism at political house parties.

In Religion

❧ The dialogue among different religions in the interfaith movement.

❧ The renewed emphasis on both contemplation and social action.

❧ The trend towards adopting beliefs and practices of several religions at once.

❧ The blending of religion with social activities and entertainment in modern mega churches.

In Psychology

❧ The integration of the conscious, subconscious and superconscious.

❧ The fusing of Eastern and Western approaches.

❧ The emergence of somatic education, integrating mind and body.

❧ The integration of the whole field of the psyche in integral psychology.

❧ The blending of psychology and ecology in behavioral ecology.

❧ The blending of traditional masculine and feminine qualities and transgender styles.

❧ The popularity of cross-cultural studies, training, tours.

In Business

❧ The new concern for doing well by doing good—profit and values.

❧ The harmonizing of environmental and economic concerns.

🖘 The merging of for-profit with nonprofit mission in social benefit corporations and social entrepreneurship.

🖘 The trend to support work/life balance in the workplace.

🖘 The blending of styles from different eras, such as retro/futuristic blends in new products.

🖘 The blending trend in banking where diverse services are offered, such as life insurance, auto insurance, mortgages, brokerage services.

🖘 The merging of economics with psychology in a new field called therapeutic economics.

In Science

🖘 The blending of physical science and social science.

🖘 The interdisciplinary approaches, such as engineering, biology and the physical sciences together tackling complex problems.

🖘 The merging of biology and ecology to create the new field of epigenetics.

🖘 The teaming of science with religion in neurotheology to study the effects of prayer and meditation and prove the existence of the soul.

🖘 The discovery of nuclear fusion which unifies atoms, rather than splitting them, as does nuclear fission.

🖘 The massive hybridization of crops.

In Technology

🖘 The creation of hybrid cars, using gas and electricity.

🖘 The open-source, free software collaboration among self-organizing communities such as Wikipedia.

❦ The hyperlinking and networking among diverse groups.

❦ The "mash-ups" that remake videos or music by splicing in diverse sequences from unusual sources.

❦ The blending of traditional journalism with citizen media, such as cell phone videos, Twitter feeds, video pods and use-news sites.

❦ The Web search engines that synthesize and connect all knowledge.

❦ The fusing of education and technology through "educasting" and online courses.

❦ The merging of real life and virtual life through online avatar games.

❦ The blending of the sacred and technology such as new spiritual apps (applications) on cell phones.

In the Arts

❦ The trend toward fusion music and world music, blending styles and cultures, such as hip hop with Indian sitar.

❦ The widespread use of mixed media in works of art.

❦ The interactive, cross-platform entertainments.

❦ The profusion of political statements in art, music, film, literature.

❦ The transforming of two-dimensional figures into multidimensional scenes called "diorama."

In Medicine

❦ The holistic approaches, which include body, emotions, mind, spirit.

- ❧ The complementary approaches of alternative and allopathic medicine.
- ❧ The integrative medicine of indigenous and contemporary modalities.
- ❧ The new "energy medicine" that relates the physical and etheric bodies.

The change in how the mainstream refers to holistic approaches of health care is indicative of the movement toward fusion and synthesis. At first, it was called alternative medicine because it was an alternative to mainstream, allopathic medicine. As it became more popular, it was called "complementary medicine," and now that it's accepted by many people in the mainstream medical profession, it's referred to as "integrative medicine."

Previous opposites, such as science and religion, have begun to fuse and complement each other. For example, scientists who observe brain changes in meditators, such as reduced activity in the parietal lobes which process someone's orientation in space and time. This research demonstrates the physical correspondence of the spiritual experience of expansiveness and connection with everyone and everything.

Embodying synthesis ultimately results in the ability to perceive the highest, the light in everything. We learn to embody synthesis by looking for the right relationship between separated parts and gathering the parts into right relationship with the living whole. Synthesis takes the best from the past and what is relevant and useful from the future and applies it in the present. Life is loving synthesis in action.

One of the unique capabilities of human beings is to embody synthesis, which is now being illustrated in quantum physics as superstring theory. This theory suggests that the universe is a series of strings capable of vibrating at multiple frequencies, each frequency representing another dimension of reality. As we become more spiritually awakened, we have the ability to vibrate to multiple frequencies or dimensions, which makes us natural synthesizers.

In meditation, it's possible to inwardly vibrate at very high spiritual frequencies and step down these frequencies when interacting with the world. Thus, an individual can become a living focal point of synthesis in action. The more consciously we recognize this, the more we can channel higher frequencies of energy to people and events that are in need of healing or transformation.

The questions for today are: How much can each of us synthesize in our consciousness—how many seemingly different realities and opposing views can we hold at once? To what degree can we identify with the whole? A good time to practice synthesizing is when we hear competing views from different political spokespeople. I highly recommend it—and it certainly makes the evening news more interesting and challenging! (For examples of how to synthesize many different political points of view on challenging issues like terrorism and international development, visit Mark Satin's brilliant Radical Middle Web site *www.radicalmiddle.com*.)

Revealing Spirit in Matter and the Inner Divinity Within All Life

Essential Divinity is a principle that helps us recognize the presence of Spirit in all life. Experiencing the inner light in each person, regardless of race, age, gender, religion or nationality, is especially helpful if we want to live together harmoniously on this planet. Today the leading edge is finding God or Spirit within your own heart. This is an experience of "God within me" — God immanent in the first person, in contrast to an experience of God as a transcendent deity — God in the second person as "You" or "Thou," the Divine Father. Lastly, there is an experience of God within all form of life: God/Goddess or Divine Mother/Gaia in the third person.

Awareness of the Essential Divinity within your own heart opens you to participation in a life greater than your own, the fundamental, universal energy or life underlying all forms on Earth. The inner revelation of this principle illuminates your interdependence with all parts of the greater whole.

The understanding of God immanent is found in all religions throughout time. Over the temple of Delphi in ancient Greece was written "Man, know thyself and thou shall know the universe and the gods." In the ancient Hindu scripture, *The Bhagavad Gita*, Krishna said, "Having pervaded the universe with a fragment of Myself, I remain." Buddha proclaimed, "Look within: thou art the Buddha," and St. Paul wrote in the Bible, "Christ in you the hope and glory." Although revealed in all of the world's scriptures, there is a far more widespread recognition of this inner divine presence in the human heart and within all life today than in times past.

Rather than seeing heaven as separate from the earth, there is a growing movement to bring heaven down to the earth, revealing Spirit in the material world in a practical way in our daily lives. More and more people are insisting that we actually embody the spiritual principles we believe in, so there is congruence between our values and our thoughts and actions.

Everyday life can be our spiritual teacher if we carefully observe the lessons we are learning as we go about our daily tasks. Doing this helps us be more spiritually awake and create more effective patterns of living—with relationships, money or power issues.

The growing recognition that the physical body is sacred, a temple of the Spirit or the Divine Mother, is also a part of the revelation of Spirit in matter. There is a new focus on caring for the health of our bodies with natural remedies and organic food and maintaining a balance of rest and exercise. Holistic centers, like The Center for Mind/Body Medicine in Washington, D.C., promote natural approaches, such as homeopathy, chiropractic, acupuncture and naturopathy for health.

Developing Right Relationship, Goodwill and Group Endeavor

Spiritual Approach is a deeper way to approach all relationships—with God, nature and other humans. It focuses on what is your next rightful, evolutionary step—where your growth lies. It's motivated by a sense of "divine discontent," wanting something beyond your current experience. A true spiritual approach maintains a balance of vertical and horizontal alignments. Horizontally, you reach out and connect with individuals, groups and humanity as a whole. Vertically, you align with your higher self or soul, to God Immanent (the presence of Spirit within you) as well as to God Transcendent (the Creator beyond you). You feel a flow of energy connecting you to these higher states of awareness. You can also align with the kingdoms of nature below, feeling connected to the mineral, plant and animal kingdoms, as we are all part of the One Life.

Too much of a vertical approach can lead to neglect of human relationships and to separatism, isolation or arrogance. Too much of a horizontal approach can lead to being absorbed in conventional thoughts or habits and being impacted too easily by others' thoughts and actions.

Right Human Relations is a keynote of the New World. It helps us recognize others as unique human beings who share a fundamental human identity with us and so need to be treated with respect and dignity. It is the Golden Rule, "Do unto others as you would have them do unto you."

Good Relationships with others begin with a good relationship with yourself. If you harbor hidden self-criticism or self-hate, you will bring the same critical or hateful energy into your relationships with others. As you transform yourself and no longer project your internal issues onto others, you can create good relationships and draw forth the highest in others.

The quality of the inner note you sound—what you actually embody in your inner being—determines what you attract into your life. Like attracts like. As we practice right human relations in our families, our neighborhoods, our communities and our nations, we create lasting peace on Earth.

Your consciousness expands as your sense of identity expands. The frequency of your vibrations increases as you move from identification and concern with yourself alone, to your family, to your community, to your nation, to your planet and beyond.

Goodwill helps you express a benevolent disposition toward others and all life. The practice of goodwill creates a sense of civility and a positive regard for other people. It nourishes the spirit of understanding, which fosters cooperation. Compassion, generosity and forgiveness are expressions of goodwill. Identifying with the good of another person or with a purpose greater than yourself develops goodwill.

Goodwill can function as a harmonizing energy and a saving force. It is an atmospheric conditioner, setting a positive vibrational field for accomplishing constructive goals. Goodwill creates a loving environment of respectful relationships that can transform difficult situations. Goodwill provides a guide for conduct in a wide variety of situations, eventually evolving into the active will-to-good and alignment with divine will.

Group Endeavor, a group conscious, collaborative approach, is a signature note of the New World. It helps us move beyond an emphasis on individual spiritual development to an emphasis on the spiritual development of groups. Group work is primarily energy work—learning to absorb, share, circulate and distribute energy from higher spiritual levels through the group and out to the world through some form of service.

Groups in the New World are gathered around ideas, rather than around charismatic people. Top-down organizational approaches and authoritarian methods are becoming increasingly dysfunctional today. To transform these old patterns, training and practice in the new methods of group consciousness and cooperative work are under way in many organizations around the world.

Unanimity is the principle of identity with others. It is a subjective union of purpose with others that is recognized in your heart. It is a cohering force that can be illuminated by your higher mind. Groups in the future will be held together by an inner, united purpose and aspiration rather than by outer, enforced rules.

The word *unanimity* comes from "uni," meaning "one," and "anima," meaning "soul." So it means "oneness of soul." Unanimity is distinct from *uniformity,* which means oneness of form, having the same form or an imposed outer unity. Unanimity is freely chosen and never imposed; it is experienced

84

on an inner, soul level. A group operating from this principle may be widely diverse in its membership—different races, religions and nationalities—yet have a powerful inner core of fiery purpose that enables it to accomplish the seemingly impossible.

Recognizing Consciousness as the Causal Factor

Consciousness, not matter, is the creative source of all reality. A key element of the New World is recognizing consciousness as the causal factor. Centuries ago, the Buddha taught, "With our thoughts, we create the world," and Christ said, "As a man thinketh in his heart, so he is." We see things, not as they are, but as *we* are. The world we see around us is what our thoughts have created. If we don't like what we see, we need to change our thinking.

To create a healthy world, we need healthy minds. Energy follows thought. You direct energy toward whatever you think about, and this focused energy, combined with your emotional desires and vital energy, gives thought the power to manifest in the world. Thought is the basic building process of the universe. With each new thought, you help create the world anew.

However, it's not just thought that creates. Your feelings and subconscious desires create as well, and you have to make sure that your thoughts and affirmations aren't trying to create one thing while your feelings and subconscious desires are undermining it.

We as humans have the incredible power for good or evil. Each moment, we are collectively creating our future as humanity—right now, even as you read this. What are you choosing to create? You can work more powerfully on spiritual and causal levels with ideas, rather than endlessly wrestling with their effects.

Scientific research by Werner Heisenberg has shown that the act of observation alters what is observed. Through what physicists, such as Dr. Rainer Blatt and David Wineland, call "quantum entanglement," particles can influence one another instantaneously despite being separated by distance. All matter in the universe is constantly interacting in the "unified field" or "zero point field."

Dr. Dean Radin's psi experiments have proven how "entangled" minds affect each other at a distance. In his book, *Entangled Minds*, Dr. Radin shows how change in one person's brain is instantly correlated with an identical shift in another person's brain, even when the people are separated by considerable distance. Actions can occur in this nonlocal way because we live in an interconnected universe. Everything is alive, and everything is related.

Dr. Candace Pert, formerly with the National Institute of Mental Health, reports on research in psychoneuroimmunology in her groundbreaking *Molecules of Emotion* and proves that neuropeptides are the link between mind and body. In his book, *The Hidden Messages in Water*, Dr. Masaru Emoto documents research on the effect of thoughts on water molecules, which make up most of the mass of our physical bodies. Thus, his research illustrates how we can create healthier bodies through our thoughts.

Our thoughts and perceptions affect our cells and shape our biology, as scientists such as Bruce Lipton are discovering in the new science of epigenetics. At the same time, environmental signals modify and fine-tune our genes through the actions of regulatory proteins. These genetic changes are passed down to future generations. As we change our consciousness and create more positive, healthy environments to live in—such as described   in this book — it will affect who we are today, and who our children's children become. This gives me great hope for our future. The next step is studying how our collective thoughts affect our collective social health.

Observing the long history of humanity, we see that changes in consciousness have resulted in evolutionary shifts and major social and political changes. When enough people began changing their consciousness about the morality of slavery, laws began to change. When enough people began recognizing their connection to one another across borders, international organizations were created. When enough people began developing real compassion, organized philanthropy was established to help the less fortunate.

Today an evolutionary priority is to elevate human consciousness from the waters of the emotional plane to the fire of the mental plane. Humanity as a whole is focused emotionally at the solar plexus center or chakra, not at the heart, the center of unconditional love and compassion. Advertising, entertainment and the news media are constantly stirring up our negative emotions — fear, anger, hatred and jealousy — which is why these businesses are so lucrative. It is essential to raise human consciousness from constant emotional upheaval to the calmer and clearer perception of the mind and the world of ideas and to eventually help people integrate their minds with their intuition.

Other evolutionary priorities are teaching people how to think clearly and educating public opinion so that informed political choices can be made and wiser leaders can be elected. Enlightened public opinion that is focused and determined is the most powerful force in the world, although it is seldom used. Sound and intelligent public opinion is one of the major factors contributing to a better world.

Supporting Enlightened Leaders

As the New World unfolds, truly enlightened, courageous leaders are becoming more widely recognized and embraced. After the recent period of postmodernist deconstructionism that took delight in tearing down famous leaders, a new honoring of authentic leadership has finally emerged.

The ageless wisdom and teachers such as Alice Bailey have long predicted the emergence and public recognition of enlightened leaders in all fields of human activity. They are the visionary builders of the new civilization who will assume high office in every land by the free choice of the people, because of their proven merit, wisdom, compassion and inclusive spirit. Their deeply lived spirituality will sweeten and clarify public life.

Today enlightened leaders with authentic spiritual qualities are beginning to be recognized and supported by the public in every arena of human life—from politics and business to science and the arts. The spiritual invocation of the people calls forth these leaders and empowers them and, in turn, they empower the people, in a mutually reinforcing circle.

Recognizing enlightened leaders is honoring the principle of hierarchy—which is essentially the evolving levels of spiritual consciousness. The word *hierarchy* is from the Greek *hieros* meaning "sacred" and *arkhia* meaning "rule." It is acknowledging that although we are all equal in potential, not all of us are at the same level of actualized expression of our virtues and talents at any given moment.

We need to recognize people who are ahead of us on the evolutionary spiral from whom we can learn. Plato called them "the torchbearers of humanity." They are more advanced in wisdom, compassion, creativity and courage. They give us   the opportunity to practice humility, which can be a difficult challenge at times!

We also need to recognize people who can serve, because they haven't yet developed certain qualities and abilities that we have. They give us the opportunity to practice spiritual responsibility. Arrogance can result from not recognizing those who are more developed, but equally harmful is being too self-effacing and not accepting the responsibilities of our spiritual status, whatever it may be.

This perspective acknowledges the Great Chain of Being, the evolutionary ladder of consciousness. Recognizing our places within it is key to our spiritual unfoldment. People ahead of us on this ladder of consciousness are more fully expressing their indwelling divinity and can be seen as our role models. Each expansion of consciousness that we experience fits us to be teachers to people who have not experienced a similar expansion. There is nothing except teachers, who are also students. All of us are learners and all of us are teachers, differing only in degree of realization.

To study people who are ahead of us on the evolutionary ladder and are more enlightened is to study our future—the guarantee that evolution is real and that we will all eventually achieve what they have. These more enlightened ones are the courageous pioneers in every field who are creating change. The examples of their greatness inspire achievement in others more reliably than any other form of education. Besides these recognized leaders emerging in every field today, all religions honor their advanced spiritual teachers who have walked among us and embodied the true Spiritual Hierarchy. To Christians, they are the saints; to Jews, the just ones; to Buddhists, the bodhisattvas; to Chinese, the lohans; and to Hindus, the rishis or avatars.

The work of these truly enlightened ones has been to anchor a dynamic truth, a potent form of thought on Earth that steadily conditions human thinking over the centuries, producing new civilizations. History is the record of humanity's cyclical reaction to some inflowing divine idea, the teaching of some great master.

These enlightened ones lived on the earth as human beings, suffered and failed, as we do, until they finally attained mastery through the purifying fires of daily life— just as each of us will eventually. In a sense, they "graduated" from the lessons of Earth and transcended the boundaries of time and space.

These enlightened ones regularly evaluate humanity's spiritual progress and transmit new energies and ideas to humanity to further our evolution. They work behind the scenes to guide and inspire humanity. They never violate our free will or dominate; they only suggest and inspire.

The spiritual ideas they offer are then picked up by the intuitive, visionary leaders of humanity, who shape these ideas into scientific discoveries and into various ideals, movements and institutions to benefit humanity. Examples are the Renaissance; the Industrial Revolution; the Scientific Revolution; the American, French and Russian Revolutions; the Red Cross; and the United Nations. History is the manifestation of divinely inspired ideas that "expand the light" and overcome some impediment in human evolution, such as slavery, racism and war.

Today these enlightened ones are working steadily to inspire and uplift humanity with new ideas and plans for helping us overcome our crises. Every individual or group who works for the common good receives their blessing and assistance in the form of unseen help. It is easier today to co-create with these helpers by asking for their assistance with projects that help humanity. They will always respond, but often in ways that are not immediately recognized.

All religions expect the return of their greatest teacher to public life: Christians look for the return of Christ; Buddhists for the Maitreya; Jews for the Messiah; Muslims for the Mahdi; and Hindus for the Kalki. Could they all be expecting the same great teacher in the trappings of their own cultures and beliefs? What if this teacher appeared in a form that people of all faiths could recognize and embrace, thus ending the separateness and divisiveness among them? The united demand of humanity, the massed intent for human betterment, could precipitate this.

This great teacher may not announce himself or herself as a great master or saint, but would arouse public interest and investigation because of his or her demonstrated wisdom, compassion and leadership. If we all worked harder on embodying the spiritual teachings of our own religions, perhaps we could more easily recognize a great teacher— without needing miracles to get our attention!

Before this can occur, we as humanity have to do our part: we need to recognize the inner light within each person, establish right human relations, create a degree of peace in the world, increase economic sharing, and clean house—removing corrupt political and religious leaders. We all have a lot of work to do!

But we can each begin by creating harmonious and peaceful relationships with the people in our lives, sharing with people who are economically less fortunate and inwardly dedicating our intention to cooperate with the higher spiritual forces.

Creating Greater Transparency and Shining Light on the Darkness

Shining light on the darkness is more urgent today than ever. You may wonder if there really is a "dark side of the force" as the *Star Wars* films call it, because it often looks as if the dark side—the retrogressive, anti-evolutionary forces—has the upper hand lately, with war, terrorism, assassinations, political and corporate corruption—not to mention vampires lurking everywhere in popular culture. What about the darkness that destroys the good work people try to do and attempts to frighten people into not challenging the status quo?

To become effective practical visionaries, we must see both light and dark in ourselves and in our society. By doing so, we won't become overly optimistic or depressed, and we will know realistically what we're up against. We each have two eyes for a reason: to give us greater depth perception and wisdom so that we can see both light and darkness for what they truly are.

What is "evil" from a deeper perspective, and what is its place in the scheme of things? Evil can be defined metaphysically as an energy that is out of place or out of timing. It is an energy that persists in something that should have been outgrown.

As humans, we are responsible for our "shadows"—our own unacknowledged harmful patterns that we should have outgrown. We must eventually mature by transforming these destructive patterns and dealing with the negative effects or karma we have created. Until we stop projecting our shadows on others, we can't clearly see the reality of darkness in the world.

God can be defined as a being who knows good without needing evil as a reference point. In the mind of God, all are one. Both light and darkness have important purposes within the divine scheme of things. God gave us free will so that we can make choices between them and learn from our mistakes. Eventually, we will all progress toward a new level of consciousness in which this duality of light and darkness, as well as all dualities, will be resolved in our understanding of the oneness of life.

As the forces of light play a necessary part in the evolutionary design, so does the darkness. The purpose of darkness is to test and strengthen us. By overcoming the resistance and opposition it provides, we grow in strength, will, clarity and love. Dark, retrogressive energy tries to enslave humanity to matter—at a time when humanity should be transforming its consciousness and infusing matter with spiritual purpose. Darkness tries to focus humanity on endless consumerism, while the evolutionary goal in this cycle is spiritual development through right human relationships.

Dark forces promote separateness and selfish power with the purpose of holding back human evolution. Weak, greedy, selfish or destructive people who "sell their souls" for personal gain are used as the instruments of darkness, as told in the famous story of Dr. Faust by Goethe. However, they often masquerade as gray and hide their true darkness.

The forces of light promote wisdom, compassion and liberation. The saints and masters of every spiritual tradition are embodiments of light. The lesser-known but heroic humans who serve humanity with compassion and wisdom are also embodiments of light.

Love and altruism are absent in the darkness. They are keynotes of the light. The margin of difference is found in motivation and intention, in the underlying purpose and concrete objectives of each. The forces of darkness work to increase fear, anger, separateness and inertia among people. They try to divide and conquer, and they use half-truths and character assassination.

In recent years, the darkness has worked effectively through the media to make people constantly frightened of pandemics, terrorist bombings, anthrax, plane crashes and economic collapse. They also make us fear any changes to the system that would make it fairer but would threaten the interests of the powerful. Have you noticed how few positive stories there are in the media about solutions to these challenging issues or about all the good people who are helping others?

The darkness has created a great public relations machine through films and TV shows to give itself a better image. For example, they create stories that glorify revenge, make the bad guys seem intriguing and the good guys boring, and make vampires seem sexy to attract confused adolescents..

Light literally reveals those who hide in darkness — transparency prevents hiding. And love, joy and laughter are potent methods of dispelling darkness — especially when you call on the power of your soul and invoke the name of a great Master.

The forces of darkness have been successful at creating moral ambiguity and clouding the issues in politics, business and entertainment. It is often difficult to tell good from bad and right from wrong. However, the fundamental choice in every decision is either self-centered, materialistic values or compassionate, spiritual values and right relationships.

Although the darkness may seem to be winning at any given time, it can only delay, not stop, the outworking of the higher evolutionary plan. Part of the change that is now occurring is that light is moving into the lower material planes and bringing Spirit into matter and into practical expression in the world. This greater light is exposing what's been hidden in the darkness for years, such as risky derivatives in the world of international finance.

Free will is the prime directive for our planet. The forces of light are always present where there is support for human free will and encouragement to learn from our choices and stand in the power of our spiritual being. Wherever there is coercion, deception or manipulation of human free choice, you will find darkness behind it.

The power wielded by those who are seeking to live as souls, aligned with Spirit, is out of proportion to their numbers and to their awareness of their contribution. Those who endeavor to use spiritual energy constructively and selflessly are far more potent than they realize. Wishful thinking, hoping and pleading are not as powerful as the mental intention of a focused mind and will that are motivated by a love of humanity. Sympathy for human pain that does not produce positive action becomes a festering sore.

By taking positive action to relieve suffering and by refusing to succumb to the fear and hatred perpetrated by the darkness, we help bring light and darkness into balance. And by exploring and transforming our inner darkness and negative patterns, we bring greater light and transparency into the world. With a broader perspective of the role of light and darkness in the higher evolutionary plan, we can act more wisely and effectively to create a joyous future for humanity.

SPIRITUAL PRACTICES

How to Keep Spiritually Sane in Challenging Times

Here are some ways to keep yourself in balance and uplift your spirit amidst the difficulties of today's world:

- ❧ Spend silent time each week in nature. The nature kingdoms are already aligned with Spirit and new energy and can be very healing and vitalizing.

- ❧ Make daily contact with the elements—water, air, earth and fire—to renew your vitality. Take a shower or swim, sit in front of an open fire or candle, put your hands in the earth, let the wind caress your body and breathe deeply.

- ❧ Meditate daily to experience the joy of your soul and to receive inner guidance for your life.

- ❧ Energize your body daily with regular walks, exercises and/or yoga.

- ❧ Regularly play music that inspires your spirit.

- ❧ Dance often to free your body and open your heart.

- ❧ Bring more color into your home and your clothing to uplift your energy.

- ❧ Eat healthful, organic foods to care for your body, the temple of your spirit.

- ❧ Step into other realities and identify with other people's lives by watching good films or reading uplifting books.

- ❧ Stimulate and expand your mind by exploring new ideas at conferences and seminars.

- ❧ Travel frequently to break out of your habitual patterns and appreciate other cultures.

❦ Create a support group of good friends and share your joys and sorrows.

❦ Learn conflict resolution techniques to create more harmony in your life.

❦ Take in only small doses of the news, since it focuses primarily on the negative, but don't close your eyes to what's happening in the world.

Meditation on the Inner Light Within Your Heart

Begin by taking a few deep breaths, breathing in peace and stillness, exhaling any tensions as you relax your body ... calm your emotions ... still your mind.

Focus your attention in your heart. Visualize your heart center as a golden lotus that slowly opens, revealing a brilliant point of light and love within.

Know that this light is the presence of God or Spirit within you, the inner light, the Master of your heart. This is your deepest essence; your radiant, eternal self, your true identity.

Visualize this point of light slowly expanding, growing brighter, radiating its love and warmth until it fills your chest and stomach area ... and then flows out into your entire body ... into your emotions ... and into your mind.

Feel yourself becoming lighter, more joyful and peaceful.

See this inner radiance, the inner divinity, within each person you know ... your family ... friends ... colleagues ... neighbors. Send loving-kindness to all of them, and then send it to the whole human family.

Recognize this radiance, the inner divinity, within all forms of life who share the earth with us. Then see the whole world radiant with light.

KEY INSIGHTS TO REFLECTON

◆ There is a higher evolutionary plan behind everything unfolding in the world today.

◆ The plan's objective is to protect, nurture and finally reveal the spiritual light within all life.

◆ There is a cyclic shift under way, moving from fanatical idealism to practical, rhythmic organization.

◆ Duality and polarization are being transcended by a new unity and higher synthesis.

◆ Fusion and convergence are the leading edge in every field today as boundaries are blurring.

◆ Consciousness is being widely recognized as the causal, creative factor.

Key #3

Make Your Livelihood a Social Change Strategy

Be a Spiritual Warrior, an Innovator, a Reformer **and/or** an Exemplar

---

Each time a person stands up for an idea, or acts to improve the lot of others, or strikes out against injustice, he sends forth a tiny ripple of hope, and crossing each other from a million different centers of energy and daring, those ripples build a current that can sweep down the mightiest walls of oppression and resistance. Like it or not, we live in interesting times, and everyone here will ultimately be judged, and will ultimately judge himself, on the efforts he has contributed to building a new world society and the extent to which his ideals and goals have shaped that effect.

— Robert F. Kennedy[1]

Applying Your Values to a Field You Are Passionate About

You can make your livelihood a strategy for social change by applying your vision in a field that you're passionate about and that needs your particular gifts. Thousands of people are making a good living while creating change. There are several key strategies for change: confronting the darkness as a spiritual warrior; creating alternative institutions as a social innovator; transforming the system from within as a reformer; and living New World values wherever you are as an exemplar.

Gordon and his colleagues at the Coalition for Environmentally Responsible Economies (Ceres) made a startling discovery about social change strategies when they met with the vice presidents of many Fortune 500 companies in 1989. They were trying to convince these executives to sign the Valdez Principles (now called the Ceres Principles), a corporate code of conduct for protecting the environment that was written after the major oil spill in Valdez, Alaska.

To their surprise, Gordon and his colleagues found these oil and chemical executives to be open to signing these principles. Why? Gordon explained: "Their companies were feeling intense public pressure, catalyzed by Greenpeace activists, over contaminating pristine Alaskan fishing grounds. They were fearful that people were so outraged that they would demand significant reduction in oil and chemical production. The companies saw the activists as 'barbarians at the gate' and were too happy to negotiate with people they perceived as more reasonable—like myself and my colleagues who were wearing coats and ties and working diplomatically within the system. Or so we seemed!"

Gordon just smiled to himself. Twenty years earlier, he had been a "barbarian at the gate," demonstrating against apartheid in South Africa in front of the student union when he was editor of the University of Massachusetts' student paper. It was satisfying to see the changes under way in the years since, catalyzed by pressure from social investors who were divesting from businesses in South Africa and in nuclear energy, weapons, alcohol and tobacco. Now the environment was their key concern.

More than 50 companies eventually signed the principles, and Ceres later launched the Global Reporting Initiative, the de facto international standard used for reporting on environmental, social and economic performance by more than 1,300 corporations worldwide.

Most startling, however, was that some company executives admitted to Gordon that their children had shamed them into signing the Ceres Principles. The children had been studying the ecological crisis in school and came home asking, "Why are you destroying our planet, Dad?" No parent wants to be a villain in his or her children's eyes. Years later, the CEO of BP (now called "Beyond Petroleum") publicly admitted in an essay in *Newsweek* magazine that pressure from his children motivated him to push BP to fund renewable sources of energy.

The Interdependence of Strategies for Change

Strategies for change can become interdependent, working synergistically in mysterious ways you may not expect. In the Ceres Principles story above, three different approaches worked together to affect public opinion and create major environmental change: political activism, reforming corporations from within, and educating the younger generation about environmental crises.

Public demonstrations confronting the problem of environmental pollution received extensive media attention and led to new environmental programs in the schools, which then helped reformers within the system negotiate changes with the company executives. The demonstrators, educators and reformers embodied aspects of New World values—such as commitment, clarity and courage—which were crucial to their success.

There are at least four key strategies for creating the New World, which are all interdependent and essential.

1. **Confronting the darkness in the old world: the path of the spiritual warrior.**
2. **Creating alternative institutions: the path of the social innovator.**
3. **Transforming the system from within: the path of the reformer.**
4. **Living the values of New World wherever you are: the path of the exemplar.**

You may have been involved in any of these strategies yourself, but tomorrow you may be drawn to a different approach because you're changing and growing or because that is what is needed at the time.

Different social change strategies synergize and mutually support one another. An example is the way in which alternative institutions can prove the effectiveness of new approaches, which are later adopted by many mainstream institutions. For example, holistic health care proved the effectiveness of herbal remedies, acupuncture and homeopathy, which were later adopted by mainstream health care institutions. Thousands of customers create a market for holistic products and services, which creates pressure for change within the system, such as insurance policies supporting preventive health care because it's more cost-effective in the long run.

Likewise, customers with environmental values who buy energy-efficient cars and other products support new businesses and transform old ones. We reform the system by what we purchase and what we invest in—as well as by what we avoid buying and investing in. And according to market research, it takes only a few letters from customers complaining about a product for a corporation to respond, because corporations hate negative publicity.

Experiencing a new alternative institution, such as a spiritual community in which you learn meditation, can change the way you live your life. You might develop a daily meditation practice, for example. Experiencing a reform within a mainstream institution, such as a school at which you learn conflict resolution techniques, can also change the way you live your life. You might use these new communication skills regularly to resolve conflicts in your family.

Changing the World and Changing Yourself at the Same Time

How can you become more engaged in changing the world as a practical visionary and, at the same time, change yourself to bring more joy and compassion into your life? Many spiritual teachers say that you must first change yourself if you want to change the world. Otherwise, you'll only create more problems, even with the best of intentions, because you'll project your unresolved issues onto others. If you're more enlightened, you will embody greater love and light and thus implement wiser strategies to solve problems that arise. In fact, a highly enlightened person will do so regardless of the conditions around him or her.

Most of us need healthy political, economic and social structures to support our personal growth. If we all wait until we're fully spiritually enlightened before we create social change, the world will continue to be a mess for quite some time—not to mention the fact that millions of people will continue to suffer!

What is the solution to this seeming dilemma? It is said in the ageless wisdom that all great truths are paradoxes. You must change the world and change yourself at the same time. The two are mutually reinforcing. What you learn in one area can help you in the other. In actual practice, your spiritual growth can refine your action in the world, and your action in the world can ground your spirituality and make it increasingly practical and effective. Working on inner and outer levels at the same time is the path of the practical visionary.

Spirituality can help you leave your ego and power trips at the door so that you can truly serve the good of others. On the other hand, social action and socially conscious workplaces can provide a practical arena for applying your spiritual principles, such as compassion. You'll grow quickly because you'll receive instant feedback if you don't "walk the talk"—if your words are not congruous with your actual deeds.

As author Andrew Harvey notes in his book *The Hope for the World*, both the spiritual mystic and the political activist have shadow areas. The mystic is addicted to transcendence and escaping the world, and the activist is addicted to doing. Bringing in a balance of the opposite approach can help heal the shadow of each. It's about balancing what we have to *do* with what we have to *become*.

Having a daily spiritual practice of some kind can help bring qualities like altruism and courage into your service to offset cynicism or obsession with power. Nearly all of the innovative solutions featured in this book were pioneered by practical visionaries who have daily spiritual practices.

I'd like to share some of what I've learned in working with each of the four strategies for creating the New World and highlight examples of practical visionaries working with each strategy.

Confronting the Darkness in the Old World: The Spiritual Warrior

The journey of a spiritual warrior into the New World begins by confronting the reality of darkness—the pain, suffering and injustice in the world—and working to stop or change it. They feel a moral imperative to take an impeccable stand against evil.

In the natural world, decaying plants are removed and become compost to nurture the next cycle of new growth. Likewise, the dark, decaying aspects of the old world have to be removed and composted to nurture the growth of the New World. This lays the groundwork for other essential strategies for creating the New World, such as reforming the system from within and building alternative institutions.

My experience in confronting the darkness began when I was an activist at the University of California, Berkeley. As I was finishing my studies in political science in 1968, my safe little world was shattered. I had been working for Robert Kennedy's presidential campaign when he and Martin Luther King Jr. were gunned down. It deepened the sense of dread that I had felt about our nation when President Kennedy had been shot five years earlier. I mourned for months.

It frightened me to realize that there were darker forces moving behind the comfort of the American dream. I was forced to deal with the problem of evil in the world. My altruistic dreams, along with those of millions of other people, crashed with these assassinations, and I knew that something was dreadfully wrong yet darkly hidden in our country. I feared that if I spoke up for justice and challenged the system like Martin Luther King Jr. had, horrible things might happen to me.

Despite my fears I decided I had to stand up to the darkness of war, racism and environmental destruction. Like so many others, I marched for peace, civil rights, women's equality and environmental protection.

I knew that I was risking arrest and jeopardizing my future career, but I believed that expressing moral outrage was the right thing to do. I somehow managed to avoid arrest, despite all of the demonstrations I participated in, but I did get severely teargassed. I learned more about politics from my activism in the streets than I did from my university classes that year.

Because of my concerns about racism and attacks against black people, I joined other white students in sitting in around the clock at the offices of a black activist group to discourage attacks against the group. It was truly scary, as we expected a violent attack might happen that evening. Fortunately, our presence there made a difference and no attack came.

Thanks to all of the courageous actions of thousands of activists, the war in Vietnam was stopped, the voting age was lowered, environmental regulations were strengthened and racial and sexual equality were expanded.

Over the years, our society has greatly benefited from battles fought by those who have been willing to take personal risks to challenge darkness and to lay the groundwork for a better world.

Today there are millions of courageous activists and whistle-blowers who are confronting injustice and destruction across the globe—from abuse of women in Africa, to the wasting of rainforests in Brazil, to corrupt banking and voting fraud in the United States.

However, I learned that overcoming darkness isn't enough to create a New World. It can be very disempowering and depressing to be constantly reacting to problems, rather than being proactive and creating something better. Activists often become polarized and angry and can easily burn out and become cynical if they don't have a vision of a positive future, a supportive community, and/or a spiritual practice.

In the '60s I was totally committed to political change and confronting the darkness. It was my whole life. I was even willing to die for the cause of peace and justice—and in fact, I was totally convinced that I would die at a young age fighting for it.

Then one day in the midst of my romantic and fatalistic ideas about martyrdom, my soul suddenly whispered in my ear something I'll never forget. It stopped me cold: "It's easier to *die* for the cause than to *live* for it!"

Wow! I had never considered that. As I reflected more on it, I recognized its wisdom. I soon made an inner commitment to learn how to live for the cause.

From that experience, I realized the importance of not only valuing physical survival but also valuing a whole and balanced life as a demonstration of spiritual values. Instead of always pointing fingers at the bad things being done in business and politics, I began to look inside myself and clean up my act.

I found that embodying wisdom, joy and compassion can attract more people to a cause than desperate, risky extremism.

As I transformed myself, I also became more effective in creating the New World in the culture around me.

The spiritual warriors who have been most effective in confronting darkness and injustice in the world are usually those who embody spiritual qualities, such as vision, commitment and courage.

For example, in 1955, Rosa Parks, a black woman, quietly refused to relinquish her seat to a white man on a segregated bus in Montgomery, Alabama, so she was arrested. Outrage over her arrest sparked the subsequent community bus boycott led by Martin Luther King Jr. and resulted in the United States Supreme Court outlawing segregation on the nation's buses.

Hundreds of volunteers from the Student Nonviolent Coordinating Committee and the NAACP risked their lives to integrate lunch counters and buses in the South in the 1960s. They changed the face of history.

Betty Friedan confronted inequality and gender stereotypes in her groundbreaking book *The Feminine Mystique* and helped catalyze the women's movement when she started the National Organization for Women in 1966.

In 1985 Randy Hayes founded the Rainforest Action Network which used nonviolent direct action and hard-hitting market campaigns to stop the logging of ancient forests and endangering of ecosystems.

Aung San Suu Kyi, a prodemocracy activist, used peaceful means to confront an unjust military dictatorship in Burma and was awarded the Nobel Peace Prize in 1991 for her heroic efforts. Jim Wallis, author of *The Great Awakening* and founder of Sojourners, a global faith and justice network, led many successful coalitions of religious people to lobby Congress to help the poor. As a dedicated and inspirational activist, he helped transform the angry dialogue between liberals and conservatives on political issues by reminding people of their moral centers.

Passionate about protecting old growth forests from destruction by lumber companies, young activist Julia Butterfly Hill sat in an ancient redwood tree for more than two years to save it. She now helps young people around the world find their service through her "What's Your Tree?" initiatives.

Today young activists from around the country are confronting the looming horrors of climate change, and thousands descended on Washington, D.C., for the 2009 Power Shift Conference which demanded changes in governmental policies. Others are setting up student Web sites like One Dollar for Life and Project Give to address poverty in Nepal and in African countries.

In just hours, volunteers with the Web site *avaaz.org* organized hundreds of nonviolent rallies around the world to prevent a genocide, sent millions of e-mails to world leaders about issues such as climate change, and raised hundreds of thousands of dollars to support a protest to stop a human rights abuse and overcome poverty. These and many other courageous, unsung heroes and heroines in every nation have been essential in dispelling the darkness and paving the way for a New World.

However, if your mission is to be the spiritual warrior confronting the darkness, it's easy to get into a mindset that the weight of the world is on your shoulders and to fall into the trap of martyrdom. To avoid burnout and cynicism, it is essential to take care of yourself physically with sufficient rest and food and to renew yourself regular spiritual practices. If you want to be really effective, you need to periodically take your focus off the bad things in the world that you're fighting against and immerse yourself for a while in positive, uplifting activities and people who bring you inspiration.

Creating Alternative Institutions:
The Social Innovator

Developing alternative institutions is another essential strategy for creating the New World, and it complements the approach of confronting darkness and injustice. People need to know what can take the place of a corrupt or unjust institution or practice. They need a sense of hope and an authentic experience of something better.

Over the years, I have learned that people like to see the application of new values in a practical and authentic way. Real-life examples of the New World make it come alive. When you can see, hear and touch a living embodiment of something, it's becomes real. Many alternative institutions are like research and development centers for society, experimenting with new approaches, discarding what doesn't work and growing what does work.

My first experience with this strategy was building a spiritual/environmental community called Sirius in 1978 in Massachusetts. Gordon and I were staying at a friend's house, after we finished a nine-month successful tour around the country giving seminars on the new holistic worldview and helping people find their part in the New World, which we called "Individual and Planetary Transformation." (With many refinements, this has been the theme of our work for all of these years.) There were 86 acres of forests and gardens for sale across the street from our friend's house, and to our surprise, one morning we received clear guidance in our meditation to buy the land. Because it came from Spirit, we knew that we had to act on it. We were really excited to create this new ecovillage, and we worked hard with hundreds of volunteers to build energy-efficient, solar buildings, composting toilets, and wind generators. We grew organic vegetables and herbs and canned and dried foods for the winter.

With much recycled material, we built a large solar conference center where we can host conferences for more than 120 people. One of the large group houses we built is totally energy efficient and feeds extra energy back to the local electric grid. We used simple, sustainable designs to demonstrate straw bale and cob house building.

We wanted to demonstrate a cooperative, environmentally sustainable lifestyle that others could replicate. However, it was harder than we thought. If you've ever been to New England, you know that you have to dig up some pretty serious rocks before trying to grow gardens there! Hauling around heavy rocks was great for keeping us very grounded (literally).

Since there was only one tiny house on the land when we arrived, we had to build everything ourselves from the ground up. There were massive amounts of firewood to cut and haul inside every winter to avoid freezing in the snow. We chopped wood and carried water while hosting thousands of visitors who were attending our seminars or helping us build community houses and gardens.

Nothing beats living with people to really get to know them and deal with conflicts. We used a variety of techniques, such as clearness committees, psychosynthesis and transformational kinesiology, to transform conflicts and heal psychological problems. We had daily meditations in our sanctuary and held many spiritual ceremonies on the land, such as Sunday services, Native American sweat lodges, vision quests, sacred dances and solstice celebrations. We also offered many innovative conferences   and educational programs, such as the School of Spiritual Science and apprenticeships in solar building and organic gardening.

Gordon and I later wrote about how to develop alternative communities, visiting more than a hundred of them and interviewing their founders for our book *Builders of the Dawn* in 1985.[2] Sirius is still going strong more than 30 years later. It has become famous as a pioneer in environmental sustainability in the New England area due to stories in major newspapers. In the beginning, when we wanted to put up a windmill for producing our own energy, local officials gave us a hard time about getting a permit. But 10 years later, town officials came to Sirius to ask for help in setting up their own windmill to power the town hall. Changing entrenched attitudes takes time. Communities like ours can be seen as way stations for the new culture; anyone can visit and stay for a day, or for years.

Gordon and I were later guided to work in Washington, D.C., where we co-founded another alternative institution, The Center for Visionary Leadership, which I described earlier. It's now based in California and North Carolina and is still going strong

I also became involved with another alternative institution in Washington, D.C., The Institute for Multi-Track Diplomacy, co-founded by Ambassador John McDonald and Dr. Louise Diamond, where I served on the board for more than seven years. The Institute mediates conflicts around the world and trains clients, such as the Tibetan government in exile, in diplomatic skills and conflict resolution. This type of alternative institution interfaces with traditional "one-track diplomacies," such as governments and international agencies, and uses a whole systems, multitrack approach to conflict, bringing all parties in a conflict to the table—activists, businesses, governments, religious groups, the media, etc.

Every social problem we face today already has an effective solution pioneered by some "civil society," nonprofit group somewhere. Civil society groups represent a powerful third force beyond government and business and embody the spirit of service. In his book *Blessed Unrest*, visionary activist and entrepreneur Paul Hawken reports that there are more than a million of these groups worldwide based on his in-depth research.[3]

Hawken says that civil society is the biggest movement in the history of humanity, although it is largely unrecognized and flying under the media radar. He says that this movement is humanity's immune response to resist and heal political disease, economic infection and ecological corruption caused by ideologies. It has no center, codified beliefs or charismatic leader. Its power is based on ideas, rather than on force. Collectively, he predicts, civil society will soon be seen as the new superpower in the world.

Since government hasn't been very effective at addressing major problems such as poverty, war, violence, terrorism and environmental pollution, nonprofit organizations and citizen activist groups worldwide, such as Doctors Without Borders and Natural Resources Defense Council, have taken up the challenge. Some of these nonprofits work to shed light on social problems and confront issues directly. Others work to create innovative solutions.

Today innovative pioneers around the world have created thousands of alternative institutions, such as holistic health centers, solar energy centers and microcredit lending institutions to provide services not offered by mainstream institutions.

For example, The Rocky Mountain Institute, started by Amory and Hunter Lovins in 1982, is a cutting-edge think tank and energy demonstration center in Snowmass, Colorado, that has pioneered energy-efficient engineering, transportation and architectural techniques to enhance financial performance. The Institute also developed a strategy for hastening the shift to a clean-energy system based on hydrogen.

Kripalu Center for Yoga and Health in Stockbridge, Massachusetts, offers a healing and retreat environment and a variety of courses in wellness, bodywork, ayurvedic medicine, intuitive development, science and spirituality.

Auroville in Pondicherry, India, a nondenominational spiritual community of 2,000 people from 35 nations started in 1968, is an experiment in human unity in diversity and in the transformation of consciousness. It is researching sustainable living for human needs of the future and experimenting with new economic, educational and governance models.

Many practical visionaries are now developing and supporting local businesses as a way to energize local economies. Business Alliance for Local, Living Economies (BALLE) leverages the power of local networks and more than 20,000 entrepreneurs to build a web of economies that are accountable to stakeholders and the environment.

Today there are many new organizations started by the younger generation that use the Internet to create social change. For example, a campaign by Bright Hope International on Facebook activates young people to invite their network of friends to provide food, clothing and education to poor people around the world and connects them to organizations for spiritual and emotional support.

Over the years, many alternative institutions have become so popular that they are now the new mainstream. Holistic health began in the early 1970s as a nonprofit alternative embraced mainly by hippies, but it's now a billion-dollar industry.

But being a social innovator can be tough in the beginning. If your life mission is to start an alternative institution, you have to be prepared to face misunderstanding, outright scorn or even worse. You'll probably also face tremendous challenges in raising money to fund your work and finding suitable co-workers who are willing to volunteer or work initially for low pay.

You'll also need to continually practice detachment from your creation so that your ego is not overly identified with it. Creating some healthy distance from your organization is a crucial spiritual practice to avoid getting obsessive about your work and driving your friends and family crazy! Also crucial for your process is staying attuned spiritually and listening to your inner guidance so that you can both avoid ego traps and develop the flexibility to make course corrections when needed.

Transforming the System From Within: The Reformer

Reforming the system is a major strategy for creating the New World. It is essential that there are reformers within the system who bring in new ideas and values and transform old, dysfunctional patterns. As Jefferson said, our social institutions must continually reinvent themselves to meet the needs of changing times. There are countless committed souls working tirelessly and creatively inside mainstream institutions to catalyze needed reforms and offer innovative ideas in response to the crises of our times.

These reformers are bringing the values of the New World into every arena of human life, from business and education to science and politics. The education department at UCLA, where I did my graduate work, for example, offers experimental programs borrowed from new consciousness programs and techniques.

Transforming the system from within was my mission for 13 years when I worked in Washington, D.C. I became seriously engaged on the front lines in mainstream institutions, bringing new approaches to challenging problems such as violence, poverty, drug abuse and environmental pollution. Washington gave me an education in how power works and how new ideas can get translated into public policy.

My first experience of working within the system for serious reform was with President Clinton's Council on Sustainable Development. The council worked to build a consensus among former adversaries and recommended policies to protect both jobs and the environment. Twelve years later, many of these policies are finally being adopted by various government agencies and businesses. Working within the system takes a great deal of patience and perseverance!

My colleagues at The Center for Visionary Leadership and I worked with the U.S. Department of Housing and Urban Development (HUD) to study what works to get people off drugs, prevent violence and develop self-sufficiency in public housing developments in the poorest neighborhoods. In interviews with hundreds of people in housing developments around the country, we found that successful projects had key values in common. The values-based dimension is what created the effectiveness in each program we researched. We wrote a guidebook for HUD based on our research called *The Spirit of Success: A Guidebook to Best Practices,* which became the most popular book HUD had ever published.

I also taught courses on leadership, team building, conflict resolution and meditation to help managers and scientists at the U.S. Environmental Protection Agency and other agencies. At American University, I taught courses on Transformational

Politics, and Spirituality and Global Politics, bringing new ideas into the university's Department of Government and its School for International Service.

In my efforts to reform institutions in Washington, D.C., I learned how to temper my idealism and deal effectively with the reality of personal power trips so that I could promote innovative ideas in politics. Working inside the system is a great learning experience for idealists—I highly recommend it. It's especially helpful for learning how to communicate new ideas and values more effectively by using nonjargon, bridging language.

Today there are practical visionaries reforming the system from within in every field of work and every profession. A major arena for needed reform is business and finance, as recent economic crises have so painfully highlighted. In addition to urgent calls for new regulations and transparency in the financial industry, initiatives to transform business have been emerging in several areas: social responsibility, social investment, environmental sustainability and bringing spirituality and ethics to business decisions.

For years I have been investing in socially responsible businesses, leading training on spirituality at work and buying environmentally friendly products. I have invited visionary business leaders to speak at conferences I've organized, and I have created salons to dialogue on Business and Spirituality in Silicon Valley and Washington, D.C. I'm also a Fellow of the World Business Academy, which promotes corporate ethics and responsibility.

Today many people are finding that there's more to life—and business—than profits. Money as the bottom line is a thing of the past. In a post-Enron, post-Madoff world, values and ethics are an urgent concern. Over the past decade, socially responsible investors, consumers and shareholders have been pushing corporations to transform and align with a "triple bottom line"—honoring people, planet and profit. This triple bottom line is creating more transparency and accountability in how companies treat their employees, their community and the environment—thus embodying New World values.

Author Patricia Aburdene calls this "conscious capitalism" or "stakeholder capitalism" in her book *Megatrends 2010* and names it as one of the emerging megatrends. She notes that socially responsible corporations tend to be well managed, and great management is the best way to predict superior financial performance. Companies who have made real changes and retooled to be more energy efficient have been able to weather the economic downturn better than their competitors. To the surprise of many, the movement for social responsibility and ethics in business is slowly beginning to transform large sectors of corporate America from the inside out, despite the economic recession.

What is spirituality in business to you? Is it embodying personal values of honesty, integrity and doing quality work? Is it treating co-workers and employees well? Is it participating in spiritual study groups or using prayer, meditation or intuitive guidance at work? Or is it making a business socially responsible in how it impacts the environment, serves the community or helps create a better world? All of these can be seen as expressions of spirituality in business.

Applying spirituality in the work environment is more acceptable than talking about religion, because it's more generic and inclusive. Instead of emphasizing belief as religion often does, spirituality emphasizes how values are applied and embodied. For example, The Container Store tells employees that they are morally obligated to help customers solve problems, rather than just selling people products.

The CEO of Vermont Country Store, a popular national catalogue company, honored, instead of fired, an employee who told the truth about a company problem in a widely circulated memo. This act greatly increased morale and built a sense of trust in the company.

Are spirituality and profitability mutually exclusive? Recent research shows that bringing spiritual and socially responsible values into the workplace can lead to increased productivity and profitability, employee retention, enhanced morale, customer loyalty and brand reputation.

A study done at the University of Chicago by Professor Curtis Verschoor and published in *Management Accounting* found that companies with a defined corporate commitment to ethical principles do better financially than companies that don't make ethics a key management component.[4]

A report released by Goldman Sachs, showed that companies in six major sectors (energy, mining, steel, food, beverages and media) that are considered leaders in implementing environmental, social and governance policies have outperformed the general stock market by 25 percent since August 2005, and 72 percent of these companies have outperformed their peers over the same period.[5] Public shaming of companies, such as Nike, for using overseas sweatshops has led to major drops in their earnings.

Growing numbers of business people want their spirituality to be more than just faith and belief—they want it to be practical and applied. They want to bring their whole selves—body, mind and spirit—to work. Many business people are finding that the bottom line can be strengthened by embodying their values. They can do well by doing good.

People increasingly want to bring a greater sense of meaning and purpose into their work lives and are pressuring   their companies to align their missions with a higher purpose and deeper commitment to service—of customers and to the local community. In today's highly competitive environment, the best talent seeks out organizations that reflect their inner values and provide opportunities for personal development and community service, not just bigger salaries.

Many business people use prayer at work for a number of purposes: for guidance in decision making, to prepare for difficult situations, when they are going through a tough time or to give thanks for something good. Timberland Shoes CEO Jeffrey B. Swartz talks openly about using his prayer book and religious beliefs to guide business decisions and company policy, often consulting his rabbi. Kris Kalra, CEO of BioGenex, uses the Hindu holy text to steer his business out of trouble.

Meditation classes have been held over the years at many major corporations, such as Medtronic, Apple, Google, Yahoo!, McKinsey, IBM, Hughes Aircraft, Cisco and Raytheon. They find that meditation often improves productivity and creativity and creates more harmony in the workplace. Google, known for its search-engine services, calls its popular meditation program *Search Inside Yourself*. Started by Chade-Meng-Tan, it helps employees bring mindfulness and inner peace to work, using neuroscience research, which is attractive to its high-tech engineering employees.

Increasing numbers of businesses are being transformed through better employee policies. Southwest Airlines says that people are their most important resource, and company policy is to treat employees like family, knowing that if they are treated well, they in turn will treat customers well.

Aaron Feurenstein, CEO of Malden Mills, which produces popular Polartec fabrics, believes that people are the best asset of a company. He says that a company has an equal responsibility to its community and to itself. Since his town has high unemployment, he kept all 3,000 employees on his payroll after a major fire destroyed three out of his four factory buildings several years ago. Workers repaid his generosity by helping him rebuild, resulting in a 25 percent increase in productivity and a 66 percent drop in quality defects.

Many companies are transforming by using more environmentally sustainable practices. Whole Foods, the world's leading natural and organic foods supermarket, made the largest renewable energy purchase to offset 100 percent of its electricity use in all 180 stores. It purchased more than 458,000 megawatt hours of renewable energy credits from wind farms, resulting in the same environmental impact as taking 60,000 cars off the road or planting 90,000 acres of trees.

By reducing, reusing and recycling, Fetzer Wine has reduced its garbage by 95 percent since 1990 while doubling wine production. Fetzer uses 100 percent renewable energy, such as solar, wind and geothermal, and has switched from petroleum to biodiesel fuel, while farming its own grapes organically.

Named the greenest company in America by *Newsweek* in 2009, Hewlett-Packard has recycled 1.7 billion tons of electronic waste in the past decade and has significantly reduced packaging materials, greenhouse emissions and energy use.

The Web sites *greenbiz.com* and *sustainablebusiness.com* both provide global news, research and resources to help the rapidly growing market of green-minded professionals and companies transform environmentally and, at the same time, become more successful financially.

The movements for socially responsible business, environmentally sustainable business and Spirit in business are all hopeful signs that business, as the most powerful institution in the world today, may be transforming from within. What is emerging is a new attitude toward the workplace as a place to fulfill a deeper purpose, both personally and organizationally. As World Business Academy co-founder Willis Harman remarked many years ago, the dominant institution in any society needs to take responsibility for the whole, as the Church did in the days of the Holy Roman Empire. Today business should take this role.

Living the Values of the New World: The Exemplar

The most important thing I learned in exploring these strategies for change—whether confronting the darkness, creating alternative institutions or transforming the system from within— is that it's essential to practice living the values of the New World wherever you are, both inwardly on a spiritual level and outwardly in your lifestyle. Living your values creates true authenticity, and people crave it. When you embody your values, your energetic presence is potent and your effect on others is transforming. This is what makes the New World magnetic and attractive to others—it seems alive and bursting with possibilities.

For example, there are many conscious people where I live in the San Francisco Bay Area who are living New World values in a practical way. They embody values such as compassion, community, diversity, nonviolence, transparency and whole systems thinking. Their lifestyles have created a different atmosphere and social environment here, even though we're all living in the context of the old world that still controls much of the resources.

This environment has created a resonant field that's magnetic to others with similar values. Far-sighted pioneers, exploring various spiritual practices, were drawn here years ago and created many changes in local culture and politics. Hundreds of acres of beautiful mountains and wetlands have been preserved as public open space, for example, by the earlier work of persistent and hard-working activists.

The conscious emphasis here on creating good relationships seems to affect most of the people I meet—from shopkeepers to bus drivers to and plumbers. There is a surprisingly common willingness to be helpful and kind. Many people here have made choices to live more simply, consuming less material stuff and thus reducing the number of hours they have to work.

Like my husband and I, many local people buy fresh, organic produce and wild-caught fish from a flourishing local farmers market and a successful whole foods market. We even grow vegetables in our backyard. Our health needs are covered by a local chiropractor and by a medical doctor who uses homeopathic and herbal remedies at a holistic, preventive medical clinic.

Most of our personal livelihood comes from people with similar values who attend our seminars, hire us as consultants and coaches, buy our books and CDs or donate to our nonprofit. We invest some of our savings in socially responsible New World businesses, such as sustainable technologies and organic foods.

For entertainment, we often attend concerts with fusion and world beat musicians and dance with friends at "barefoot boogies" and circle dances—community dances that are smoke and alcohol free. I organize monthly spiritual film gatherings with a community of local friends who like to watch DVDs together and discuss the spiritual dimensions of the films.

We subscribe to a number of magazines that feature positive solutions to problems and hopeful visions of the future, and we read books exploring the frontiers of consciousness in many fields. We also participate in online conferences and teleconferences with inspirational leaders who address the whole person—

body, mind and spirit—and the whole planet. We are members and supporters of dozens of nonprofit organizations co-creating the New World by promoting solutions to global problems.

Like many people here, we've found that a daily meditation practice helps us develop a greater sense of inner peace and connect with a clear source of inspiration and guidance for our lives. We host monthly meditations in our home and offer guided meditations on national teleconferences. We attend spiritual seminars and conferences to learn new techniques for personal growth and resolving conflicts, and we have found an effective approach for transforming our subconscious issues, which Gordon also uses with his consulting clients.

Anyone can live the values of the New World right now; it begins inwardly with a willingness to open your mind and change your consciousness. The more people discover the New World within themselves, the more they will create New World initiatives in the culture around them. Most of the activities and services I've described are publicly available in any moderate-sized city in the United States, Europe and other countries. All of the businesses and services expressing New World values in my town and elsewhere have grown from scratch in less than 30 years.

But as I said earlier, you might hardly notice any of this New World in the society around you unless you've discovered the New World within yourself and worked on transforming your consciousness through spiritual practices. If you become an active participant in the creation of this New World, your thoughts and activities will help energize and nurture it.

There is a unique way that each of us can make our livelihood a social change strategy and play a part in the New World— whether it's confronting the darkness in some arena, starting a new organization or business, reforming an already existing one, or embodying New World values wherever we are.

Hope for the Future

I am optimistic about the future, because I'm old enough to have been involved in early efforts for social change that created huge impacts on the world, such as the civil rights movement, the peace movement, the women's movement, the environmental movement, the holistic health movement, the socially responsible business movement and the social investment movement.

The best part about all of my efforts is knowing that I'm not alone in holding a positive vision of the future. Over the past 30 years I have traveled and lectured in many countries around the world and met with literally thousands of people who are experiencing a new culture and civilization growing right in the midst of the old. These practical visionaries have given me a wider perspective and a sense of hope for the future—a tangible experience of our interconnection as a human family and our endless capacity to create solutions to any problems that emerge.

SPIRITUAL PRACTICES

Personal Spiritual Practices for Creating Change Within Organizations

If you want to be more effective in creating change within an organization, welcome the opportunity to more fully embody your spiritual values in each moment.

- Begin by leaving your ego at the door so that you are detached from praise or reward and are not overly identified with any particular outcome.

- Purify your motives for creating the change you're committed to so that you can do it from a place of true helpfulness and service, rather than ambition.

- Observe with detachment. See clearly and objectively what is going on, rather than getting hooked emotionally or taking criticism personally.

- Communicate more clearly by using simple, bridging language rather than jargon, and people will pay more attention.

- Be respectful and appreciative of others, and be a good listener so others feel heard.

- Practice honesty, transparency and integrity in all of your dealings with people. Not only is it more ethical, but it also makes life a lot less complicated.

- Avoid self-righteousness and demonizing people with different opinions, and instead look for common ground with mutual benefits.

- Be courageous in standing up for what you believe in, speaking truth to power when necessary, but also be wise and realistic in knowing what you can accomplish.

- Take initiative and leadership, rather than passively hoping that someone else will do what you see needs to be done.

- Be flexible, open and flowing so that you can respond quickly and creatively when opportunities for change arise.

- Stay attuned to your inner spiritual guidance and "coincidence" so that you can be guided to do what is needed at any given time.

- Be fully present in each moment, letting go of old thoughts and opinions. Life may surprise you!

Spiritual Techniques for Energizing the Workplace

Here are some approaches that managers and staff of various companies around the country are using to make their companies better places to work:

Purpose and Values

- Help people align with a higher purpose and service to others to provide a deeper sense of meaning and fulfillment in their work.

- Engage people in creating a consensus around what values are shared, and create a mission statement together.

Inner Work

- Design quiet time for creativity, meditation and/or prayer on a daily basis, and if possible, set aside a special room for this.

- Encourage spiritual study groups and discussion groups in the workplace during lunch breaks.

- Reflect, write about and/or discuss lessons learned from difficult experiences.

- Develop a process for eliciting people's intuition and inner guidance in decision making.

- Create positive affirmations, and display them prominently in the workplace to inspire people.

Relationships and Community Building

- Show frequent appreciation and gratitude toward co-workers.

- Structure work to draw out the best in people so that they are fully engaged.

- Actively elicit people's concerns and creative ideas.

- Model telling the truth to free up energy and build trust.

- Pay employees to do volunteer work in the local community.

- Invite input from key stakeholders in the community.

- Mentor new employees and partner them with experienced ones.

- Hold regular organizational retreats to build deeper connections.

Creativity and Inspiration

- Focus on what's positive and on solutions rather than problems.

- Encourage humor, playfulness and role-playing.

- Invite people to post inspirational messages and pictures in the workspace.

- Use visioning exercises and imaging of future scenarios.

Stress Reduction

- Encourage people to take regular three-minute breaks for deep breathing and relaxation.

- Create a healing environment with softer lighting, plants, pictures, harmonious sounds and pleasant fragrances.

KEY INSIGHTS TO REFLECT ON

◆ We can change ourselves and change the world at the same time because these changes can be mutually reinforcing.

◆ Confronting the darkness, creating alternative institutions and reforming the system are all interdependent strategies for change.

◆ Most important, however, is embodying the values of the New World wherever you are because you will help create a magnetic environment.

◆ The new triple bottom line of "people, planet, and profit" is transforming the marketplace.

◆ Bringing spiritual and ethical values into your workplace helps transform it.

◆ Socially responsible business practices improve productivity and bring financial rewards.

The Practical Visionary

Key #4

Invoke the Magic of Your Soul

Explore the New World Within You and Make Friends With
Your Subconscious

Be a Columbus to whole new continents and worlds within

you, opening new channels, not of trade, but of thought.

— Henry David Thoreau[1]

Having a Consciousness Makeover

To be a practical visionary, it is most essential that you call on the wisdom of your soul, or superconscious, and at the same time, develop a collaborative relationship among your superconscious, conscious and subconscious parts. People are unsuccessful in manifesting their vision because they neglect their superconscious, their subconscious or both.

When I began my search for enlightenment more than 30 years ago, I had a significant dream that helped my development as a practical visionary. I remember the dream clearly and cherish its wisdom, although I'm still trying to embody what I learned. It has become a cornerstone of my spiritual path, because it helped me dissolve the duality in my spiritual perspective between my ideals and everyday life. It helped me experience a sense of unity between my inner, subjective life and the world around me.

In the dream, I went to hear a lecture by a spiritual teacher whom I admired and had heard speak many times in real life. There were hundreds of students attending his talk. They all saw him as a great guru and brought him flowers and fruit. He gave a wonderful and inspiring lecture, full of deep, spiritual truths.

When I blinked, the scene suddenly shifted, and I traveled into the future. I knew somehow that I had advanced spiritually, and I was now attending another spiritual lecture. This time it was held in an unusual, futuristic building. I noticed that there were few students in attendance compared to the previous lecture.

I realized that it was because this time the teacher was a black man. Racial prejudice kept people from hearing the same deep, spiritual truths from him as from the white man. I was told inwardly that any type of prejudice could prevent someone from hearing great truths. Some people couldn't hear truths from a woman or from someone of a different religion, for example. Since I was more spiritually advanced in the dream, I could accept teachings from an authentic teacher, regardless of how he or she appeared.

Remarkably, the scene shifted again, and I knew that I had advanced even further on the spiritual path. Now I saw myself standing in the kitchen of an ordinary house, but there were hardly any other students left. I knew that I was there for the same profound spiritual teachings, but where was the teacher?

The realization suddenly hit me: the spiritual lesson at that moment was washing the dirty dishes in the sink and doing it with love! It was about noticing what was right in front of me and doing what needed to be done in the best way possible. This dream was my first lesson in being a practical visionary. I had to become more aware of my subconscious and my resistance to doing mundane things if I wanted to learn the deeper spiritual mysteries.

I don't like doing dishes very much. So this teaching made me feel sick to my stomach and I had to lie down. I just couldn't believe it! Could this really be the advanced teaching? I felt a lot of resistance. Yes, I was told in my dream that the more-advanced approach is about finding your inner Teacher rather than always looking for an external teacher or teaching. It reminded me of what the Buddha said: "Look within: thou art the Buddha. Be a lamp unto your own feet."

I realized that your true Teacher is your soul, the divine Presence within you. In your soul, you will find the most reliable source of guidance for your life. When you work with your inner Teacher, you learn to do everything with love, even mundane tasks like washing the dishes. You learn to be more fully present, awake and aware in each moment.

The dream reminded me of the ancient wisdom of the East: Before enlightenment, chop wood, carry water. After enlightenment, chop wood, carry water. However, now you do everything with love and greater awareness and consciousness. You are more fully present in the moment.

Spirituality is a part of everyday life, and there's no real separation between Spirit and matter. Eventually you transcend the duality of your everyday self and your spiritual ideal. You become the ideal; you embody it. You no longer search for the way; you become the way, the spiritual path itself. This is the goal of the practical visionary.

Discovering the New World within you is about connecting with your soul, or inner Teacher, and integrating your soul with all dimensions of your being. Living from this deeper reality will transform how you perceive the world around you, and amazing things will be revealed. You'll begin perceiving the New World growing everywhere and wonder how you could have missed it before. In truth, there is no separation between the inner and outer worlds. The entire world as you know it exists within your own instruments of perception. When your lenses are clean and clear, you see the world in a new and beautiful light.

Although everyone is unconsciously on a spiritual path of learning and growth, more and more people are waking up and realizing that life is really all about spiritual growth. By consciously embracing the spiritual path, we grow more rapidly.

The Science of Transformation

Spiritual isn't something unattainable and removed from Earth. A broader and wiser definition of the word spiritual is that which represents your next step in evolutionary development. It is the embodiment of the vision lying beyond your present point of attainment, urging you toward a further goal. What might be spiritual for me, because it's my next step in development, may not be spiritual for you—because you've already achieved my goal or because my goal is beyond your current next step.

I've found that spirituality includes both vertical and horizontal aspects. It includes a vertical channel that connects me to my soul or higher self—Spirit, God, Universe, Ground of Being, Life Force or whatever name you use—which is part of the transcendent reality. This vertical channel also connects me down to my subconscious, and to the earth and the kingdoms of nature. To me, the earth and all of life are sacred, and my connection to the earth keeps my spirituality grounded.

I also see spirituality along a horizontal line of outreach—our relationships to family, friends, co-workers and humanity as a whole. The horizontal line is where we often find the greatest challenges in embodying our spiritual beliefs. If we think we're being spiritual because we pray or meditate a lot but we don't treat people or nature well, then our spirituality is shallow. The vertical and horizontal dimensions need to be balanced for true spiritual development.

The key for rapid development is to balance study, meditation and service. Study is needed to understand key spiritual principles. Meditation is helpful for going beyond your mind, experiencing the presence of Spirit within you and receiving a clear sense of guidance for your life. Service is most essential because you need to apply the spiritual principles you've studied to make them real in your life. You'll receive instant feedback about how well you're doing. In some Christian traditions it's said that, "Faith without works is dead." You can certainly see the problems created in the world by people who believe that faith alone is sufficient and think that it's okay to be mean to their neighbors!

The Soul: Your Essence and True Identity

Have you ever experienced an unexpected glimpse of something new and wonderful inside yourself? Have you ever felt a fleeting moment when you suddenly found yourself in a timeless space of boundless joy and tremendous well-being? Or have you felt a sense of vast spaciousness, luminous clarity and oneness with all life?

Have you ever had a peak experience—a profound sense of compassion and connection to everyone or a deeper understanding of the meaning of life and your higher purpose?

Have you ever felt as though you'd awakened to a radiant, hopeful future for humanity and a whole new life ahead of you? Have you heard the whisper of the eternal?

These experiences are tastes of the New World within you, the realm of your soul, your higher self, the realm of the good, the beautiful and the true. It's a world of timelessness, the eternal now. It's a world of profound harmony and optimism, singing of infinite possibilities to explore.

Imagine meeting an incredibly wise and radiant being who looks directly into your eyes with such overwhelming compassion and wisdom that you experience total bliss. But then it suddenly dawns on you: This is your true self—your soul! You can't believe how uplifted, peaceful and joyful you feel. Time seems to expand into eternity.

The first time I experienced this incredibly wise part of myself during a meditation, I felt like I'd finally come home. It was liberating and joyful. It reminded me of the end of *The Wizard of Oz* when Dorothy suddenly wakes up and realizes that everything she was looking for was right there in her home all along! To find your soul, you must find the unique expression of God or Spirit that is *your* expression of divinity.

Moments of heartfelt kindness, courageous daring and deep inner peace are experiences of your soul—your deepest essence, your highest self—who you truly are. Forgiving someone who has harmed you, inspiring others with deep insight, and bravely doing what is right, but not popular, are expressions of your soul. Your soul embodies not just loving compassion but also purposeful will and clear-sighted intelligence.

Your soul is the key to the New World within you. Experiencing this inner New World helps light up more circuits in your brain and awakens you to the outer New World unfolding in the surrounding culture. It is like the rising sun of a new dawn revealing a previously dark landscape. A whole New World suddenly lights up all around you. It's been there all along, but it becomes much more visible and vibrant when you live more fully in the reality of your soul.

As you develop spiritually, you raise your frequency—the rate at which your physical, emotional and mental bodies vibrate—to the frequency of your soul. Each of your bodies has a higher correspondence in the soul. Your personal will and physical action eventually align with the higher spiritual will of your soul. Your emotions become purified and calm as your heart opens and expresses your soul's unconditional love and intuition. Your concrete, rational mind opens to the higher mind of your soul and abstract, whole systems thinking develops.

The higher and finer vibration of your soul brings you a clearer vision and puts you in resonance with the current unfolding of the higher evolutionary plan for our world. It's all about resonance. Your soul embodies the forward thrust of evolution.

Your soul is the observer within you, the higher part of you that watches the world and your life with compassionate detachment. It is the part of you that is willing to serve and help others.

In scientific terms, the soul is nonlocal—meaning that it has no location in time and space, unlike your local skin-encapsulated personality. Your soul is essentially energy vibrating at a higher frequency than your personality. When you study the soul, you are studying the science of energy.

Your soul is the mediating principle of consciousness, linking the higher, spiritual world with the material world and resolving the seeming duality of Spirit and matter. Opening to your soul is the key to resolving all other dualities.

Your soul reveals a grand design—a magnificent evolutionary plan unfolding behind the scenes today despite escalating crises. As your frequency changes with your soul's unfolding, you can see more clearly your part in this evolutionary plan. You discover more skillful means of expressing your higher purpose and making your contribution as a practical visionary.

Your soul is a compass for your evolutionary journey; it is a source of reliable guidance for your life that is always available when you request it. Your soul embodies not just loving compassion but also purposeful will and clear-sighted intelligence. The signature of your soul is a balanced expression of love (heart), light (intelligence) and will. Practical visionaries embody this balance.

The soul is referred to as the "causal body" in the ageless wisdom teachings because it is the ultimate cause and director of spiritual growth in your life. Every spiritual tradition honors a source of innate wisdom and power within you. In the Christian tradition, the Bible says that "the kingdom of heaven is within you." In the Jewish tradition, the soul is sometimes referred to as "the vital principle." In the Hindu tradition, it's called the "atma" or "self." In the Buddhist tradition, it's referred to as "the Buddha nature" or "the mind of enlightenment (bodhichitta)." As you begin to understand your soul, the microcosm, so you will begin to understand the mystery of the universe, the macrocosm.

Plato saw the soul as the mediator between your higher and lower natures, between your immortal and mortal selves. He believed that the soul precedes form and is the life principle animating your physical body, which cannot exist without it. "There is an eye of the soul which is more precious than 10,000 bodily eyes, for by it alone is truth seen," he wrote in *The Republic*.[2]

Physicist Gary Zukav notes in *The Seat of the Soul* that the goal of your evolutionary journey is to align your personality with your soul, the part of you that is immortal.

In *Your Sacred Self*, best-selling author Dr. Wayne Dyer calls the soul "your sacred self," a divine energy that permeates your entire being. He says that the inner aspect of this energy is dormant but that it can be awakened when you discover your sacred self and let it guide your life.

Waking up spiritually is likely to end your world, as Adyashanti notes, and to awaken you to what he calls "a new world, a state of oneness."

Ken Wilber notes in *The Integral Vision* that your soul can be understood both as a *state* of consciousness—a fleeting experience of wisdom, compassion and oneness with all life—and a *stage* of consciousness—a sustained level of spiritual development beyond the self-centered stage. There are practices and techniques to expand a glimpse of the soul to a regular, ongoing experience of the soul.

Wilber says that you can develop from an egocentric stage to an ethnocentric stage (concern with only your own family, your community and your nation) to a world-centric stage (a post conventional concern for all humanity and all sentient life) to even a cosmic-centric stage (an authentic sense of oneness with the entire universe as embodied by the great spiritual masters). Your awareness moves from "me" to "us" to "all of us." Each stage transcends and includes the previous stages. The more you experience authentic higher states of consciousness, the faster you will grow and develop through any of the stages of consciousness.[3]

You are a spiritual being having a human experience, rather than the other way around. Although you might initially think that you *have* a soul, it is more accurate to say that you *are* a soul who has a personality. This personality is your instrument of expression in the world.

In any given lifetime, your personality is only a small portion of your larger identity as a soul. For ages your personality tries to run your life on its own but eventually discovers that it's not very successful at creating a lasting sense of peace or happiness.

Your personality is often unaware of the higher truths about how life works. Therefore, it creates pain and suffering through unwise choices. Once your personality realizes that it is creating suffering and recognizes the need for greater wisdom and understanding, it will invoke your soul's help. From then on, spiritual evolution is about integrating your soul and your personality.

We know that the human body is the endpoint of the evolution of form. However, evolution doesn't end with the perfection of physical form. Consciousness continues to evolve. Soul expression is the next evolutionary stage in consciousness for most of humanity. The stage beyond soul-personality integration is the nondual state of identity as pure being.

Although some popular modern writers see the soul primarily as your deep unconscious or as some fragile thing that your personality needs to care for, the truth is quite the opposite. It is your soul that cares for your personality—if it is invited to do so. Are you sending an invitation yet?

The Soul as Link Between Spirit and Matter

Your soul is neither Spirit nor matter; it is the relationship between them. Your soul is the energetic, connecting link between Spirit and matter, between God and your human personality, between the ultimate, formless Ground of Being and your individual self. Your soul is the bridging principle of consciousness. Being in soul consciousness helps you transcend the seeming duality of Spirit and matter and experience a higher synthesis.

Spirit and matter aren't really separate. They are merely different frequencies along the same spectrum of energy. Spirit is matter at its highest frequency; matter is Spirit at its lowest frequency.

Your soul is the attractive force that holds all forms together so that the life of God, or Spirit, may express through them. Technically, your soul is a unit of light colored by a particular ray vibration.

Your soul is anchored in two places in your body: the consciousness thread is anchored at the top of your head, and the life thread is anchored in your heart. You can sense the energetic presence of your soul most easily at the top of your head and in your heart.

When you sleep, the consciousness thread in your head withdraws and an aspect of it travels to other dimensions that you experience as dreams. Near-death experiences occur when the consciousness thread withdraws dramatically but the life thread remains connected in the heart. Actual death results when both the consciousness thread and the life thread are permanently severed.

Your personality is an extension of a portion of your soul into form—physical, emotional and mental substance. Therefore, your personality seems separate from others in time and space. Spiritual growth builds a bridge of consciousness between your personality and your soul, which is much greater and more potent and inclusive than your personality.

Your soul is the observer or witness, the higher part of you that watches your life with detachment. It watches your life as if it were a movie, with your personality playing the star. Is your life movie a tragic melodrama, a comedy or perhaps a thriller?

Your soul draws to you tailor-made experiences and lessons for your spiritual growth—as you are ready for them—leading to progressive growth and unfoldment. Crises, such as illness and accidents, may be calling cards from your soul, suggesting that you need to reflect deeply on your life and your purpose and perhaps make some changes. Have you had any calling cards like this?

I received one when I landed in the hospital years ago with a major illness and almost died. It provided the impetus for a major re-evaluation of my life. I realized that I'd been repressing emotional parts of myself that needed expression, and they were trying to get my attention in a rather dramatic way through my illness. I had a powerful dream in which my soul reminded me to pause throughout the day and become fully aware in the present moment, noticing the beauty of a flower, a person's smile or a breeze swaying the trees.

Qualities of the Soul

The only difference between a saint or master and the rest of us is that a saint expresses his or her soul more of the time. Most of us express mainly our personalities and only occasionally our souls.

Being in soul consciousness is experiencing a sense of timelessness, of being in the eternal now. Christians call it "practicing the presence of God," and Buddhists call it "nirvana." When you're in soul consciousness, you feel expansive and liberated, a sense of pure being, without having to do anything. You often help and heal others just through the qualities that you radiate—joy, grace, strength and inner peace. Sometimes when I feel emotionally upset or tired, I am uplifted by interacting with someone who is radiant with soul energy.

Your soul deals with the world of causes, not effects. It is aware of the higher evolutionary plan and strives to contribute to that larger purpose. For example, your soul may realize that peace on Earth is a part of this plan. So you work on first healing any conflicts within yourself to be sure that all parts of you are in loving harmony. This harmony then helps resolve your conflicts with others—in your family, workplace and local community—and eventually contributes to peace among nations.

Your soul is also the source of the clearest and most reliable guidance for your life; it holds the spiritual blueprint for your life. Through meditation and prayer, you can ask your soul for help in making important decisions. Meditating on a question and asking for guidance from my soul has been an important spiritual practice for me.

The soul within you is the source of your restless searching; it constantly pushes you to grow spiritually. Have you noticed that shortly after fulfilling a desire or accomplishing a goal, you can't just rest on your laurels and feel satisfied? You feel restless again and seek another goal or another experience that you hope will be more fulfilling. This constant searching is actually your soul pushing you from within to expand yourself and grow in new ways, to keep evolving spiritually. Your soul will not let you settle for anything less than fully realizing that you are a spiritual being, here on earth to make a contribution to life.

Your soul is a magnet that draws to you all of the good to which you can respond, such as people, resources and opportunities.

What Is Your Personality?

What gives you the unique quality we call personality? What makes you who you are? Did you know that you are a multidimensional being?

According to modern psychology, once you have worked through your biggest psychological complexes or issues, such as pain from past experiences, general unhappiness or blockages in your ability to realize your desires, you are a whole person. At that point, you are free to go out into the world and achieve whatever you want, such as becoming a billionaire, a rock star or a famous athlete.

But in many cases, people find that even after 10 years of therapy, they don't seem to be resolving their issues and they are still limited by inner conflicts, fears or repetitive, self-destructive patterns. Modern psychologists often don't know what to do, frequently resorting to prescribing a variety of pharmaceuticals, hoping for a medicinal cure.

One of the reasons for this dilemma is that most psychologists have too simplistic a view of the human being and   don't recognize that the human personality is much more complex and includes transpersonal, spiritual dimensions. Each of us is a multi-dimensional being with layered levels of simultaneous functioning, a composite of three interpenetrating bodies—a physical/etheric body, an emotional body and a mental body.

When these three bodies are integrated and moving toward a common purpose, they create a unique identity that we call the personality. A healthy personality acts like a musical conductor for your life, inviting various expressions—mental, emotional or physical—when needed for a specific purpose or to complement each other so that they can produce a harmonious melody.

Once your personality is integrated, it is ready to begin invoking the soul. You need to have some degree of an integrated personality to be a practical visionary, or you'll have trouble being inspired and effective.

Your personality is not integrated if there's no functioning conductor and your emotions are going in one direction while your mind or body goes in another direction. If your personality isn't integrated then your personality is divided and your soul cannot work effectively through it. For example, if your mind is insisting that you have a career as a manager who must sit in an office all day, but your body can't sit still and you're feeling emotionally bored or angry most of the time, you won't be very effective.

Your soul is like the sun. It is always present, but it may be hidden behind the clouds of an unintegrated personality, where you can't experience its warmth, radiance and power. You have got to dispel the clouds and let the sun shine in.

Your Physical/Etheric Body

The first aspect of your personality is your physical body—the dense, material form you use to move through the physical world. Did you know that you also have an etheric body, an energy body that is like a double or a template of your physical body? Another name for it is the "life force body," and it is composed of energies slightly less dense than the physical, that create a circulating system of life force flowing throughout your physical body. The etheric body gives you energy and vitality and keeps you healthy.

The rate of vibration of your etheric body reflects the development of your soul. The will of your physical/etheric body eventually becomes aligned with the higher will and purpose of your soul.

Your etheric body is the network of flowing energy called meridians. Where there are major intersections of these energy flows, vortices called *chakras*, or centers, are formed. Acupuncturists and other energy healers use meridians to stimulate chakras to remove blockages and balance energy circulation throughout the body.

Many people can see the etheric energy of various life forms, which radiates as a subtle, white glow around plants, animals and people. You can see this by unfocusing your eyes and staring at a person against a dark background or at a tree against a blue sky. Etheric energy emanates from them and is a part of the web of life that spans the entire universe.

It is important that you love and honor your physical body, regardless of its appearance and perceived imperfections. It's the temple of your Spirit, and it needs to be kept healthy, clean and rested, with good food and adequate exercise. It is also essential to appreciate your body for all that it does for you—like a good horse that carries its rider from place to place.

Your Emotional Body

The next more subtle body of your personality is your emotional or astral body—your feelings. This body interpenetrates your physical/etheric body. Your emotional body radiates as an ovoid-shaped aura from your physical body. The aura of an undeveloped person can be seen extending a fraction of an inch from his or her body. The aura of a spiritually advanced person can radiate for miles.

The astral body is composed of a finer-grade than the physical/etheric body. To people who can perceive it, it appears similar in form to the physical body and radiates an aura of changing colors. The emotional body perceives and expresses a wide range of human feelings, passions and desires. Next time you're yelling in anger at someone, remember that it's only your emotional body, not all of you, that is expressing.

Each feeling results in a change in the aura that can be observed by people with inner vision. They can observe the dull brown and gray of selfishness, the red and black of anger and the pure violet and gold of spiritual love and aspiration. An emotional pattern of ongoing self-hate, guilt or anger can have severe effects and eventually cause damage to your physical body.

The aura's brilliance and definiteness of outline become stronger as the evolution of the individual proceeds. This astral body is what many psychics who read auras are registering. However, since the psychic perceives the aura of another person through his or her own aura, what he or she sees may be distorted. So don't believe everything a psychic tells you!

Your emotions and astral body can have a powerful effect on other people. You might hear people say that they feel wounded or drained by someone. This can be confirmed by those with psychic sight who can see holes in their auras. Fiery arrows of uncontrolled anger shoot out like flashes of lightning that can penetrate the astral bodies of others, and they actually create psychic wounds in the emotional bodies.

When you find yourself getting angry and upset in response to the emotional reactions of others, your astral body is resonating to this outside influence. When you start firing back thoughts about how you are right and the other person is wrong, your mental body becomes engaged in the process as well. Once you're aware of what is occurring, you have a choice about how you respond. A simple, daily practice of loving-kindness, as a key theme for your life, can help transform negative emotions.

Likewise, if you sit near a person who is surrounded by a fog of gray depression and you're not conscious of this, you may also become depressed before long because their emotional body is affecting yours.

Because the emotional body is sensitive and responsive to outer stimuli, it occupies a dominant position in the lives of most people—until the effort is made to bring it under the loving direction of the mind and the soul. Your emotions become purified and calm as your heart opens and expresses your soul's unconditional love and intuition.

The goal is not to suppress your emotions but rather to find healthy and appropriate expressions for emotional energy, especially joy and enthusiasm, which will make you more effective in your work and your relationships.

For example, I realized that I started suppressing my natural enthusiasm and joy when I was about 12 years old and my mother became very ill. I picked up the message from my father that it was not okay to be happy and make noise when someone else was sick and unhappy. I learned to bottle my emotions, and this was reinforced by other people I spent time with over the years, and by the professional environment where I worked in Washington, D.C. In recent years, I've been working on reowning and expressing the more exuberant part of myself.

A healthy expression of your emotions and a sensitivity to the emotions of others is often called emotional intelligence, which is different from mental intelligence and cognitive development. From an integral perspective, you need to eventually develop multiple intelligences along many different lines of development, which give you a more complete picture of reality.

Your Mental Body

Your mental body is the next subtle body of your personality, composed of an even higher-grade matter than the emotional and etheric/physical bodies. Unlike the etheric and emotional auras, the mental aura has a spheroid shape that does not reflect the form of the physical body. Your mental body grows in size and activity as you mature and develop mentally. Within it are contained the forms of thought that govern how you think and what you think about. Using a computer analogy, you can say that the hardware is your brain, the operating system is the structure and capacity of your mental body, the software programs are how you think and your data files are what you think about.

Your mental body grows through the thoughts that you formulate. If you are receptive only to others' thoughts and not thinking your own thoughts, then no growth of your mind will occur. Much of what you call thinking is the registering of the thoughts and emotions of other people, which flow through your mind, depart, and are replaced by new ones.

When you observe your thoughts, you may be amazed at the mental trivia in your lower mind and how easily it goes off on irrelevant tangents and doesn't stay focused on the task at hand. When you, as the soul and observer, begin to carefully watch your mental processes, you may be surprised to discover how few of your thoughts are original! Once you recognize this, you can begin a process of choosing which thoughts you will download and develop and which ones you will delete from your mind.

Your mental body includes a lower, rational mind and a higher, abstract mind and develops from simple, concrete thinking to abstract, whole-systems thinking as your soul illuminates it. As the soul, you can set high-frequency mental matter into motion by thinking elevated and uplifting thoughts. This thinking can vibrate similar quality matter in your astral/emotional body, which then affects your physical/etheric body.

Researchers in psychoneuroimmunology, such as Dr. Candace Pert, have discovered that your thoughts affect your health—through the action of neuropeptides. The fundamental truth is that when you hold a positive idea in your mind, such as "loving-kindness toward everyone," that idea resonates through all of your bodies and positively affects your physical health and behavior. Of course, negative thoughts do the opposite, creating illness.

In *Dynamics for Living*, Charles Fillmore wrote, "Every thought clothes itself in a life-form according to the character given it by the thinker ... The mind of man marshals its faculties and literally makes into living entities the thoughts that it entertains."[4] With your thoughts you create the world, the Buddha taught. Your thoughts are powerful and create the reality you experience.

Do you want to have positive, uplifting experiences or negative ones? If you want to be an effective practical visionary, study your thoughts, observe the effects you create in the world around you, and create more beneficial thoughts.

Each of your bodies—physical, emotional and mental—has its own tendencies. Each body tends to pull your consciousness toward its energetic field of activity and would prefer to be the premier focus of attention. For example, your physical/etheric body would like to have all of your attention focused on physical plane life, doing physical activities, such as eating, running, having sex, etc. Your emotional body, on the other hand, would like to satisfy all its desires, such as needs for affection, recognition, power, excitement and stimulation. Your mental body would like you to spend more time in your head intellectualizing, planning, analyzing and judging.

Working on your emotional body helps you grow up and become more mature, while working on your mental body helps you wake up and experience a greater reality.

Integrating Your Personality

When your physical, emotional and mental bodies are working together fairly harmoniously and are going in the same direction, with no major conflicts among them, your personality is becoming integrated and synthesized. But if your integrated personality does not start to become illumined by the light of your soul, you can be powerful in worldly terms but you may not be very happy or peaceful.

Your self-centered personality can weave such a smothering veil over your eyes that you see only the material world of physical forms and emotional excitements. You may then obsessively strive toward power and status, constantly greedy for more and more of everything to fill that gnawing, empty space inside you. A personality lacking soul influence can be like a black hole,   an insatiable set of desires that obsessively consumes everything in its path to fill its emptiness. Such a personality is always grasping—things, people and experiences. It can be very self-centered and unethical, harming everyone in its way to get what it wants. Fortunately, each of us is more than this aching hole. In essence, we are the soul, the creator and generator of light and joy. Interest in the inner life of the soul is the necessary antidote to the toxic consumerism and materialism that has poisoned so many people's lives.

To progress spiritually, you shouldn't just go with the flow of whatever is happening, as some people mistakenly advise, as some flows of energy are good and some are harmful Some flows lead toward Spirit, and other flows lead toward matter and greater materialism. These latter flows are the most powerful for the average person, because they are personality energy and the path of least resistance. So if people go with this flow, it will most likely take them deeper into self-centered materialism.

Going with the flow toward Spirit requires an understanding of what life is really about. You must learn to love yourself and others, develop a clear mind, and strengthen your spiritual will. In doing so, you will feel a sense of joy in being alive in your body and your feelings, while using your mind creatively to fulfill your soul's purpose in the world.

Until your personality has exhausted its obsession with running the show, your soul isn't given the space to express itself. Your personality can be threatened by your soul, because your personality has controlled your life for a long time and doesn't want to give up control. Your personality is like a wild horse that tries to throw off the rider trying to tame it. The rider is your soul. Often it takes a major crisis, like an illness, divorce or losing a loved one, to open your personality to soul influence.

There is a stage in spiritual development in which a battle for control is waged between your soul and your personality. One minute, you may be expressing the altruism of your soul and the next minute, retreat into a cynical self-centeredness. This battle goes back and forth until you have clearly experienced the difference between personality separateness and soul unity and you are invoking your soul more often through regular spiritual practices, study and service.

How to Tell Who Is in Charge

How can you tell the difference between when you're in expanded soul consciousness and when you're in a more-limited personality consciousness? The first sign of the presence of the soul is feeling a sense of responsibility for yourself and others. A soul-infused person doesn't play the victim but works to change his or her consciousness to create better experiences and outcomes.

Your personality usually thinks of only itself and its own needs, rather than the needs of other people; it looks out only for number one. When you are in soul consciousness, you experience your greatest joy in serving others. Your soul, by nature, is group conscious and identifies with others. It is fundamentally concerned with what is the highest good for the whole, not just for yourself. In your deepest essence, you are one with the whole. The outstanding characteristics of your soul are the sense of responsibility, the urge to serve and a loving wisdom that includes everyone.

Your personality often feels separate, while your soul experiences a sense of connection with everyone and everything. Your personality is primarily a consumer, while your soul is a creator

153

and generator of energy. Your personality acquires, while your soul shares and gives.

Your personality becomes obsessed with competing; your soul is more naturally cooperative. Your personality expresses self-will; your soul expresses a higher spiritual will. Your personality may be aimless and obsessed with its latest desires. Your soul has a clear sense of meaning and purpose.

Eventually, fuller soul contact and fusion are achieved, and the personality becomes the beautiful instrument of your soul's purpose, love and creativity in the world. The duality of soul and personality is transcended in a new unity.

Making Friends With Your Subconscious

A large part of spirituality is learning to love as fully and unconditionally as possible. This means first loving yourself—your soul, personality and subconscious, including all of its parts and subpersonalities, such as your inner child, inner judge and/or inner victim. These subconscious parts of your psyche often operate out of old, dysfunctional patterns that no longer serve you. With certain outer stimuli, these subconscious parts and their patterns can hijack your personality, making you do or say things that you later regret.

Even after people strive for years to connect to their souls and live by their soul's guidance, it is not unusual for them to find that they still have strong subconscious tendencies that are antithetical to their souls' purpose. Most of us have been taught that our subconscious is the place where our darker tendencies and desires are found and that we should keep a lid on this part of ourselves at all costs.

However, you eventually will discover that the subconscious part of your being is having great, hidden influence on your personality. Traumas from childhood or even past lives, such as sexual abuse, may be buried in your subconscious; your subconscious attempts to avoid repeating these traumas in your current life experience. These traumas can be physical, emotional and/or mental, and can affect you when they are not resolved and released, creating, for example an irrational fear of heights or fear of water. Unconscious anger at someone who has hurt you in the past, for example, can make your stomach upset or your jaw tight when you meet someone in the present who reminds you of him or her.

The increased light that you invoke through spiritual study and practice will inevitably reveal more of these hidden aspects of your personality. Problems and flaws that were previously unknown or unacknowledged are suddenly seen with painful clarity. You may feel that you've fallen from the state of grace— the previous spiritual high you experienced.

If you hold anger, self-hate and criticism toward any part of yourself, you will often unconsciously project these vibrational frequencies onto others, accusing them of your own faults. They become the "evil other," whom you hate and fear.

Trying to suppress or beat up your subconscious parts only backfires; they will only resist and increase their covert influence. Sooner or later you will realize that you must begin the process of acknowledging and loving these parts of yourself so that they may be healed and integrated. By making friends with your subconscious and understanding its motives and positive intentions, which are to keep you safe and to avoid further suffering, you can transform negative patterns into supportive energy to assist you, the conscious personality, in fulfilling your soul's purpose.

As you work cooperatively with your subconscious parts, you'll soon discover the gift that each part has to offer you. For example, a harsh judgmental part of yourself can become a wise, compassionate evaluator of people and situations. You'll also be able to shine more light and love on what's hidden within each part and to work with your subconscious to find better ways to respond to difficult situations. It's important to recognize that these shadow parts of yourself served you in the past in some way and played a positive role in protecting you. However, you've outgrown the need for them to act in this way and you need to transform how they function.

It helps to appreciate that everything you experience is a movement by some part of yourself that is seeking to feel better. Appreciate the positive intent of your subconscious—that its key strategy has been to help you feel safe and secure. But realize that it does the best it can with what it knows at any given the time, based on what it has experienced in the past.

Your role as the conscious self is to help your subconscious learn more effective strategies for making you secure, happy and able to fulfill your soul's purpose, as it has the soul as you, the conscious self. This process is a core foundation for authentic healing, integration and transformation, as well as for having truly compassionate and supportive human relationships.

It helps to have an inner dialogue with different parts of yourself. For example, tell your physical body that you appreciate it for how it helps you experience the world and move around easily. Pay attention to it when it's uncomfortable and needing something. Ask your subconscious how it is feeling and why it's feeling that way. You might find, for example, a subconscious inner victim who feels that everyone is always intentionally harming you. Be alert to these messages from your subconscious, rather than ignoring them. Help your subconscious find new ways of operating in the world. This is the type of work that my husband

Gordon does to help his clients transform negative subconscious patterns into positive ones.

Until you love every part of yourself and find the gift in every rejected and suppressed part of yourself, you will continue to treat your neighbors, consciously or unconsciously, exactly as you treat these parts of yourself. It's true that you always "love your neighbor as yourself."

As you confront and re-own parts of your "shadow", you are helping transform part of the collective shadow of humanity and making it easier for others to do the same. Since human consciousness is one, any change in a part of that consciousness affects what Ruper Sheldrake calls the "morphogenetic field" and thus repatterns the whole of human consciousness.

Eventually, as you advance on your spiritual path, you will confront the accumulated negative patterns you've created over a very long period personified in what the ageless wisdom calls "the Dweller on the Threshold." This dweller may appear to you as a fearful monster from a horror film or book and appears to bar the doorway to your further spiritual growth. In reality, this frightening image is only the accumulation of elemental energy from your fears, failures, hatreds and illusions. As you learn to lovingly embrace it and understand its gifts for you, you can turn it into a positive ally on your spiritual path.

Have you ever wondered why the natives of Hawaii seem so happy? It's not just because they live in a beautiful paradise (though that sure helps!); it's also because their native religion, Huna, incorporates an understanding of their three selves—their higher self (soul), their conscious self (personality) and their basic self (subconscious). Hawaiian people are taught from childhood how to communicate with and love their basic self. Kahunas, traditional practitioners, believe that the subconscious provides all of the energy needed for the conscious self's activities and for making prayers effective. Kahunas work with their basic self in their daily spiritual practices in order to reach their higher self, and this makes them more joyful, as Max Freedom Long notes in *The Secret Science Behind Miracles* and Charlotte Berney describes in *Fundamentals of Hawaiian Mysticism*.

Building the Rainbow Bridge to Your Soul

A key technique for strengthening your connection to your soul and helping transform negative subconscious tendencies is to consciously build the "rainbow bridge" (or *antahkarana* as it's called in the Eastern teachings) between your personality and soul through meditation. Using a process of visualization, you build a line of rainbow light between your lower, rational mind and your higher, abstract mind. You visualize another line of light between your emotional body and your heart, the center of unconditional love and higher intuition. Then you visualize a third line between your personal will and your higher will that's aligned with God's will. This process strengthens the integration of your personality with your soul so that you can express a synthesis of light, love and will.

A regular practice of meditation can help you reflect on and identify with the qualities of your soul. You can begin your meditation by visualizing the emotional energy in your solar plexus center rising up to your heart with each breath you take, transmuting it into universal love. You can also meditate on an image of your soul as the Master in your heart by visualizing a wise person or a symbol, like a star or a flame in your heart..

Another powerful technique is dialoguing with your soul in a daily evening review, in which you reflect on your thoughts and actions of the day, beginning with the most recent hour, and then review in reverse to the beginning of the day. It helps to honestly examine your motives and work to purify them. In a difficult relationship or situation, you can ask yourself, "What is the lesson I am learning in this? What do I need to see more clearly? How can I develop more detachment from this? How can I bring more love to this situation and to this person?"

You can also practice the powerful "act as if" technique, imagining that you are already embodying your soul. This acting will help it become a reality.

Practicing harmlessness in thought, word and deed is also effective for spiritual growth. It may sound simple, but see what you learn when you practice it!

Positive thinking is another tool for invoking the soul, as energy follows thought. The Agni Yoga teachings suggest, "Behold as under a magnifying glass the good, and belittle the signs of imperfection tenfold, lest you remain as you always were."[5]

You can also experience soul consciousness by honoring it in others. The Hindu practice of the "Namasté" greeting—bowing to the inner Divinity in each person you meet—helps remind you that we all contain this Divine spark. By studying the lives of those whom you honor as heroes—the famous and the unsung—you can recognize the higher qualities that your soul is encouraging you to develop.

Serving others, as well as yourself, is a powerful practice for invoking your soul. Scientific research has shown that altruism and helping others create a "helper's high"—a euphoric feeling of well-being. Thus, an evolutionary strategy operating through our immune and endocrine systems is assisting our spiritual development.

Your Chakras and Spiritual Development

To understand the mechanism of how spiritual development unfolds and how your soul infuses your personality and energizes your life purpose, it helps to understand the energy centers in your body and the stages of spiritual growth. The ageless wisdom teachings of the East, such as Buddhism and Hinduism, have taught about these energy centers, which they call chakras, for centuries. Western teachers, such as Helena Blavatsky, Charles Leadbeater and Lucille Cedercrans, and modern teachers, such as Michelle Lusson, Carolyn Myss and Andodea Judith have helped modern students understand the chakras more fully. Especially helpful in understanding these energy centers is the book *Esoteric Healing* by Alice Bailey.

There are seven major chakras or energy centers in your etheric body, which is the inner pattern of energy that affects the corresponding physical glands. The glands, in turn, affect your physical, emotional and mental well-being. Here is energy expressed by each chakra:

- **The crown center** located at the top of your head (pineal gland): higher purpose and vision, spiritual will and synthesis.

- **The brow or ajna center** in the middle of your forehead (pituitary gland): intuitive analysis, planning and directing.

- **The throat center** (thyroid gland): creativity, communication and personal will.

- **The heart center** (thymus gland): unconditional love and compassion, good relationships skills and group consciousness.

- **The solar plexus center** at your navel (pancreas gland): emotional power, desire and enthusiasm.

- **The sexual center** below your hips (gonads): vitality, sexuality and attraction of money.

- **The base or root center** at the base of your spine (adrenal gland): life force, survival and practicality.

Each center opens gradually and radiates energy through the process of spiritual growth and expansion of consciousness. Becoming a practical visionary is learning to express energy in a balanced way through all of your chakras and bringing your higher purpose and vision (perceived through your crown center) down through each chakra and each stage in order make it practical and grounded in the world.

Stages of Spiritual Development

Although the following stages of development are outlined in a consecutive way and tend to build on one another, you might be working on more than one stage at the same time. These stages reflect movements of energy flows between the chakras and can be seen as initiations along the spiritual path.

First Stage: Purification and Control of Your Physical Body

Obsession with pleasure, physical desires and the material world is released, and sexual energy is transmuted and raised up to the throat center to express a higher creativity. Rather than being the controlling force in your life, sexual energy is expressed in moderation and as appropriate, in balance with other aspects of your life. Often there is a focus on diet and/or physical discipline, such as yoga, to purify and strengthen your body. Your heart center is vivified, and love for humanity grows.

Second Stage: Transformation and Control of Your Emotional Body

Solar plexus (emotional) energies are transmuted or purified so that they become less harmful and more heartful, and they are raised to the heart center. You may engage in psychological therapy to transform your emotional body. There is a release of negative feelings and obsessive emotional desires, and your mind is strengthened. Enslavement to ideas and fanatical reaction to any truth or teacher is overcome. The keynote of this stage is freedom, and the motivation becomes harmlessness and service to others. Group consciousness and a sense of inclusiveness develop. Your life purpose or mission is discovered, and fellow co-workers are found. Spiritual progress becomes more rapid.

Third Stage: Illumination and Control of Your Mental Body

Your mind becomes enlightened, and attachment to ideas and beliefs is overcome. All personality energies—physical, emotional and mental—are purified, transmuted and raised to the crown chakra at the top of the head, where they are controlled by the higher vision of the soul. The personality is flooded with light from above, and the soul becomes dominant in your life. The intuition is developed, and all sense of duality is resolved into unity. A degree of mastery of time is achieved, and there is a growing awareness of the higher evolutionary plan.

This stage is the most difficult because the mind doesn't want to give up control—it's been running your life for eons. This stage is also challenging because it involves confrontation with the "Dweller on the Threshold" (the embodiment of accumulated and unacknowledged shadow personality traits), which bars the gateway to further growth and must be embraced, educated and redeemed.

Fourth Stage: Renunciation of Personality Life

Your heart center becomes fully opened, and you become adept in working with angels and with the significance of color and sound. Suffering and sacrifice may be experienced because this stage entails renunciation of all personality goals. Family, friends, money, reputation and even life itself are sacrificed for the greater good of humanity. The word *sacrifice* means "making sacred." There is great joy in this sacred process, and that which is released is replaced by great wisdom, peace and true bliss.

Fifth Stage: Mastery

This stage is the achievement of mastery and permanent nirvana. You work primarily through the heart and crown chakras on the intuitional plane, and the evolutionary plan for humanity is fully revealed. You are totally dedicated to helping humanity and all kingdoms of life evolve.

Karma and Spiritual Growth

To become an effective, practical visionary, it helps to understand your past karma, which you bring to your work in the world. Karma provides a key to your life purpose. You are sometimes drawn to work in a certain field in order to learn something important and to transmute past karma. Studying how karma works may also help you understand why you are powerfully attracted to or repelled by a particular profession or a particular person or group. You are helped or hindered by how much positive or negative karma you've accumulated.

Karma is the Eastern term for the popular wisdom that says, "What goes around, comes around," and what the mainstream press refers to as "poetic justice" or "the chickens coming home to roost."

The Bible says, "Whatsoever a man soweth, that shall he also reap." In the East, it's said that "the wheels of karma grind slowly, but exceedingly fine." While people seem to focus on bad karma, there is actually more positive karma in the world than negative. Positive karma is referred to as grace in the Christian tradition and merit in the Buddhist teachings. Grace or merit is the reason you might experience things flowing smoothly and successfully, such as doors of opportunity opening easily and people generously helping you.

The purpose of karma is not to punish but to educate, so that we can make better choices next time. Some of us seem to have a full curriculum! Karma is called the law of balances because you are responsible for balancing the consequences of your actions. You must balance the results of the causes you have generated that are out of harmony with the law of love. You may draw a difficult situation to yourself because of past karma—in order to learn that what you did was harmful—even if you don't consciously remember its original cause.

Karma is actually the law of empowerment. You can change your destiny by changing the causes you set into motion now. You are creating your future in the present. So wouldn't you prefer a happier life that makes a contribution in some way? Start creating positive, loving thoughts and actions right now to set new causes into motion!

A sincere desire for change and forgiveness of self and others is the key to releasing negative karma. Once a lesson is learned through experiencing its karma and practicing real forgiveness, you no longer have to suffer from its negative effects. As you invoke your soul and dedicate your life to helping others, you transmute negative karma.

You can change your past by changing how you think about it today. Your thoughts will create new causes that will, in turn, have effects. Time is not linear; it's spherical, so you can affect both the past and the future in the present. All learning is stored in your subconscious and gradually integrated to become your character.

Karma can be instantaneous—or it can take a long time to unfold. Assigning a specific cause to a specific event is an over-simplification, as everything is interconnected. The Buddhists call this interconnectedness "co-dependent origination." If you are open to considering that your karma might result from experiences in your past lives, your soul may reveal information to you that's important to your current life purpose. However, trying to uncover your past lives from a sense of curiosity can create delusions or open a Pandora's box that you may not be prepared to handle wisely.

There is also collective karma—group karma, such as family karma or national karma—in which every member of a group experiences both positive and challenging effects of collective past actions or the actions of their leaders.

What kind of world do we collectively want to create for ourselves, our children and our children's children? What contribution would you personally like to make to the New World that is emerging? Are you ready to invoke the magic of your soul to help you become more effective and help create a better world?

SPIRITUAL PRACTICES

The Art of the Observer

The observer or witness is the soul within you, your Divine essence. When you become too caught up in your problems—feeling angry, fearful or sad—you can practice detachment by stepping back and becoming the observer. This detachment can restore your balance and help you experience inner peace. You can shift your perspective and become an observer of your emotional state, rather than being in pain from overidentification with anger, fear or sadness. Here are some techniques for viewing your problems from different perspectives and developing a supple quality of mind:

- Step back and imagine that you're watching a fascinating movie in which your personality is the main actor.

- Put your problem in perspective by looking at the bigger picture, the larger context, and realize everything is relative.

- See your problem from a distance so that it appears smaller and not so overwhelming.

- Compare your problem with a greater event or what someone else has gone through that might have been worse.

- Focus on the details of the problem, rather than on overgeneralizations. You may discover new insights and a subtle internal change.

- Look for the positive qualities in a person whom you dislike or in an event that is distasteful. You'll soon realize that no person or event is 100 percent bad.

- Look for opportunities presented in the action that made you become emotionally upset. Is there something new that you are learning about yourself?

Meditation for Invoking Your Soul

Begin this meditation with a dedication to serving the highest good of all and to the awakening of humanity. Then, take a few slow, deep breaths, breathing in peace and stillness with each inhalation, and slowly exhaling, releasing any tension, worry or irritation.

As you inhale, visualize the energy in the solar plexus center at your navel as a ball of energy rising upward to your heart. See your heart center transmuting negative emotional feelings into universal, unconditional love as you exhale.

Inhale again, visualizing the energy rising up from your heart to your head, and in the interlude before exhaling, dedicate the energy to service to helping others in some way.

Then exhale, visualizing this positive energy flowing out through your throat center to release creativity and energy, and see positive energy also flowing down to your solar plexus center.

Repeat this sequence a few times. See the energy rising all the way up to your head. Lift your consciousness higher and affirm your intention to align with your soul, visualizing it as a star or lotus above your head, if you like. Affirm your soul as your essential identity, the presence of God or Spirit within you.

Hold the silence for 10 to 15 minutes, listening inwardly to the voice of your soul—the still, small voice that provides inspiration and guidance for your life.

Close the meditation by visualizing love, light and spiritual power flowing through all of your chakras. From your head and heart centers, radiate positive, healing energy into the world to where it is most needed for peace, healing and transformation. Write down any insights or guidance that you experienced as a way to help remember them.

Techniques for Strengthening Your Heart

Begin with a meditation on loving yourself, because you can love others only when you love yourself. Visualize a fountain of love within your heart, pouring forth healing waters of compassion to nurture and support you and all whom you contact.

Reflect on a past experience of unconditional, universal love, and allow the energy and magic of that memory to fill you.

Meditate on forgiving yourself and others for any harm they have done you. Invoke the fire of forgiveness to burn away past wrongs and suffering.

Visualize lines of light and loving-kindness connecting you to everyone: first to your family, then to your friends, to your co-workers, and finally to everyone in your town, your state, your nation and the world. Experience a deep sense of peace and connection to all humankind.

Express your gratitude often: write down five people whom you would like to thank and do so as soon as you can.

Find something positive in a person with whom you're having a conflict. What do you appreciate about him or her? Communicate your appreciation to him or her.

Act as if you are loving. Practicing loving behavior will help you develop authentic love.

Create a positive affirmation for yourself and repeat it many times a day. For example, "I am filled with love and share it with everyone I meet." Write it down, and post it where you will see it frequently.

KEY INSIGHTS TO REFLECT ON

◆ To find the New World within you, invoke your soul, or higher self, to guide your life.

◆ Your personality is a consumer of energy, but your soul is a producer.

◆ Your soul is the connecting link between Spirit and matter and is the inner observer or witness.

◆ Your soul expresses a balance of love, intelligence and will.

◆ It is essential to make friends with your subconscious and engage its help in transforming your life.

◆ The key for spiritual development is to balance study, meditation and service.

◆ The purpose of karma is to educate you so that you can make better choices next time.

Key #5

Turn Within to Find a Source of Spiritual Strength

Develop a Regular Meditative Practice to Receive Clear Guidance

---

Meditation isn't sufficient to change the world.

You must have a plan, but to make the plan work, you

must meditate.

— The Dalai Lama[1]

Developing a Regular Meditation Practice

Taking time for quiet reflection each day amidst your busy life can greatly strengthen your spiritual life and bring important insights about your higher purpose and contribution to the New World. Meditation or contemplative prayer helps you wake up to a greater reality and create a peaceful and healthy life for yourself. It also helps you develop a greater sense of detachment from your work so that your ego doesn't become overly identified with your work and outer success.

In the silence, you'll discover the wisdom that illuminates all things. Here you'll find a deep source of intuitive wisdom to guide your life and a surprising joy and peacefulness that stays with you despite outer circumstances and difficulties. You'll see glimpses of the big picture—of both your own life and the life of the larger world. You'll understand more about why you are here on Earth at this time and what your higher purpose is. You'll see life with a whole-systems perspective—how everything is connected to everything else

Meditating daily for the past 30 years has been the most transforming thing I've done. It has helped me clarify my life purpose, accelerate my spiritual growth, and increase my effectiveness in the world. I have always had a lot of nervous energy and could never sit still. I drove my teachers crazy when I was in high school. Meditation helped me become much calmer. Even old friends who hadn't seen me in years noticed the positive change in me. And I really knew something had changed when my mother commented on how peaceful I'd become!

I first learned to meditate by making a commitment to sit in silence for 20 minutes each day. Meditation is called a practice because it improves with practice. It's like exercising an inner muscle. Unlike sports, you can't try too hard or push it, because pushing undermines achieving a sense of inner balance.

I didn't have a meditation teacher. However, in the beginning I sat with a group who meditated each morning and that helped me resonate with the states of consciousness they were accessing. After about a month of sitting still and working on calming my mind during meditation, I noticed a subtle shift in my consciousness. For the first time, my mind wasn't busy running all over the place with a million thoughts. As physicist Amit Goswami noted, meditation is an experience of "quantum nonlocality," or infinite space and eternal time.

The first inner message I received in my meditation was a classic one that many people have heard from the inner divinity: "Be still, and know that I am God." My meditation practice developed naturally, and soon I was teaching meditation to people from around the world who'd come to visit the spiritual community where I was teaching.

I started using meditation to make major decisions in my life, and I worked with groups using meditation for group decision-making, which is very effective. For the past 15 years, my husband and I have organized regular meditation conferences in cities around the world.

If you want to explore your soul, the New World within you, meditation is the golden key that unlocks the door to this amazing world. It is very helpful for discovering your contribution to the New World growing all around you. When you become still enough, outwardly and inwardly, you can hear the voice of your soul giving you guidance for your life. Meditation is key for strengthening your intuition—your inner wisdom.

I'd like to share with you some of what I've learned about the types, benefits and techniques of meditation. If you're already using a meditation technique that helps you calm your body, emotions and mind, then you might want to skip to the fifth step in the "Creative Meditation Techniques" section presented on page 179.

What exactly is meditation?

Meditation is an inward journey to your true self, your true home. Meditation is for everyone, whether your spiritual path is Eastern, Western or none at all. Meditation is about bringing your attention inward and allowing your mind to settle into stillness. It is withdrawing your attention from the periphery of your consciousness into the center.

Meditation is your mind's power to hold itself steady in the light and become aware of your higher purpose, your life's mission. Meditation is sometimes called the science of light because it works with the substance of light. Visualization is said to be the secret of true meditation work in the early stages.

Meditation is the science of bridging between your personality and your soul, your eternal self. It is becoming one with all that is, dropping the sense of separateness and duality.

Paradoxically, meditation is also an experience of emptiness—letting go of all thoughts, feelings and sensations. It helps you realize the impermanence of all forms—physical, emotional and mental. You become aware that everything is constantly changing—nothing is static or permanent. It thus helps you learn detachment from forms and discover your true essence, which is beyond all form.

In the Western traditions, prayer is often called "talking to God," praising God or requesting something, while meditation is called "listening to God," deep inner listening. "It is in the silence of the heart that God speaks," Mother Teresa said.

Types of Meditation

There are several types of meditation that can be helpful to your spiritual growth and your service to the world.

- **Concentration**—steadying your mind and focusing energy and attention on an issue or task.

- **Contemplation**—reflecting on the deeper meaning of an idea or seed thought, such as compassion, by holding it gently in your mind and allowing its meaning to unfold.

- **Mindfulness**—observing with detachment any sensations, feelings or thoughts that may arise in order to deepen your insight into the nature of reality.

- **Receptive**—inner listening to receive impressions, ideas and spiritual guidance from your soul, or higher self.

- **Creative**—using your mind to build positive pictures and thoughts, energizing them with life and vitality and giving them direction with your will, such as creating a visualization for self-healing or sending healing energy to a place of crisis in the world.

- **Invocation**—calling in higher energy or beings, such as invoking the Christ or the Buddha.

Benefits of Meditation

Meditation develops a sense of inner peace, joy and strength. On a spiritual level, meditation helps strengthen your intuition, open your heart, and clear out negative emotions. It helps you develop detachment from physical and emotional reactions to outer events. It helps purify and discipline your mind, awakening and freeing it so that it can more directly perceive reality, or truth.

Most important, meditation strengthens your alignment with your soul and helps you discover your higher purpose in life.

Scientific research at the Center for Mindfulness in Medicine, Healthcare and Society at the University of Massachusetts Medical School has shown that meditation helps you cope with stress. It can also repair or compensate for damage already done to the brain. Other studies have found that meditation can help lower your blood pressure, improve your memory and creativity, strengthen your immune system, and reduce depression and hostility.

Research by Professor Richard Davidson at the University of Wisconsin found that meditation alters the brain itself by creating enduring gamma waves, which relate to positive feelings, such as happiness and indicate heightened perception, insight and problem solving. Buddhist monks who had been experienced meditators for years had a much higher level of gamma waves than beginning meditators—not only while they were meditating, but also during rest periods. Harvard psychologist Sara Lazar also found that meditation causes changes in the physiological structure of the brain by increasing cognitive and emotional processing and a sense of well-being.

Andrew Newberg, M.D., and Eugene d'Aquili, M.D., of the University of Pennsylvania studied Tibetan Buddhist monks and found that meditation caused the prefrontal brain lobes, which relate to focused attention, to be more active than normal. Less activity than normal occurred in the parietal lobes, which process information about space, time and our orientation to space and time. This finding is consistent with meditators perceiving themselves as unlimited and interconnected with everyone and everything.

In a study on the effect of meditation on crime rates in Washington, D.C., Dr. Audrey Lanford found 22 percent fewer homicides during the weeks when 400 people practiced meditation together regularly. More than 600 scientific studies in the classroom have verified that 10 to 15 minutes of meditation twice a day improves students' academic achievement, reduces stress, promotes creativity and decreases substance abuse.

The late physicist Itzhak Bentov found that a good meditator can charge the electrostatic field surrounding his or her body so that it will be resonant with the frequency of Earth at 7.5 cycles per second. This enables the meditator to affect any other body vibrating at a similar frequency.

Group meditation with experienced meditators is especially potent, because it creates a resonant field that makes it easier for everyone to access a deeper meditative state. The spiritual energy generated grows exponentially with the number of people meditating together.

The resonant field created by experienced meditators is noticeable. Gordon and I once invited a Congressman to meet with a group of our friends, who meditated together just before he arrived. When he walked in the room, he exclaimed, "This is a resonant field! I've experienced this only once before." He used those actual words, so he must have known something about this.

Establishing a Regular Rhythm and Place

For daily meditation, it's important to find a comfortable place where you won't be disturbed. Meditating in the same place each day builds up a vibration there and makes it easier to meditate each time you use this place. It can be a special room or just a corner in a room that is dedicated to this purpose. Clean and decorate this area to create a sacred space, adding inspirational pictures, flowers, candles or incense.

Establishing a regular rhythm with your meditation is essential. Ten minutes each day is better than an hour every once in a while, because it creates a regular habit pattern and rhythm. I generally have meditations of 20 to 45 minutes a day, since I've been meditating for many years, but 10 to 15 minutes daily is a good way to begin.

Most people find that the morning is the best time to meditate, because they are fresher at that time and are not yet caught up in the day's activities. It sets the right tone for the day and connects you with higher spiritual energies and a sense of purpose. Meditation is better before eating or at least an hour after eating. Wait several hours after drinking alcohol before meditating, and reduce its use as much as possible. Alcohol tends to interfere with meditation. It is best to take a scientific approach to meditation. Experiment with different techniques, and study the results to find what works for you. Proceed slowly with caution. Meditation should be in balance with the rhythm of your daily living. Observe the effects on your life, and make sure that you're not getting ungrounded, neglecting the physical world or acting too spaced out. If so, reduce your meditation time.

An especially powerful time to meditate and invoke higher spiritual energy is at the time of the full moon each month. Spiritual energy can flow in unimpeded during the full moon, because the moon is on the far side of Earth, away from the sun, and the full light of the sun (symbolic of Spirit) can radiate to the earth. Thousands of groups around the world hold special meditations at this time and link inwardly with one another. They visualize a network of light around the world and dedicate their meditations to the benefit of humanity. Gordon and I have been hosting these monthly meditations regularly for many years now.

Creative Meditation Techniques

Align your posture and relax your physical body. It's best to sit up straight so that your chakras are perpendicular to gravity. If you lie down, you may become too relaxed and fall asleep. Your hands can be folded in your lap or with palms up or down on your thighs. Your eyes should be either closed or staring straight ahead with a relaxed gaze, turning your sight inward. (If your body is tense or restless, you may want to do some relaxing, stretching exercises or yoga before you meditate.)

Appreciate and send loving energy to your physical, emotional and mental bodies before you begin the meditation. Hold an attitude of cooperation with each of these aspects, rather than trying to suppress them. It's important to stay relaxed yet aware and awake during your meditation.

Focus on your breath. Inhale peace and stillness, and exhale any tensions or worries. Deep breathing helps energize you as you bring in more *prana* or life force. Create a regular rhythm of inhaling, holding the breath, and exhaling. Count to seven (or whatever number works for you) as you breathe in, hold it for a few moments and exhale to a count of seven, releasing any tensions or worries each time you exhale.

If your mind wanders and you become distracted, always come back to awareness of your breath. With each breath, feel yourself becoming lighter and more expanded. Experience the pause between your breaths expanding into infinity.

Calm your emotions. Observe your feelings as if you're watching a movie of your own life. Become a detached observer, noticing what's going on without reacting.

If you're experiencing fear, anger or other negative emotions, you can help transform them by visualizing them as a ball of energy in your solar plexus chakra (at your navel). Visualize this ball of energy moving up to your heart and transforming into positive, loving energy, and then send this positive energy back to your solar plexus. You can see it as a ball of energy, or just feel it or hold the intention of moving the energy to your heart and that will also have an effect.

Another technique for calming your emotions is to visualize a calm, clear lake reflecting the sun on a beautiful day. The water symbolizes your emotions; the sun symbolizes your soul, or higher self. Visualize the lake becoming still so that it can reflect the sun of your soul clearly.

Still your mind. See your mind becoming calm, yet poised and alert. In meditation, you are quieting the lower, rational mind and working with the higher, abstract mind. You are learning to focus your mind like a searchlight into the higher realms in order to receive impressions and new ideas that can help you and help humanity in some way. Your mind is held steady in the light, perceiving a still greater light, the light of your soul that infuses it.

A good technique for calming your mind is to become a detached observer, noticing your thoughts without trying to stop or change them and without judging them. Simply label thoughts that arise as "thinking," label emotions as "feelings" and label physical experiences or discomforts as "sensations." In the East this is called Vipassana meditation, and in the West it's called Insight meditation.

You can also use a psychosynthesis technique to disidentify from your thoughts, feelings and physical sensations by saying to yourself, "I have sensations such as hunger or cold, but I am not my body. I have feelings that swing from one extreme to the other, but I am not my feelings. I have thousands of changing thoughts, but I am not my thoughts. I am far more than any of these aspects of myself. I am the soul, my true essence."

It is helpful to focus your attention in the present, letting go of any worries about the past or future. Be here now. Be fully present in this moment.

Another technique for stilling the mind is to listen inwardly to the sound inside your head and keep your attention focused on it. Or you can repeat a mantra, a simple word or phrase, over and over, such as *peace, love* or *Om* (a sacred word that helps still your physical, emotional and mental bodies and align them with the infiniteness of the universe).

Visualization is effective because energy follows thought. You can visualize pure white light pouring in through your crown chakra, the energy center at the top of your head, and see the light circulating throughout your body as you begin feeling lighter and more expanded.

Align with your Soul or Higher Self. Many meditation techniques end with stilling the mind, but the creative meditation approach goes a step further. It uses the mind and the will to penetrate into the higher spiritual realm, the realm of your soul, and to align with the great enlightened Teachers of humanity found in many spiritual traditions, such as Christ, the Buddha, Moses and Mohammed.

This creative approach is called building the rainbow bridge or *antakaranah* as it's called in the East. You literally build strands of light from each of your bodies—physical, emotional, mental—to their higher counterparts—the spiritual will, compassionate heart, and enlightened mind, respectively. You raise your consciousness to the vibratory frequency of your soul.

If you're new to meditation, a simple way to build the rainbow bridge is to visualize a line of light connecting your crown chakra (the energy center at the top of your head) to a star above your head that represents your soul and the higher spiritual realm. Then, dedicate your meditation to serving the highest good for all. This dedication to a higher purpose is like a magical incantation that purifies your consciousness and lifts it higher, bringing you benefits as well.

If you're a more experienced meditator, you can focus your attention in your *ajna* center (the brow chakra in the middle of your forehead) and visualize a line of light connecting your lower, rational mind with your higher, abstract mind (the manasic plane, as it's called in the East. Then, visualize another line of light connecting your emotions to your heart and intuition (the buddhic plane). Lastly, visualize a third line of light connecting your physical body and your personal will with a higher will, aligned with God's will (the atmic plane). Your higher will, heart and mind are aspects of your soul.

If you would like, you can then align your soul with a great master, such as Christ or Buddha, visualizing a line of light making this connection.

Then you hold open this higher alignment with your soul for a few minutes in silence, being open to receive any impressions, ideas or guidance. This stage is referred to as the higher interlude in meditation. After a period of silence, you can start bringing the energy down and enter what's called the lower interlude, where your brain is impressed with ideas received in the meditation and is stimulated into activity. Allow your lower mind to shape the ideas or impressions you received into usable thoughts for your life and for humanity and to plan action, if appropriate.

End with a blessing. The last step is the circulation of the energy contacted in meditation as a blessing. The spiritual energy you received can be released and directed into the world to bring healing and transformation to individuals in need or to humanity as a whole. You can visualize light, love and healing energy radiating out from the ajna center or through your heart to where it's most needed in the world. It's important to share and circulate the energy you've received in meditation. The meditation should make a complete circuit of receiving and giving energy so that you won't experience congestion.

Lastly, visualize light, love and healing energy pouring through your whole being, energizing and balancing your physical, emotional and mental bodies. Let the energy flow through you and out the bottoms of your feet into the earth, to the Divine Mother, helping you ground yourself.

Some people like to begin and end their meditations by sounding three Oms, which can be done silently if needed. Closing the meditation this way helps distribute the energy out into the world.

After you end, you might want to write down anything you've received in meditation— ideas, visions, inner guidance—as a way to remember it and apply it in your daily life. This is a key purpose of meditation. If you don't receive any guidance or messages, that's perfectly fine. You will still experience the benefits of meditation, such as greater inner peace or clarity about your purpose, and useful ideas or guidance may spontaneously come to you later during the day.

Meditation for Social Change

If more people would meditate regularly, we'd have a more peaceful society with fewer violent crimes and fewer wars.

Research shows that there is a reduction in crime rates when groups of people meditate together in an area. Also, having trained meditators present whenever important negotiations or political decisions are being made could create a positive energy field of goodwill that could lead to greater insights and wiser decisions.

A number of spiritual groups are now hosting live meditations and prayers over the phone and on the Internet to link people globally. The Center for Visionary Leadership and many others have organized regular meditations for peace in the Middle East, for example. A major meditation vigil around the world in 1995 helped support the peace process in Bosnia at a crucial juncture. Another vigil in 1997 mobilized prayers to prevent war with Iraq over a United Nations weapons inspection. Many groups, such as Pathways to Peace and Meditation Mount, promote meditation on the International Day of Peace, September 21, each year. National prayers and meditations are held each year around the world to ask for the highest good in major elections.

Sarvodaya, founded by A.T. Ariyaratne in 1958 in Sri Lanka, has engaged more than 2 million people in dozens of peace meditations that it has convened over the years. Its members do daily "loving-kindness" meditations. Its mission is to build a new society, and it has created social services, village banking systems and training in job skills and conflict resolution.

Many people are "Adopting a Leader"—finding a national leader who has potential but needs help spiritually. They pray or meditate for this leader to help him or her align with higher spiritual principles and truly serve the good of all.

We can invoke help from higher spiritual forces in meditation. As humans we do not have to struggle with our problems alone. Help is always available from Spirit if we ask for it.

There are many examples of guidance by higher spiritual forces throughout history: George Washington's vision of an angelic presence at Valley Forge, the help received by the Allies during the Battle of Britain in World War II, and Egyptian President Anwar Sadat's vision of Mohammed inspiring him to create peace in the Middle East. Even ordinary people are reporting experiences of invoking spiritual help and receiving it. In a poll reported in *USA Today*, 55 percent of Americans polled said an angel had protected them from harm and 20 percent said that they had heard the voice of God speaking to them.[2]

We can also invoke the soul of our nation and its higher purpose in our meditations. Once a nation's higher purpose is more fully understood, it can be shaped into a clear, effective thoughtform and widely communicated so that it can be more fully expressed in the world.

We can envision a better future through our meditation work. Trained facilitators are leading policy makers and citizens in guided visioning exercises on key issues, such as health care and transportation. In the exercises, people imagine themselves five or 10 years in the future to see solutions to current problems and they visualize what steps were taken to achieve that future.

Meditative Group Decision-Making

Meditation can be used to help a group make wiser decisions than it would using ordinary decision-making methods, if group members sincerely want to serve the highest good of all. Meditative group decision making is something I've worked successfully with in several nonprofits over the past 20 years. Following is a description of the process that Gordon and I wrote with our colleague Michael Lindfield, who has also used it effectively in corporate settings.

The basic agreements for this process to work are that everyone must do the following:

- Decide which decisions need to be meditated upon.
- Be willing to deeply discuss issues with everyone in the group using the agreed-upon process.
- Have an agreement to listen lovingly and respectfully to others and to give honest, calm and loving feedback.
- Go into the process with a willingness to change his or her views.
- Be willing to support 100 percent all decisions reached by meditative consensus.

Step 1: Laying the Question and the Facts on the Table

The group outlines and frames carefully the question(s) to be considered. A summary of the background and key components of the issues around the question is given and members define what the question means for the group. (Preliminary work can be done by sending out basic information before a meeting.)

Step 2: Clarifying Questions on Key Points

Members ask about any factual points they need clarified so that everyone understands what they are deciding.

Step 3: Discussing the Issue

Various perspectives and reasons for deciding one way or the other are presented by participants. These statements and opinions from each person are not trying to convince others of his or her position. It's important that each person share honestly, in a nonemotionally charged way, so that differences can be heard by all. This sharing is an opportunity for deep listening to the intent and true contribution behind the words spoken.

Step 4: Releasing Opinions

Members consciously let go of their individual views and prepare for meditation on the question. This release allows for inspired new perspectives and possibilities to emerge. The assumption is that if the truth of your position is still there after the meditation, it is likely to be authentic truth.

Step 5: Meditatively Aligning and Invoking on the Question

A member of the group leads the group in a releasing process, unifies the group energy, aligns with higher spiritual levels and invokes the decision that is for the highest good of all concerned. The assumption is that the right decision exists and that the group's task is to discover and reveal it.

Step 6: Engaging in Silence for Inner Listening

There is a period of silence for five to 10 minutes in which members attune to the highest level of consciousness that they can and remain open to receiving insights of any kind regarding the decision. Insights can be received in the form of words, images, feelings or an inner knowing. Then each participant takes two to three minutes to write down his or her insights.

Step 7: Sharing Insights

Each member sets aside his or her insights from the meditation and listens to others' insights without inner judgment or outer comment. (Not everyone has to make an input, and it is not necessary to make up something if you did not receive anything.) Participants take turns sharing their impressions with the group, whether these impressions are thoughts, words, visions or simply changes in perspective. Everyone listens for how the individual views indicate the collective impression.

Step 8: Synthesizing Views

The group reviews the various insights received and looks for any new perspectives, for the overall impression of the group and for points of synthesis and consensus. Differing points of view are explored to determine their essential truth and whether they reflect personal issues that are affecting the insights received. Objections are carefully considered, and synthesizing alternatives are proposed.

Step 9: Making or Postponing a Decision

The group decides whether it has consensus, or near consensus with no one blocking, or if there is a divergence of opinion that can't be synthesized. If no consensus is apparent, the group needs to meditate further or postpone the decision, returning to it when the time is right. Now may not be the right time to make the decision, because more information is needed or because other actions need to occur first.

Step 10: Supporting and Committing to Action

Participants clarify the implications of the decision and its value for the group goals. Once a decision is made and written down, it is important for the group to affirm and celebrate the decision, with all individuals agreeing to support the decision 100 percent. (The assumption is that the decision will drive the action and the goal will pull the work toward it.) The group agrees on and writes down what each individual needs to do by what time to implement the decision.

Receiving Guidance in Meditation

For more than 30 years, Gordon and I have been making major decisions in our lives based on guidance we've received in meditation. Our first dramatic experience of making a decision this way was when we suddenly received clear inner guidance in a meditation in 1978 to purchase land to start a spiritual community in Massachusetts. Only six months later did we learn why we were guided to that particular piece of land.

The local historical society informed us that the land had been sacred to three tribes of Native Americans who came there to do their ceremonies, so a strong spiritual energy was already anchored there. Then we learned from local dowsers that many important ley lines (meridian lines of energy in the earth) flowed through the property from all over New England. We realized how important it is to follow your inner guidance—even if the reasons aren't obvious at first.

We also received inner guidance to call the community *Sirius* after the brightest star in the heavens. Sirius Community is still going strong today and continues to be a trusted beacon of spiritual light and practical sustainability in New England.

I've also benefited from other people's experiences of guidance, such as an experience of our editor at Ballantine/Random House for our second book, *Spiritual Politics*. I met her at a conference that Gordon and I organized at the United Nations Plaza Center, and she encouraged us to write the book. She later confided to me that "a little voice" inside her had told her to publish our book, even though she already had too many books to edit. An inner voice also prompted her to offer us almost twice the book advance as we had asked for, because she "misheard" the figure we initially requested!

Guidance can come in many forms. Our friends, Ambassador John McDonald and Louise Diamond, trained the Dalai Lama's government in exile, and through them we had asked the Dalai Lama to write the foreword to our second book. But we did not hear anything from His Holiness until the last possible minute.

Just an hour before the book was sent to the printer, the Dalai Lama's foreword arrived from India to our editor's office. She was just about to quit the publishing business, because her eyes were seeing double from the strain. As a Buddhist, she interpreted this arrival as spiritual guidance to keep publishing new consciousness spiritual books, as few other editors at big New York publishing houses seemed interested.

Receiving this foreword also explained an unusual experience I had when I suddenly heard Tibetan chanting one evening at home. I hadn't been able to find where it was coming from, so I'd just shrugged it off. I later realized that the chanting had occurred at about the same time that the Dalai Lama was writing the foreword. Perhaps he had been chanting as a blessing for the book and I heard it on an inner level, even though I'd thought that it was a physical sound at the time. We're all more connected than our rational minds recognize!

Evaluating Spiritual Guidance

As a practical visionary, how can you be sure that you are receiving reliable inner guidance about your life and your part in helping create the New World? How can you evaluate the messages or visions you receive in your meditation? These questions are crucial, because many good people have been led astray and good projects have been harmed through false or misleading guidance.

Some people believe that anything received in meditation must be truth from on high. They mistake what may be a distorted vision or message for true spiritual wisdom and may even let their ego become inflated about it.

Receiving spiritual messages can be compared to receiving signals on a radio. While a good radio can easily pick up clear signals from distant and nearby radio stations, a cheap or old radio can pick up from only nearby stations and will receive a lot of distortion and static. Likewise, a relatively pure and developed spiritual person will pick up clear messages coming from a distance—the higher spiritual planes and the soul—which happens less frequently than one would hope. A more self-centered or emotionally unbalanced person will pick up a great deal of distortion and will get messages from only nearby sources—the psychic, or astral, planes closer to Earth, where there is more static from the lower thoughts and emotions of humanity.

It is important to learn how to objectively evaluate any spiritual messages or guidance that you or others receive. Here are some guidelines that might be helpful.

First, remember that your most reliable source of information is your soul, or higher self. This is the highest source of guidance for most people, and contacting your soul should be your goal. It's best to consult someone else for spiritual guidance only if you're feeling totally stuck and not getting any clear answers from within.

Guidance from another person is not meant to take the place of your relationship to your soul or Spirit, and it should never create dependency. It is merely meant to provide guideposts along the path and to help you develop your inner guidance. Do not depend on someone else's guidance or become passive and surrender your will. Your most precious gifts are your intelligence and your will—and thus your ability to make your own decisions.

Also, it's not healthy to take an attitude of "just following orders" when your inner guidance tells you to do something with which you don't agree. It's wiser to take responsibility for your life and challenge the guidance, especially if you suspect that it may be coming from an emotional or astral level that's not as clear as your soul.

Remember that the relative purity of your life will attract guidance of similar vibration through the law of attraction or resonance. An emotionally uncentered person who's motivated by ego and a need to control others could attract a harmful message in meditation, as could someone who's feeling anger, fear, greed or boredom. Negative emotions, wrong motivations and confused thinking will distort any guidance received. Drug or alcohol abuse will also distort guidance.

Ask yourself whether the information you've received in guidance is being applied in your daily life and whether it helped you live a more-spiritual life. "By their fruits you shall know them," the Bible says. If you don't work on purifying yourself, use a lot of discrimination and accept full responsibility for what comes through you, you can easily become deluded and harm others. This has happened many times and is why most spiritual traditions caution against lower psychism, where someone is open to any kind of message coming through him or her.

Sources of Spiritual Guidance

According to Alice Bailey in *Esoteric Psychology II*, there are several different levels that guidance can be coming from — and some levels are much clearer and more reliable than others.[2] Most guidance comes from a person's subconscious wish life or from what he or she has read in traditional religious sources. Thoughts can also be picked up telepathically from a teacher or others on the physical plane. A great deal of guidance also comes from the lower psychic plane, which is full of confusion distortion, glamour and flattery.

The clearest guidance comes from our soul or inner divinity. Once that guidance is firmly established, guidance can eventually be received from a more advanced teacher on the inner planes or from a true spiritual Master, such as Jesus, but receiving guidance from these sources is rare.

You can evaluate guidance by examining its content. True spiritual guidance never flatters or chastises the receiver and never demands obedience. It merely recommends a choice or course of action and leaves the person free to choose whether to follow it. It is intelligent and inspirational, and usually it is short and to the point. Guidance from the soul is often described as a still small voice.

On the other hand, guidance from the lower psychic levels is often long and flowery and/or confusing and contradictory, with many voices competing for attention. It can be harmful to others. It often flatters the ego of the receiver, creates glamour, specialness and separation and appeals to greed and desire for power. It can create fear, negativity or feelings of unworthiness. It often demands obedience and surrender of your will and can conflict with your personal ethics. It may claim ultimate authority for itself and not recognize any Higher Power.

Lower psychic guidance is received through the solar plexus chakra, rather than through the higher chakras, and is often unconscious, mediumistic and received in a trance state. It usually presents a rehash of platitudes that are generalities and can be found anywhere, and it may contradict the essential teachings of the major religions.

Another tip-off that guidance is from a lower psychic plane is when it disparages the physical plane and practical living, claims

that spiritual growth happens with no personal effort or pro-
claims the half-truth that we are gods and perfect just as we are.
It helps to get a reality check and honest feedback from trus- ted
friends about guidance you're receiving. Practical visionaries
maintain a balanced life of involvement in the inner worlds and
in the everyday physical world. They don't try to live totally in
the inner worlds as an escape. Whatever wisdom is gained from
the spiritual worlds must be applied in daily life, or it's useless. If
guidance is not integrated in a practical way, it can lead to living
in fantasy worlds and ultimately to psychological breakdown. We
are in this world to learn the lessons that physical life has to teach.

Also, it's important to recognize that the spiritual worlds are
different from the physical world and that time and space are
experienced differently. Messages can be misinterpreted, especially if they predict the future and if the interpretations are made
too literally, rather than symbolically or psychologically. For
example, a message about a tidal wave could refer to being overwhelmed by a wave of emotions, rather than a warning about an
actual tidal wave.

How to Download Reliable Guidance From Your Soul

If you are concerned about getting reliable guidance about
your life, you can prepare for it by asking from your heart for the
highest good and by making sure that your motivations are pure.

Which techniques are most useful in seeking guidance from
your soul? The most effective technique is a regular meditation
practice. Although there are many types of meditation, it's always
good to focus in your higher centers, your heart and head
chakras, rather than in your solar plexus center. If your energy
stays focused in your solar plexus level and you become too pas-

sive, opening yourself to anything that comes into your awareness, you may pick up the feelings and thoughts of others. Or you may pick up an astral spirit who wants to influence you and who may not intend your highest good.

It's best to stay alert and aware and to consciously seek contact with your soul, or higher self. This can be done through prayer, visualization, invocation or the focused attention of your higher mind. The important thing is to have the intention of contacting your soul for guidance, and not being open to just anything that wants to communicate with you.

Regular meditation, study and service will help purify your body, emotions and mind of negativity. You can work on strengthening your mind and developing your will to consciously cooperate with God's will. Practice releasing your preferences and opinions, and then ask your soul, the inner Divinity, for guidance. It is also important to purify your motivations so that you release any need for recognition and popularity.

On the other hand, if you're concerned that you never receive guidance—no words or visions, even when you ask a question in your meditation—don't worry. Many spiritually evolved people don't receive guidance in this way. Rather, they are guided in the moment, in action. The true goal is to *be* the guidance, to embody it moment to moment.

In the end, the most important thing about guidance is learning how to think as wisely and broadly as more enlightened spiritual beings do. The more you ask yourself, "How would a higher being or master answer this question? What would Jesus or Moses or Buddha do?" the more you are developing wisdom within yourself and becoming enlightened.

Strengthening Your Intuition in Daily Life

Practical visionaries often have a well-developed intuition to guide them. You can receive guidance not only while meditating but also through dreams and intuition during the course of your day. Guidance can be received in both ordinary and unusual ways.

You can develop your intuition first by setting your intention to be more open to insights and by meditating regularly. You have to practice setting aside your rational, linear mind to listen inwardly. You can test your intuitive ability on small things, when there's no pressure to perform, and monitor how your body feels when your intuition is accurate and when it is wrong.

It's helpful to write down any insights that appear in your meditations or dreams. Keep a journal of intuitive experiences, and record daily hits and misses in order to see patterns and notice what affects accuracy. Verify your intuitive experiences with objective facts. Continually practicing truthfulness will help you be true to your inner experience.

Also, you might want to notice the unusual coincidences that pop up in your life and see if they offer any messages for you. Whom do you happen to run into on the street, what book falls off the shelf as you browse, etc.? You can also be guided by ordinary signs in your environment like highway ads and bumper stickers, by a random line in a book or magazine that grabs your attention or by the conversations of complete strangers that you may overhear.

Gordon asked for spiritual help when he took an exam to get his broker's license for social investment work, and he was guided by seeing light around the correct answers in the multiple-choice exam.

There are many inspirational and useful messages for us that we miss because we're not paying attention. So while practicing regular meditation is helpful for receiving guidance for your life and clarifying your part in creating the New World, don't miss the guidance available all around you in your everyday life!

SPIRITUAL PRACTICES

Meditative Techniques for Receiving Clear Inner Guidance

- Clarify and affirm your intention before you begin.

- Purify your motives for receiving guidance.

- Release ego needs, such as pride, greed, fear, anger and any doubts that you can receive clear guidance.

- Relax, and take a few deep breaths to calm your body, emotions and mind.

- Align yourself with the highest source within you (God, Spirit, Universal Mind, etc.).

- Invoke your soul, or higher self, and ask your question(s).

- Listen quietly for the answer from your soul, and write it down to remember it.

- Avoid becoming too passive. Stay conscious and aware.

- Be aware that the answer may come in many forms: direct knowing, words, pictures, symbols, inner light, energy sensation in the body, synchronistic events, a message from a friend or a passage in a book.

- Challenge your guidance as to its spiritual source and authenticity—make sure that it is coming from your soul, not from the lower psychic or astral planes.

- Make a commitment to follow through on the guidance you've received (use it or lose it), and take full responsibility for it.

- Dedicate yourself to living a life of service to others, because this will help create a field that attracts clearer guidance.

Meditation on Discovering Your Vision and Contribution to the New World

This can be done as a quiet, meditative exercise. Write down your answers to the following questions:

What values would like your work to express?

What field of service, social problem or area of crisis today concerns you the most? Why? What is needed in this field?

What are your natural abilities that might contribute to this area, and how can they be put to the greatest use?

In what way have your past experiences and training been a preparation for fulfilling your part in co-creating a New World?

How can you make your contribution bring the greatest joy to yourself and others? How can you feel most authentically aligned with Spirit?

How can you purify your motives and cultivate a spirit of selfless service? Are you willing to align your personal will with a higher purpose?

Take some time to meditate on these questions, and ask for guidance from your soul. You can use the Meditation for Invoking Your Soul at the end of Chapter 4, or you can imagine going on an inner journey in which you climb a mountain and meet a wise person who represents your inner Teacher at the top. Ask him or her for guidance about your higher purpose and contribution.

KEY INSIGHTS TO REFLECT ON

◆ Meditation is a key to exploring the New World within you and discovering your higher purpose.

◆ Meditation alters the brain itself by creating enduring gamma waves, which relate to happiness.

◆ Visualization is the secret of all true meditation work in the early stages.

◆ Creative meditation is using the higher mind to build positive thoughtforms for helping yourself and others.

◆ To still the mind, you can become a detached observer of your thoughts without judging them, and align with your soul, or higher self.

◆ Guidance in meditation can come from various sources, so wise discrimination is essential for distinguishing reliable guidance from astral nonsense.

◆ Set your intention to be more open to dreams, intuitive insights in your daily life and messages in your environment.

Key #6

Clarify Your Higher Purpose and Vision

Create a Mission, Practical Strategy and Right Timing

I am not a visionary. I claim to be a practical idealist.

— Mahatma Gandhi[1]

The Need to Embody Your Vision and Values

Being a practical visionary is all about application and embodiment. It's about creating positive change in the world while making a living. To fulfill your higher purpose and make your vision a reality, you can shape it into a specific mission and an achievable strategy with practical steps to take in right timing.

On a book tour for *Spiritual Politics,* Gordon and I and were scheduled to do a major radio interview in San Francisco. We knew that our higher purpose was to promote spirituality in politics, and part of our strategy was to respond to invitations to speak about it, such as the one from this radio show.

As we were driving from Oregon on the main north/south highway in California toward San Francisco, we suddenly saw smoke and flames leaping high into the sky ahead. A huge forest fire was raging right in front of us. Soon it filled the whole sky, and smoke choked our throats. The cars ahead of us slowed down and came to a complete stop. The four-lane highway became a parking lot, and people were getting out of their cars and trying to figure out what to do.

We asked a policeman if he knew when they'd have the fire under control. He said that it could take hours or even until the morning. He suggested that we leave our cars, get some coffee or food at a nearby restaurant for a few hours, and maybe find a hotel for the night. Most people followed his advice.

We were really upset because we had only had a few hours to make it to San Francisco for our interview. We couldn't believe that there was no alternative. We went into the local town to find a map and talk to locals about other routes to San Francisco. Sure enough, there was another road that went through the mountains. It was a little longer and windier than the main highway, but we decided to give it a try.

We thought that the road would be packed with other cars taking a detour from the fire on the main highway. However, it was empty! We couldn't believe it. The beautiful, scenic drive took a little longer than the main highway, but we made it to our interview in plenty of time.

So why had none of the other cars had taken this alternative? Gordon explained: "We've always been practical visionaries, looking for alternative ways to express our vision—such as getting around blockages and traditional ways of doing things—so we naturally looked for an alternative route. The other people on the main highway seemed passive, like cows contented to be herded into a blocked pasture, waiting for the authorities to tell them when they could move. They reminded me of the 'muggles' in the *Harry Potter* movies."

This experience symbolizes some important points. A practical visionary has both the vision to imagine another reality (an alternative route to take instead of being stuck for hours) and the practicality to find a way to make it happen (looking for maps and getting advice from locals). A practical visionary synthesizes the duality of being visionary and being practical.

It is not enough to rage against the problems and evils in the world. You need to understand the larger context of what's unfolding today. You need to study what's already being done that's effective and appropriate to address the problem you're passionate about. Then you need to get in touch with your higher purpose and do an honest inventory of your gifts and abilities. You need to shape your purpose into a specific mission to address the problem, and you need to design an appropriate strategy for achieving your goals. Most important, you need to make sure that you'd really enjoy taking on the challenge that you're considering so that it's sustainable for the long run.

Vision in Your Leadership or Leadership for Your Vision?

In the Visionary Leadership training I offer, I begin by asking participants these questions. Do you need more vision in your leadership—or more leadership for your vision? Do you need to incorporate new ideas and inspiration, or do you need to make your vision a workable reality? Where are you in this journey?

Visionaries talk endlessly about their beautiful visions. Practical visionaries are not good with just words; they're also effective with actions. They can actualize their visions using effective strategies with achievable goals. Even in today's economy, a practical visionary knows how to attract resources to execute his or her vision.

Many visionaries fail in their efforts because they're too far ahead of what humanity is ready for. Their challenge is to envision the next step needed—an attractive, pragmatic vision for the near future—not something that will take a hundred years to manifest. It's more effective to focus on a vision that can be achieved in the foreseeable future, outline the steps needed to manifest it, and work on each step in turn.

Many visionaries are good communicators of the vision but are poor managers. Several years ago, Gordon became involved with an idealistic Silicon Valley entrepreneur who had a great vision for developing a business around a breakthrough solar technology. A former executive at a major technology company, he had initiated several start-ups after he left the company, and seemed to know a lot about business. He had a sincere   spiritual commitment to creating a triple-bottom-line company honoring people, planet and profit.

However, he was a poor manager who lacked practical skills, and he didn't hire and empower people with the abilities he lacked. Every time something didn't work, he would create a whole new strategy and business plan and look for new investors.

The business failed, and we lost much time and money. However, we learned some painful but useful lessons about the need to be *practical* visionaries. Over the years, I've seen many inflated visionaries with grand ideas and few skills to achieve them. I've become inoculated against this kind of ungrounded idealism that often runs rampant in circles of innovators and visionaries.

A truly effective visionary leader is rare. We're each stronger in one area or another, but we can learn to develop what we're lacking—or at least hire people with complementary skills to ours—if we first have the humility to admit what we're lacking.

I was inspired to write about being a practical visionary because I'm a veteran of many hard-fought battles to make visions more grounded and effective.

Too often I've been in group meetings in which someone dramatically states an ideal with such passion and inspiration that they sway the group, while being totally dismissive of practical considerations and the actual reality on the ground. This type of person leads people into disastrous failures and wastes much time and resources, which then gives that ideal an undeserved bad name.

Being a practical visionary is about first embodying your vision and values. When I was teaching about spirituality in business, a good friend pulled me aside to rant about how evil capitalism was. I had to point out the obvious that he was over-looking—that he owned several rental properties in Los Angeles and was a capitalist himself! Actions speak louder than words.

Life has been my teacher in helping me become more practical and disciplined in daily life, instead of always just talking about ideals. When my father became very ill a few years ago and passed away, I had to take on many responsibilities for my family—financial, legal, insurance, health care, etc.—and engage with numerous government and corporate bureaucracies that often frustrated me.

However, I learned that I could accomplish a lot more by standing in the shoes of the people I was relating to and understanding the structural limitations of what they were dealing with in their organizations. This helped me figure out a way around roadblocks so that I could get things done more skillfully. Like many people, my family responsibilities take up large amounts of my time, but they also keep me focused, disciplined and practical.

Other life experiences have also shaped my appreciation of the practical side of being a visionary. When I lived in Washington, D.C., I was often invited to give Visionary Leadership training in government agencies, and the real-life problems I needed to address there helped me infuse my training with practical advice and techniques.

For example, when the Office of Sustainability was created by President Clinton in the U.S. Department of Commerce, many people there didn't have a clue what to do. Since their representative co-chaired my national task force on Sustainable Communities, I realized that my best contribution would be to invite more than a hundred practical visionaries already   doing sustainable projects around the country to join the task force and advise them.

Qualities of Practical Visionaries

Successful practical visionaries lead from the inside out while employing skill in action. They are pioneers who bring a new, compelling picture of the future to the present to meet people's needs. They courageously follow an inner sense of direction and stand for core values and clear principles. They think outside the box and embrace challenges and change. They focus on opportunities and solutions, not problems. They see mistakes as learning opportunities, ensuring future success.

Practical visionaries anticipate change; they're proactive rather than reactive. They think systemically—seeing processes and interconnections. They're aligned with their inner essence, or higher self, and link people's current needs to their deeper, spiritual needs. They radiate energy and vitality and express a balance of will, heart and mind, which can be seen as essential points on a triangle that need to stay in balance:

- **Will:** Expresses purpose, courage, focus, vitality and perseverance.

- **Heart:** Expresses compassion, harmony, mutual respect in relationships and empowerment of others.

- **Mind:** Expresses creative intelligence, whole systems thinking, intuition, thoughtful planning and problem-solving.

From a broader, integral perspective as described by author Ken Wilber in *Integral Psychology* , practical visionaries work in four quadrants: interior/individual (personal values); exterior/individual (personal behavior); interior/collective (collective values); and exterior/collective (collective behavior).

To be a practical visionary, you need to strengthen your inner spiritual life to receive a clear vision (interior/individual dimension). You also need to adopt effective external behaviors, such as developing a clear strategy to manifest your vision and pursuing achievable goals (exterior/individual dimension). To be successful and engage the support of others, you need to develop good relationship skills (interior/collective dimension). You also need to relate your individual vision to the needs of the world and adapt your behavior to the social/political/economic environment (exterior/collective dimension).

Practical visionaries are engaged in right livelihood. This is work that is in alignment with your deepest values and nourishes your soul. It's based on your higher purpose and expresses your inner self and your full talents. It is work that is done with awareness and mindfulness.

Right livelihood serves the true needs of others and does no harm to the earth. You could say that it expresses love in action, because you serve from a deeper state of *being*—not just *doing*. It requires that you purify your motives and be willing to serve with detachment from the fruits of your action—from either praise or blame.

Recent scientific research has found that altruistic service is good for you. Researchers at Harvard University and at Brown University Medical School found that people who help others and serve the world experience a profound sense of "helper's high"—a sense of well-being from their service.

Overcoming Short Circuits in Your Energy Flow

Right livelihood and manifesting your vision in the world work much like an electrical energy system. There needs to be a source of energy to plug into, a conductor or good wiring to carry the energy and a grounding outlet for the energy. To be a successful practical visionary, you have to have a good flow of energy from your spiritual source, through your personality and to a grounding outlet of service that receives the energy.

You have to be plugged in to become energized spiritually. Your personality has to be kept clear emotionally so that the energy can flow through unimpeded. You need to have a place of service where you're meeting a true need. Otherwise, you'll experience short circuits in your energy flow and be unable to express your vision effectively in the world.

The Law of Balanced Interchange: Energy Flowing in Equals Energy Flowing Out

You will have the energy and resources you need to carry out your work when you do the following:

- Connect to a power source (align with your higher spiritual purpose).

- Have a clear conductor (develop a loving heart, an intelligent mind, and release emotional blockages).

- Have a grounded connection to humanity (meet true needs with detachment from results).

All three aspects need to be in balance for you to become an effective server. Otherwise, there will be a short circuit—no connection—in the energy flow.

Types:	Over-Charged	Closed Circuit	Grounded Out	Balanced Flow
	Spaced out	Obsessed with personal growth	Martyr	Server
Spiritual Source (Power)	Over connected	No connection	No connection	Connected
Channel (Conductor)	Clogged	Clear	Clogged	Clear
World Need (Grounding)	No connection	No connection	Overconnected	Connected

Sounding a Clear Note of Purpose

Plugging into a spiritual energy source awakens you to your higher purpose in life and your vision for a better world. You can lay the groundwork by doing an inventory of your unique gifts and abilities. Research which fields of work need the passion and skills you have to give. Identify a need that is not currently being met and that you could help provide for. In *The Hope*, author Andrew Harvey suggests that you ask yourself what breaks your heart—what problem in the world do you find the most painful? This is where you'll find the passion to act, because you care so deeply. Follow your heartbreak. Purpose is connected to the sacred fire of your heart.

For example, Judy Wicks, founder of the highly successful White Dog Café in Philadelphia, was very concerned about the poverty and environmental destruction she found all around her. So she reframed the purpose of her restaurant as "a tool for the common good" and used it to raise money for the hungry, support local organic farmers, and sponsor seminars on racism, the environment, and social change.

Is there a burning vision within you that urgently wants to be expressed in the world? Turn within, connect to a spiritual energy source and ask about your soul's unique purpose: "What do I have to give the world that is really needed and that no one else is doing right now?"

Focusing on your purpose is like sounding a clear note on an inner level. A clear inner note calls everything around it through the law of resonance and attraction. Your note mysteriously draws people and resources that are in resonance with it to help you carry out your purpose. When you're in alignment with your purpose, you're more joyful. You're also more in tune with a higher plan—the Divine plan or the evolutionary design for humanity.

Why is having a clear purpose and vision so powerful? Quantum science provides some insights through research on the impact of invisible fields on human activities. Scientists are finding that matter is affected by nonlocal causes, that elementary particles are affected by connections that exist unseen across time and space. Creating a clear purpose and vision broadcasts a coherent field of intention, and this affects your (as well as other people's) thoughts and actions. It results in the unexpected synchronicities that bring wonderful possibilities to our lives and open new doors.

When there is a clear vision and purpose in an organization, there is tremendous coherence and energy. Things seem to happen effortlessly and magically. In fact, focusing on vision and mission is one of the latest trends in management. Clear purpose and commitment create a unified field of shared intention that produces the most productive, creative and high-energy organizations, because the resulting coherence creates a powerful, energetic vortex that aligns everything around it. And having a clear mission, in alignment with your soul's purpose, makes you more effective and productive in your own life.

For example, a key expression of my soul's purpose is to educate people about practical, spiritual approaches to leadership, business and politics. Hence, I've written books and articles on these themes, founded a leadership institute, and offered hundreds of public seminars on these ideas. I feel creative and excited about my work because it's aligned with my deeper purpose.

When I honestly examine my intentions and motives for doing something, it helps me eliminate things that aren't in alignment with my purpose. My *intention* helps me focus my *attention*. Examining my intentions acts as a powerful sorting system around all of the information that comes in to my awareness and all the possible activities I could choose to engage in. Therefore, I don't become distracted by so many unimportant externalities.

I've found many interesting activities in my area that I enjoy doing. But if I don't focus on my intention, my attention (and time and money) gets captured by a million diversions. They may not be bad in themselves, but they divert my energy from something more important and fulfilling that I want to accomplish.

Honest examination of my motives helps me purify them, so they are positive and loving rather than selfish or harmful to others. This examination is an incredibly difficult but powerful discipline.

Whether your vision is a part-time avocation or a full-time vocation depends on three things: your karmic obligations (the responsibilities you may have to your family or others), your previous experience and skills that may need developing, and the evolution of humanity in relation to the aspect of the evolutionary plan that you seek to serve.

In other words, are people ready to receive what you have to offer? Can you actually make a living in this profession, or is it so new that there is not an easy way to produce income from it yet? Are the colleagues whom you need to work with ready and available? The answers to these questions can affect the timing of expressing your higher purpose.

Your life purpose is your reason for being on Earth at this time. It's an expression of your soul and an integrating vision for your life that illustrates how everything fits together. It's the theme or quality around which you shape your life and work. Your life purpose is your shared mission to stand in the conscious presence of Spirit, and do what you can, moment by moment and day by day, collaborating with others to make this world a better place.

Your life purpose may be about learning to embody a new quality of *being*, such as compassion or courage. Or it may be mainly about *doing* something, such as starting an organization for peace.

Your life purpose is your unique contribution to the world that both serves a true need and expresses your natural talents. It gives you a profound sense of who you are, why you are here, where you come from, and where you are going. It often involves working on something bigger and more enduring than yourself. It's what you most enjoy, as it fills you with love and a sense of giving. It's about making a difference in the lives of others.

For example, Bill George, founder of Medtronic, said that the real purpose of his business is "to contribute to a just, open and sustainable society." Each year, he asks six customers to share their personal stories with employees, describing how the company's medical equipment has saved their lives or the lives of loved ones. This inspiration fuels the passion and commitment of his employees.

Discovering your life purpose is an ongoing process in which one thing can lead to another. As you step through one door, another opens. You have to learn how to work where life has placed you and make it a better place before you can move on. Look at your life, and see how everything you have experienced so far has been training and preparation to fulfill the current manifestation of your purpose.

Your purpose can be any number of things. For example, your purpose could be to learn about selfless love by raising a good family. Or it could be to write a book or produce a work of art, to invent a new technology, or to help someone create a new organization. At any particular time, it could also be to learn a spiritual lesson, to pay off karma, or to fulfill or balance out a relationship.

Your life purpose is often revealed by accidents or coincidences. Life is what happens to you while you're busy making plans. Pay attention to the signals you receive from life. Your soul often puts your personality in a position where you have to draw on the resources of your soul to get through it. Allowing your soul to express and radiate more completely through you generally happens more easily as you age—thank goodness! It probably becomes easier because you've tried everything else and found that being in soul consciousness brings the greatest joy.

What You Have to Unlearn About Your Purpose

You need to unlearn the idea that everything about your purpose must be unique to you. Some parts of your purpose are shared by other human beings; it is always a group mission of some kind. You must also unlearn the idea that your purpose   is something that Spirit orders you to do without any agreement from your soul, mind and heart. You always have free will to cooperate with Spirit or not. Your purpose is about receiving guidance from God or other spiritual beings and co-creating together.

You also need to release the idea that your unique purpose must consist of some achievement that all the world will see. In reality, no one may ever know about your purpose or achievement, so be detached from recognition and fame.

Lastly, let go of the idea that what you have accomplished is only your doing. Acknowledge and appreciate the help you receive from other people. Thank friends and colleagues who have helped you or laid the groundwork for you to take the next step. And inwardly give thanks to the help you've received from the spiritual dimensions. We all have many spiritual guides who open doors for us and arrange for seeming coincidences in people we meet and for resources and support that come our way.

How to Use Your Chakra Energies to Manifest Your Vision

This section is one of the most important sections in this book. There are seven steps in expressing a vision effectively in the world, related to your seven chakras or etheric energy centers. In becoming a practical visionary, it helps to understand how energy flows through your centers and where there are blocks or imbalances. The ideal is to have visionary energy from your highest chakra (at the top of your head) flowing unimpeded through each chakra until it is grounded in a practical way through your lowest chakra, the root chakra. The following steps will help you realize your intention.

1. Align your vision (crown, or pineal center). The first step is to focus your attention in your crown chakra at the top of your head. Affirm your intention to align with your soul, your higher purpose and your core values, guided by concern for the common good. Then take some time in the silence to turn within and ask for an intuitive vision.

A vision is a specific, compelling picture of a desirable future that is achievable and appropriate. It includes a long-term, whole-systems perspective. Vision can be described as a field that brings energy into form. It may come in words, pictures or symbols, or just as a sensed energy. It may be about embodying a quality of energy and/or doing something.

For example, my friend Daniel Greenberg is an educator who is deeply concerned about global warming and the destruction of the environment. He wanted students to learn how to create a more sustainable future and receive university credit for living and studying in ecovillages around the world. So he created a nonprofit called Living Routes through which students can do this.

Your vision may be learning how to be more loving toward your family, for example, or it may be promoting Spirit in business. When you're clear about your vision for the future, it helps to constantly reaffirm and articulate it to create a coherent and magnetic field of energy around it. Having a clear vision will start magnetizing people, resources and ideas toward you.

2. Shape your vision into a clear mission with strategy and goals (brow, or ajna, center). Focus your energy and intention in the intuitive brow center in the middle of your forehead. Think clearly, and create a specific mission to describe how you will achieve your vision. Next, create a strategic plan and clear goals as steps to achieve your mission. Your goals will provide focal points for your attention and will attract energy, because energy follows thought.

Create SMART but flexible goals: Specific, Measurable, Achievable, Realistic, Timed. Then prioritize your time and commitments, which is like creating a magic circle to work within — inscribing boundaries that contain and harness your energy. Without clear boundaries, you will be tempted to take on too much and dissipate your energy. You have to be able to say no to some things and prioritize others.

If your larger vision is learning how to be more loving toward your family, your specific mission might be to appreciate each family member daily and express gratitude more frequently. If your vision is creating Spirit in business, your specific mission might be to create an organization that hosts a monthly public forum with dialogues among local business leaders to create mutual support.

3. Communicate your mission creatively and sound a clear note (throat center).

Your throat center is your creative will center and can help you be disciplined, imaginative and innovative in how you express your mission. It focuses and directs your will to accomplish your goals and project a clear thoughtform of your mission. It helps you focus on opportunities and solutions, not problems. Get feedback from others about how clear and compelling your communication of your mission is. You may want to employ new media technologies, for example, as well as face-to-face communication. Research the best ways to get your message to others, and if appropriate, develop a public relations strategy.

For example, if your mission is creating Spirit in business through socially responsible business forums, you might want to develop a colorful, interactive Web site, social media site, and an e-mail list to attract potential participants. You might also want to attend business mixers at the Chamber of Commerce and Rotary clubs to meet potential participants and invite them to your forum.

4. Develop good relationships to ensure support (heart center). Reach out to other people to enlist their support and collaboration in helping you create a harmonious environment to manifest your vision. The best way to reach out is from the heart—by being sensitive, respectful and appreciative. Express gratitude on a regular basis for help you've received.

Marc Lesser, founder of Brush Dance, said that he learned to take a few minutes each day to appreciate an employee, to thank them for a job well done or to just listen to their concerns. Simple things like this can make people feel supported. He found that generosity with his time can be as important as generosity with his money.

It's important to develop good listening skills so that people feel heard. Don't make communication a one-way street. Encourage team spirit, and build a sense of community and trust with people who are drawn to your vision. Agree on a process for resolving any conflicts that might emerge so that your relationships will be harmonious.

If your mission is creating Spirit in business through public forums, you might want to invite others to co-sponsor and/or co-host the dialogues, or you might want to invite guest speakers from local businesses. If you hire staff in your business, you can express heart energy by offering supportive and generous benefits.

5. Energize your mission with emotional enthusiasm (solar plexus center). To generate emotional power, confidence and enthusiasm for your mission, you need to energize your solar plexus center at your navel and express the dynamic "fire in the belly" needed to ignite others and attract allies and supporters. You need a burning desire to make the vision manifest and the passion to do whatever it takes to see it through. Enthusiasm is contagious and ignites others. Risk-taking and playfulness bring excitement to your project.

Many good spiritual people try to keep their attention out of the solar plexus center and the next two lower ones, wrongly thinking that these centers aren't spiritual. Or they may repress the energy in their solar plexus center or it may be depleted, and they wonder why their visions don't manifest.

To kindle your passion and enthusiasm about your Spirit in business forums, for example, you could brainstorm and write down the reasons you want to do this project, whom it will help, and what you enjoy about it. You can also talk to other people about why you want to do your mission and what inspires you about it and ask for their feedback and support. You can also read about similar initiatives around the country and attend conferences on this theme, because this can energize you.

6. Attract resources (sexual/financial center). The sexual center is the life force center of vitality. It's not only concerned with sexual procreation and attracting people but also with vitality and attracting prosperity. Madison Avenue clearly knows this as they use sex to sell everything. If this life force energy is inhibited or blocked, financial resources may be lacking. Scarcity consciousness around money and lack of generosity also block the flow. Focusing energy in this center will make your mission vital, attractive and compelling—even if it's a public forum on business. It will attract investors, donors and/or paying customers.

7. Ground the vision with practical, sustainable strategies (root/survival center). Here is where the rubber meets the road—

where your vision and mission meet real human need and where you need clear strategies for survival, security and safety. The root center at the base of your spine is the life-giving principle. Honoring this grounding energy, you create a basic survival strategy, interface carefully with local bureaucracies, make sure that you are following legal, financial and health requirements and deal with physical-plane realities such as buildings and transportation. You also make sure that you've created a healthy, comfortable and safe environment for people.

You can't have successful dialogues on Spirit and business, for example, without renting a meeting room or at least finding a comfortable living room, setting up a business or nonprofit to receive money and pay bills, keeping records of your expenses and income and filing yearly taxes. Too many visionaries come up with great ideas and announce their events or projects, thinking that the rest will magically fall out of the sky without them having to do the hard work to organize it or pay someone else to do it. Some spiritual types seem to be allergic to the physical world!

Through the process of spiritual growth and expansion of consciousness, each chakra will open eventually and radiate balanced energy. Your inner world affects your outer expression in the world. The key is to appreciate and love each chakra; each one is equally spiritual and important. Remember that Spirit and matter are simply different frequencies of energy along the same spectrum. Your crown center and root center are different frequencies, each with a specific, sacred function that is essential to your overall well-being and that of your mission or project.

Spiritual Stages in Creating a New Organization

If your mission is to create a new organization with others, a 15-step process of translating your vision from creative inspiration into an organism and finally into an organization can be helpful. The process is about translating energies from one frequency to another, materializing Spirit and spiritualizing matter.

The Creative Inspiration

1. Contacting the Vision: A new organization or project begins as an inspired idea or vision in the mind of its initiator, who aligns spiritually, penetrates into a higher realm of spiritual purpose and energy and then transmits that energy through himself or herself to the intended creation. The founder holds the purpose of the proposed project, evaluating its alignment with the higher evolutionary plan and its place within it. The greater the alignment with higher purpose, the greater are the power and life force of the project.

2. Clarifying the Mission and Inscribing the Circle: After meditation on the perceived purpose, the founder mentally formulates a plan to manifest the higher purpose through a specific mission and goals. He or she visualizes this plan in detail, creating thoughtforms that embody the purpose and are suitable for the consciousness and needs of the times. He or she defines the circle within which he or she will work. Boundaries are established for focus and for clarifying who can participate. The founder needs to hold a point of spiritual and mental tension with a pure motive so that manifestation will be inevitable.

The Emergence of an Organism

3. Sounding a Clear Note in the World: The founder sounds forth words of creative power describing the new organization and communicating the vision and mission clearly. This sounding of the integrated note of Spirit and matter radiates from the center to the periphery and attracts those who resonate.

4. Balancing Core Qualities: To successfully manifest, the founder balances will, love and light (clear mental energy) within himself or herself individually or within his or her core group. This balance can be created by developing the needed qualities personally or by attracting individuals who embody each quality.

5. Aligning of Incoming Members: As new people are attracted (members, staff or volunteers), they are given the vision of the group's purpose and mission as well as methods to achieve an alignment with the soul of the group.

6. Invoking Energy: The group invokes the appropriate energies, enthusiasm and commitment to accomplish the next stage of the group's work and to manifest its mission.

7. Defining the Roles of Leaders: A triangle of a central leader, a director of internal affairs and a director of external affairs is eventually created. These leaders are people who have already taken on responsibilities and have the needed abilities and qualities. Leadership rotates based on experience and wisdom related to the function needed.

8. Outlining the Group Process: The leaders (with other group members if appropriate) develop flexible and fluid processes for carrying out the work needed. The decision-making process, criteria for membership and task groups for specific work are established and assigned.

- **Establishing Circles of Commitment:** As the group attracts additional members, concentric circles of involvement and commitment are defined. Members taking most responsibility for the group work closest to the center and have the most authority.

222

- **Defining Roles of Group Members:** Members find their own levels and niches in relation to the center and in taking responsibility and are then given authority as appropriate.

- **Dealing With Shadows:** A process is established for how the group handles problems—the shadow elements and conflicts that emerge in both leaders and members.

The Development Into an Organization

9. Elaborating Energy Flow Systems: As the organism grows, energy dynamics become more complex and require more attention, as increasingly complex communication systems and organizational structures are established.

10. Balancing Livingness and Structure: A challenge arises as the demands for more structure to deal with complexity require vigilance to balance structure with the livingness and flexibility of the organism.

11. Passing on Leadership: As the organization matures, leadership/inspiration is passed on to a larger group, which holds the vision and carries out responsibilities.

12. Maintaining Life Force: As time passes and flows of energy solidify, the need for creativity, renewal and livingness become important issues to address.

13. Resisting Bureaucratization: As the original founders depart and inspiration fades, bureaucratization can take over and ultimately dominate.

14. Crystallizing Into Rigidity: An organization can become so encrusted with rules and structures that it becomes rigid and unable to respond to evolutionary changes.

15. Allowing Death: An organization that has fulfilled its purpose and outlived its time has the right to die, so that the life can be released and new forms can be created. Unfortunately, many organizations are kept on artificial life support far past their time.

Finding the Right Timing for Your Vision

To be a successful practical visionary, it is important to choose the right timing to bring your vision into the world so that it meets a current need and receives the best reception. In other words, you have to connect your passion to give with the capacity of others to receive. Conditions in the world and in your immediate environment need to be auspicious.

Every spiritual tradition honors right timing. The Bible states, "To everything there is a season ...," and the Chinese *I Ching* says, "A wise man knows when to wait and when to act." Even popular astrologers help people choose the right time to begin something.

Many visionaries are intuitive and creative but have big issues with time. They value the future, but they are impatient with the past and the present. The future seems to be so real and present in their lives that they are always pushing things to hurry up. They see the future outcome and are anxious for the present process to catch up, so they create greater stress for themselves. Their impatience can lead them to miss key opportunities and synchronistic events.

By studying synchronicity (an unusual alignment of events in time), you can recognize an important opportunity presenting itself. Someone may show up with the exact ideas or experience that you need at that moment. A physical space may suddenly open up somewhere that provides the right environment.

You can choose the right time to bring your work into the world through careful study and research, following your intuition and responding to synchronicities that present themselves.

Your intuition comes from alignment with your soul, which expands your consciousness and helps you think more clearly and synthetically. It helps you see the big picture and larger context so that you can make better choices and be more efficient.

You need to pick the right moment in the collective consciousness to offer "an idea whose time has come"—something fresh that meets a real need in the world. You need to do your homework and make sure that it's neither too radical nor too old and hackneyed. Research what's already being done in the arena in which you're interested. Find out if the climate is right. Are people ready to receive it and respond positively?

You also have to be sure that the people who could help you are ready to become engaged. Maybe they have to finish up some other work, or learn something first, or move into your area. Often, a wave of energy moves in a new direction and many people pick up on it intuitively and look for a way to get on board.

Notice the various alternating cycles in our collective consciousness—politically, from liberal to conservative; economically, from expanding to contracting; culturally, from restrictive to free; etc.—and match your offering to the times. The wise person knows when to act and when to wait.

Managing Time Efficiently to Manifest Your Vision

If you think that you are too busy and don't have enough time to make your vision a reality, how can you release your scarcity consciousness around time? How can you make time your friend, rather than an enemy you have to beat? How can you fill your time with magic and meaning, rather than with stress?

Time management is not about getting more things done or working harder. It's about prioritizing what's important—your higher purpose and what your heart values.

Focus on essentials, on your purpose and values, and put first things first. When you focus on the results you want to achieve, rather than on activities you are doing, you'll accomplish more. Ask yourself what you hope to achieve with each activity. Write down each major activity you plan to do tomorrow, and ask yourself, "What result do I hope to achieve from this?" Write down the goal next to the activity, and ask yourself if doing the activity is worthwhile.

Prioritize important activities that may not need to get done immediately but are quality-of-life issues that are central to your purpose and goals. What gives your life meaning, what inspires you, what is your passion, and what is your life mission? You might want to post a mission statement for yourself where you can see it each day to remind you to organize your time around it.

Don't respond to urgent activities that seek your attention if they don't relate to your goals or help you make a significant contribution to the world.

The key is to develop the right rhythm and pace in your work and create a balance between work and rest so that you don't burn out. Avoid rhythmic entrainment, that is, allowing your rhythms to fall into synchronicity with the people around you. Research has shown that nature likes harmonization. You're unconsciously influenced by the speed of people and activities all around you, so beware if people in your environment are too speedy or too lethargic and slow, and make adjustments. Their rhythms may not be appropriate for you.

Simplify your life, and release some activities. Less can be more—more quality and more fulfillment. Avoid multitasking and scattering your focus, which usually results in a much-reduced quality of life and tasks not being done well. It's also disrespectful when you don't give people your full attention or when you have to ask them to repeat things because you were focusing on something else.

Plan your activities more effectively. Are there ways you can eliminate steps, combine operations, shorten procedures, stream-line paperwork and remove bottlenecks? Analyze recurring crises to see if there is any pattern involved that can be planned for bet-ter.

Flexibility is crucial to successful planning. Allow time for the unexpected—a traffic jam or a jammed printer. Life is what hap-pens to us while we're busy making plans.

Schedule your activities. While planning is an intention, sched-uling is a commitment. The key to scheduling is the belief that there is a time and a place for everything. Give important activi-ties large blocks of time when you're at your best. You might also want to schedule an interrupted block of quiet time so that you can concentrate on your work. Getting an early start will give you more lead time and a more relaxed feeling of spaciousness.

Take your passion and make it happen. You need not only an inspirational vision but also skill in action. Working with your vision in a step-by-step process can help it take tangible shape in the world and benefit others.

Join the legion of practical visionaries worldwide creating new solutions to our problems by manifesting their visions. As President John F. Kennedy said in his Inaugural address, "Here on Earth, God's work must truly be our own."

SPIRITUAL PRACTICES

Practical Visionary Worksheet

Create Your Vision Statement

Create a vision statement for your life and/or your organization. It should be a clear, compelling picture of the future. You can use the Meditation on Discovering Your Vision and Contribution from Chapter 5. When you are ready, write your vision statement in this format:

1. My vision for_____is:_____.

2. I care about this vision because_____.

3. I will enlist the help of others to achieve this vision

by_____.

4. Share what you've written with some trusted friends. Give a short, enthusiastic speech, and elicit their honest feedback: Was your vision clear? Did it inspire and motivate them? How could you refine your vision statement?

5. Develop clear boundaries for yourself in order to focus your energy, time and resources. List what's *not* included in your vision and what you will *not* do:

_____.

Shape Your Vision Into a Mission and Strategy

6. Write a specific mission to express your vision:

_____

7. List the SMART goals you would like to achieve. (SMART goals are Specific, Measurable, Achievable, Realistic and Timed)

_____

8. Create a step-by-step strategy for achieving your mission and goals (on another sheet of paper). Think clearly about the next step you need to take, and build on that.

9. What is the next step you need to take tomorrow or next week to actualize your strategy?_____

10. On another sheet of paper, make an inventory of your resources (both tangible and intangible) as well as your allies and friends. Then reflect on how to make the best use of each resource and each friend to help you achieve your goals.

Overcome Barriers to Success

11. Explore the self-created barriers to your success as a leader. The first step toward overcoming them is to name and face them. Circle the emotional reactions listed below that apply to you.

- FEAR—of success, of failure, financial ruin, what others may think, etc.
- LOW SELF-ESTEEM—lack of confidence and belief in yourself.
- OVERSENSITIVITY—overreacting to criticism.
- GUILT—feelings of unworthiness because of past actions; concern that you do not deserve the best.
- VICTIMIZATION—blaming others for your lack of success.
- ISOLATION—not relating to others.
- REJECTION OF RESPONSIBILITY—not wanting to be visible, take a stand publicly, or fulfill commitments.
- IMPATIENCE—needing immediate results; unwillingness to wait.

- RIGIDITY OF THOUGHT—closed-minded to considering other possibilities.
- LACK OF CREATIVITY—inability to imagine a different way.
- LACK OF FOCUS—scattered energies going in many directions.
- LAZINESS—lack of discipline to do what's needed.

12. Use these techniques each week to overcome one of your barriers to success:

- **Explore the cause of the barrier.** Trace the negative pattern to where it was created (in childhood or more recently), and answer these questions: Why did I create this pattern, what good did it serve (then), and why have I continued with this pattern?

- **Develop the positive.** Write the positive quality that is the opposite of each negative barrier you circled in question 11 (e.g. courage instead of fear)

  _____

- **Affirm the positive.** Pick the most difficult barrier that you listed above and write an affirmation for yourself using the positive quality. I express _____
  when I_____.

- **Visualize.** Relax and breathe deeply. Visualize yourself expressing the positive quality that you listed above. See yourself embodying it in daily life. Use your breath to energize it, desire it and commit to it.

- **Act as if.** Practice expressing this positive quality in your daily life and soon you'll experience it as a reality.

A Diagnostic Tool for Balancing Energy Flows

This assessment tool is based on the seven chakras and can be helpful in analyzing the energy flow in an individual or organization, because organizations operate through energy centers just like individuals. It will help you understand which areas are positive and strong and which are blocked, dysfunctional and need attention.

Rate how often you or your organization expresses each quality.

0 = never 1 = rarely 2 = occasionally 3 = average 4 = often 5 = always

Positive/Balanced Expression   *Blocked/Dysfunctional Expression*

1. SURVIVAL ENERGY

___ Safety and security	___Anxiety about survival
___ Realism and groundedness	___Disconnection from reality
___ Practicality	___Lack of practical sense
___ Consistent follow-through	___Weak or sporadic follow-through
___ Physically supportive environment	___Tense, unsafe environment
___ Ability to protect and defend	___Fight-or-flight tendency
___ TOTAL	___TOTAL

2. SEXUAL/FINANCIAL ENERGY

___ Prosperity	___Poverty; indebtedness
___ Balanced money management	___Obsessive pursuit of money
___ Generosity	___Stinginess; scarcity consciousness
___ Attractiveness; magnetism	___Blandness
___ Vitality; stamina	___Depletion; exhaustion
___ Respect between the sexes	___Sexual harassment; disrespect
___ TOTAL	___TOTAL

3. EMOTIONAL/POWER ENERGY

___ Empowerment of self and others	___Stifling control
___ Dynamism; enthusiasm	___Emotional numbness; inertia
___ Positive, can-do attitude	___Depression
___ Confidence	___Hesitancy; low self-esteem
___ Risk taking	___Risk aversion
___ Passion; playfulness	___Overseriousness; boredom
___ TOTAL	___TOTAL

4. HEART/RELATIONSHIP ENERGY

___ Harmonious relationships	___Conflict; resentment
___ Trust	___Suspiciousness
___ Respect for others	___Exploitation; overwork
___ Teamwork; collaboration	___Excessive competition
___ Attitude of service	___Selfishness; egotism
___ Commitment; loyalty	___High turnover
___ TOTAL	___TOTAL

5. WILL/CREATIVE ENERGY

___ Discipline; focus	___Laziness; unruliness
___ Steadfastness; perseverance	___Diffusion of energy
___ Balanced, regulated action	___Out of control; over-controlled
___ Clear communication	___Miscommunication
___ Creativity; originality	___Lack of imagination
___ Innovation	___Conformity
___ TOTAL	___TOTAL

6. MENTAL ENERGY

___ Clear, strategic thinking	___Lack of strategy; chaos
___ Good management of people and resources	___Waste of resources; disorganization
___ Proactive planning for the future	___Reactive responses
___ Intelligent, effective strategies	___Poorly designed strategies
___ Efficiency	___Duplication and bureaucracy
___ Clarity	Vagueness
___ TOTAL	___TOTAL

7. VISIONARY ENERGY

___ Alignment with a higher purpose or mission	___Lack of direction; confusion
___ Long-term, whole-systems thinking	___Narrow, short-term thinking
___ Universality	___Parochialism
___ Openness to progressive change	___Rigidity; crystallization
___ Commitment to ethics and values	___Lack of ethics; neglect of values
___ Guided by the common good	___Guided by self-interest
___ TOTAL	___TOTAL

_____ OVERALL TOTAL   _____OVERALL TOTAL

Scoring

A high overall score of 141-210 in the left column indicates that you and your organization have a healthy and balanced expression of energies and are likely to be positive and successful. **A high overall score in the right column** indicates blockage, dysfunction or underperformance that needs attention.

A medium overall score of 71-140 in the left column indicates an average expression of positive qualities that could be improved. **A medium overall score in the right column** indicates some blockage or underperformance that should be addressed.

A low overall score of 0-70 in the left column indicates blockage, dysfunction or underperformance that needs attention and support. **A low overall score in the right column** indicates a healthy and balanced expression of energies.

Noticing which areas in each column have the highest scores will reveal strengths and weaknesses. Awareness of imbalances in each area is the first step toward correction. Weaker or blocked qualities can be transformed by cultivating the positive quality in the opposite column. An individual or an organization that expresses New World qualities will tend to have higher scores in the left column, indicating positive expression in each area, and lower scores in the right column. Note whether the higher scores are in practical areas, such as survival and financial energy, or in visionary areas. An effective and inspirational individual or organization will have a balance between the practical and the visionary energies.

Reflective Exercises on Managing Time

Reflect on the following questions, and write your responses on another sheet of paper.

In the past week, when did you say to yourself, "I don't have time for_____"? What types of activities did you not have time for?

In the past week, when did you say to yourself, "I can *always* make time for_____"? What types of activities did you make time for? Can you see any pattern here?

In the coming week or month, what are some urgent but unimportant activities you need to deal with?

What are some important activities, which may not need to be done immediately but are key to your personal goals and values?

What are some important activities that are also time urgent?

What are some unimportant and nonurgent activities?

What changes can you make to reorganize your schedule to honor what's important?

How can you better prioritize your activities to more effectively achieve your goals? What changes in your scheduling process will help you achieve your goals?

KEY INSIGHTS TO REFLECT ON

◆ A practical visionary develops a clear mission and an effective strategy with achievable goals.

◆ A practical visionary leads from the inside out, employs skill in action, and embodies a balance of will, heart and mind.

◆ Right livelihood is work that is in alignment with your deepest values and nourishes your soul.

◆ Having a clear life purpose broadcasts a coherent field of intention and attracts people and resources.

◆ You can manifest your vision through each chakra by visioning, creating a clear mission, communicating creatively, connecting from the heart, energizing emotionally, attracting resources, and developing a practical survival strategy.

◆ You should find the right timing to bring your vision into the world so that it meets a current need and receives the best reception.

Key #7

See Money as a Spiritual Asset

Trust in the Abundance of the Universe and Be Practical and Wise

---

We make a living by what we get,

But we make a life by what we give.

— Winston Churchill[1]

Developing Trust and Creating a Harmonious, Attractive Field

To attract financial abundance to fulfill your higher purpose, it is important to have faith in the abundance of the universe and to practice generosity. It's also important to appreciate money as a spiritual asset and to be a practical custodian of it.

My most amazing experience with manifesting abundance was when Gordon and I were inwardly guided in a meditation to buy 86 acres of land in Massachusetts to create a spiritual community and ecovillage. We needed a large amount of money to buy the land, so we prayed and worked very hard on trusting the benevolence of the universe and God's abundant supply.

We didn't expect money to fall out of the sky—we knew that we had to do our part by not only praying but moving our feet. So we went to a local bank to ask about borrowing the money. But when they found out that we had no permanent address and no permanent jobs, they laughed us out the door.

So we went to a conference on New World ideas in New Hampshire and asked several people whom we knew had money if they would be interested in helping. To our amazement, three out of the four people we asked said yes right away! We raised the whole down payment for the land in one day. The next day, one of these angels called us and offered us even more money! Then, the owner of the land generously agreed to give us the mortgage himself—at half the going rate.

We learned that when you follow your inner guidance and have trust in God, miracles do happen. We gave a prayer of thanks for all of this amazing help.

But we discovered that trust in God and the abundance of the universe is not the only thing needed to manifest money. Several months after we bought the land, a dozen people had joined us and we faced a new challenge. Our monthly mortgage payment was due in two days, and we had no money to pay it. We'd been meditating and affirming our faith in God to provide, but we were also fighting and arguing with one another about what to do.

We finally realized that we had to work out our conflicts and create harmony among ourselves if we wanted to attract financial resources. So that's what we did.

Literally the next day, a visitor arrived and spent the day with us and, as she was leaving, she said, "Oh, by the way, I have a donation for you. I was going to send it a couple of weeks ago, but I forgot." It turned out that the donation was the exact amount we needed for the mortgage! But the really interesting part was that she could have sent it weeks earlier, but we weren't ready to receive it then. We hadn't done our part in resolving our conflicts and creating a harmonious, loving group field to attract the money.

Appreciating Money

Money is neither good nor bad in itself. It's simply a neutral instrument for measuring exchange based on a community agreement. It's a tracking and scoring system for production and transactions among people. Money is an energy that communicates between material things and facilitates human relationships. It has the values we each give it through our attitudes and how we use it. It's also a way to examine how well we're applying our values—such as fairness and honesty— in our transactions.

On a deeper, metaphysical level money is concretized energy or *prana* (life force). If Spirit is matter at its highest vibration and matter is Spirit at its lowest vibration, money is actually Spirit vibrating at a slow frequency. Money can be seen as both a particle (a coin or bill) and a wave (a flow of financial energy). Seen as a particle, money can create attachment—either desire or fear of lack. Seen as a wave, money is a stream of flowing energy that should circulate widely. When it's freely given, more can be received from the abundant supply of the universe. This wave is called the divine circulatory flow.

Did you know that the word *money* is from the Roman fertility goddess Moneta, an aspect of Juno? The first money was minted in her temple. Money is a spiritual energy and a sacred trust to be used wisely for ourselves and the good of all.

The word *money* has an "m" before the word *one*, followed by a "y," so I like to see it as a lens to observe "my one-ness" with all that is. When I examine my discretionary spending by looking at my check stubs and credit card bills, I see a clear statement of what I actually value among the things that cost money. The stubs and bills show me what I'm willing to spend my accumulated life energy on.

Why Spiritual People Have Money Problems

Many visionaries and good spiritual people often lack the money needed to manifest their visions and make their work effective. While many people in our society are obsessed with and greedy about money, many spiritual people do not value it and even ignore it. Thus, their projects don't thrive or contribute to the New World.

Spirituality and financial abundance are not mutually exclusive. It all depends on what you do with your money—whether you selfishly hoard it or use it to help others. Can you hold money as a sacred trust and responsibility?

Many good people seem to experience an inner split or dualism, believing that money is connected only with worldly things, pleasure, comfort and desire, and that spirituality is a world set apart. Many spiritual people are often too detached from the material world, focused primarily on higher mental, abstract levels and not very connected to Earth. They may also have a sense of distaste or laziness in dealing with the material side of life.

Since money is a medium of exchange, if you are not involved in exchange with the world, you may not be able to attract money to yourself.

You may also have ambivalence toward money—about earning it, asking for it, or even having it, and therefore, you don't attract it easily. Your selflessness may result in an inappropriate sense of shame in needing to manifest money.

As author Eric Butterworth noted in *Spiritual Economics*, any person who is experiencing lack is living in opposition to the universal flow. Financial problems may be the outer manifestation of inner states of consciousness.

If you are having problems attracting money, you may have experienced a wounding from negative experiences around money, such as dysfunctional family patterns when you were growing up, that left you with a sense of fear, worry or scarcity. How many of us were told that money is the root of all evil or that money doesn't grow on trees? Do you subconsciously believe that you have to have to nearly kill yourself through hard work to earn money?

Chakra imbalances and blockages in your lower centers, especially in the sexual chakra, can also be the cause of a lack of financial resources. You may have been surprised by discovering that your sexual center is also your money center, but advertisers know this quite well. It is why they use sex to sell products. You need to honor and appreciate your lower chakras, as well as your higher ones, and visualize energy circulating to your sexual chakra.

If you have trouble with money, another possible cause is a lack of education and training in how to rightly handle money. Know your flow. Count your money carefully, and know exactly how much you take in, how much you spend and exactly where it goes. You need to know not only how to balance your checkbook, but also how to invest your money wisely and in a socially responsible manner.

There's another reason you might have trouble attracting money: you may have experienced one or more past lives in a religious order, an ashram or a monastery, where money was ignored or seen as evil. If this is something you'd like to explore, you could begin a deep dialogue with your subconscious mind, telling it that a vow of poverty may have been appropriate in the past but it isn't relevant today. It's also important to release the attitude that money always taints spiritual endeavors, because this attitude is no longer appropriate for today.

Another possibility to consider is that you might have a subconscious memory from a past life when money was misused through greed, selfishness or dishonesty, which creates a deep lack of trust in yourself to use money rightly today. To transform a past experience such as this would require dialogue with your subconscious to forgive what was done in the past so you can move on.

Recognizing and Transforming Unhealthy Attitudes

You may have noticed that a part of your personality is perpetually a consumer—always hungry to be filled. The hunger can seem like an insatiable hole, a craving to own, possess and accumulate in order to feel happy. However, this hunger can never be fully satisfied materially. It can be truly filled only by your soul.

Take time from the frantic busyness of the modern world to turn within and become quiet enough to hear the voice of your soul, and you'll discover what will truly bring happiness. The soul is like the sun, a producer and generator of energy, rather than a consumer of energy. Identifying with the soul will help you drop the sense of scarcity and fear that there's not enough to go around.

Having enough means having what is needed to fulfill your life purpose, which may vary depending on the nature and scope of that purpose. Today many people are affirming that what they already have is sufficient and are joining suffiency networks and simplicity networks to support one another in this approach.

Each of us has a karmic bank account. Your good deeds or contributions (deposits) are balanced by your harmful actions or unjustified takings (withdrawals). Debt is one measure of how much more you have taken from life rather than given to life.

Pay off whatever debts you can, because there is an etheric link between you and any person or institution you owe money to. It's difficult to attract money if you're not free of unnecessary debt. House mortgages and car loans may be necessary debts for most people.

I learned an important lesson about debt many years ago when I didn't have the money I needed to stay at the spiritual community that I was visiting in Scotland. An insight came to me when I realized that the college loans and other debt I had were pulling on my energy and getting in the way of being able to attract the money I needed. I made a deep inner commitment to pay off the loans, no matter what it took to earn the money. I was ready to work hard and even do administrative work (which I really disliked at that time), if that's what it would have taken.

When I made that decision to finally take responsibility for my debts, something shifted inwardly. I released the energy that was blocking my financial flow, and I was finally able to manifest money. Out of the blue, my grandmother (who usually gave me only small gifts at Christmas and birthdays) suddenly decided to write me a large check to pay off all of my loans so that I could stay at the spiritual community—even though she didn't quite understand what it was about.

You can experience many spiritual tests around the issue of money. For example, are you willing to compromise your key values for money? I was given this test when a major donor for our nonprofit didn't like some political statements made in our e-newsletter and said that she wouldn't fund our newsletter if we continued to make strong political statements that seemed too partisan to her. Free expression of political views is very important to me, so I said, "No, thanks." I won't compromise my values to gain financial support. Fortunately, an abundant Universe soon provided the needed finances from other sources.

How Money Can Be a Spiritual Asset

Needing to attract money to sustain yourself and your work keeps you grounded and connected with meeting the true needs of society. Money creates relationships with the people you share it with, and relationships can help your spiritual development. Money can also be a wonderful mirror for you to see yourself more clearly; your spending patterns show what you really value, beyond the necessities of life.

Money is very useful for buying spiritual resources, such as books, seminars and counseling, to aid your development. It can buy time for spiritual study, practice and quiet retreats. It can provide for your physical health and the sense of well-being necessary to be of service to others. How can you help others and change the world if you're sick, tired or stressed out?

Some people think that spiritual service shouldn't be tainted by money, but most service work in the world, including spiritual teaching and healing, does require money and sometimes a great deal of it. Money can help people be more effective in their service and help their service expand. Charging for services, for example, can provide a spiritual teacher with the money to rent a larger facility to help more people, print more literature, hire extra staff, or buy advertising space to let people know about a book or a class.

With the new practical approaches to spirituality today, many spiritual teachers, healers, and counselors are charging reasonable fees for their classes and services in order to support themselves so that they can devote their energy full-time to their spiritual service. Charging for their services is preferable to working at regular jobs and trying to squeeze in their spiritual work when they have the time and are not too tired. Service isn't more spiritual just because it's volunteer work. It's great for all of us to have more full-time healers, teachers and counselors. The problem is when someone gets greedy and charges exorbitant fees to satisfy his or her ego or to keep score with others. There's plenty of this greed in the spiritual movement today. You can't measure your spirituality by how much you earn from your service work.

Having money can also enable people to move at whichever levels of society are needed for their spiritual service. If someone's service is working with major business leaders, for example, where a great deal of travel is required, he or she will need the kind of money that enables this.

As a spiritual person, it is important to realize that physical living, when motivated from the spiritual levels, is equally important to spiritual practice. One of the greatest gifts you can give to the world is the example of a well-balanced life of giving to others, where you balance Spirit and matter. You can do well by doing good. Spirituality and financial abundance are not mutually exclusive when you do work that helps others.

Attracting Money to Meet Real Needs

Need, love and magnetic power are the three things that must be present to attract money for your service work. You must have a clear need for the money. You must have sufficient love—of yourself, others, your work and life itself. You must also be magnetic through your positive energy and faith in the abundance of the universe. As you focus on thoughts that are for the benefit of the wider community, your magnetic attraction of money will become stronger.

The Bible says, "Seek ye first the kingdom of heaven, and all things will be added unto you." Recognize that God, or the Universe, is the source of all abundance, and develop an attitude of gratitude for what you've already been given. See yourself as a custodian, rather than an owner, of money and material things. As you give away things you no longer need or use, you create a vacuum for money to flow in. Clean out your closets and drawers. It is amazing how much stuff you accumulate that you no longer need.

By maintaining detachment and avoiding obsession with money and possessions, you retain your inner freedom and dignity. To be a spiritual master of money, you must resist using it to indulge your sensual desires out of indolence, or to gain personal power over others. You can then hold money as a sacred trust to be used for the good of humanity.

Right Circulation: Tithing and Blessing Money

Circulation to all parts of the whole is the key to the health of our economic system. Clinging to money, rather than circulating it, indicates a poverty and scarcity consciousness. It creates congestion, stagnation and spiritual and physical illness, because you place yourself outside the universal flow.

As you give, so shall you receive. Tithing 5 percent to 10 percent of your income to good causes is a powerful way to overcome your fear of lack and to open to the flow of abundance. By consistently giving, you move universal substance, forming a vacuum that substance rushes in to fill with a new supply. When you give money freely for spiritual purposes, it automatically redeems you from past negative karma with money. Give with absolute release, detachment and generosity, and without expectation of thanks, self-gratification or control. When you give, communicate appreciation for the recipient.

Bless money as you donate it and use it to pay for goods and services. Blessing money helps purify it of negative influences and adds the positive, life-giving energy of Spirit. If you're paying in U.S. cash, hand people the bill with the words "In God We Trust" face up and affirm your trust in God's abundance as you do.

You can also affirm the spiritual power in the metaphysical symbols on a one-dollar bill. On the left, there are a pyramid with the all-seeing eye of God above it and the words *Annuit Coeptis* (He favored our undertakings) and *Novus Ordo Seclorum* (New order of the ages). On the right, a star of David symbolizes the union of Spirit and matter, "as above, so below." Written above an eagle who faces the olive branch of peace and looks away from the arrows of war are the words, *E Pluribus Unum* (Out of many, One—the One Life). These symbols are on the two sides of the Great Seal of the United States. Our founding fathers were pretty tuned in!

Socially Responsible Investing

It's important to make your money work for you, not just by saving money for emergencies but by saving for opportunities. By investing in socially responsible businesses that embody values you care about—social, environmental, ethical—you are helping create the New World. Despite the ups and downs of the stock market, you can give thanks to God and a benevolent universe as the source of your supply. You can bless your investments as a channel through which your supply can manifest.

More and more people want to invest in companies that embody New World values, and this trend will grow exponentially in future years. By early 2009, social investing had already become a $2.7 trillion industry, growing 40 percent faster than the overall fund universe. My husband was the executive director of the Social Investment Forum when it started in 1987, and he would often field questions from major media, such as *The Wall Street Journal*, who were skeptical until they saw the stellar financial performance of socially responsible funds and companies.

Socially responsible investment (SRI) includes four strategies: screening, shareholder advocacy, community investing and socially responsible venture capital.

Screening subjects stocks to a set of "screens" or criteria, asking for example, "Does the company protect the environment, use fair labor practices, promote women and minorities and display integrity in advertising?" Many SRI funds avoid companies that produce firearms, nuclear power, tobacco and alcohol. Some of the leading funds that have been pioneers in the field for more than a decade are Calvert Funds, Pax World Fund, Parnassus Funds and Domini Social Funds. Domini offers a range of social funds and an index comparing social funds to the S&P 500.[2]

Shareholder advocacy is a second SRI strategy in which shareholders have pressured major corporations, such as McDonald's and J.C. Penney, to be more socially responsible through shareholder resolutions and divestment campaigns. The Interfaith Center on Corporate Responsibility (ICCR) has been a leader in shareholder advocacy and corporate social responsibility for more than 37 years. ICCR's membership is an association of 275 faith-based institutional investors, including national denominations, religious communities, pension funds, foundations, hospital corporations, economic development funds, asset management companies, colleges and unions. Each year ICCR institutional investors sponsor more than 200 shareholder resolutions on major social and environmental issues. Green America, As You Sow, and Proxy Democracy also provide helpful information on shareholder activism.[3]

Community investing is a third strategy that encourages people to invest in valuable local projects that might not qualify for funding, such as rehabilitating abandoned buildings, which creates good jobs and safe neighborhoods for the economically disadvantaged. ShoreBank of Chicago was an early pioneer in this type of investing. It rehabilitated many blocks of abandoned buildings on the south side of Chicago. It has received many awards for its work, and its banking model has been adopted in many other cities. RSF Social Finance is an effective model with an innovative mix of investments in social enterprises, direct loans and donations to nonprofits in areas such as ecological sustainability, food, education and the arts.

Socially responsible venture capital is the fourth SRI strategy. Socially conscious capital is key for getting start-up businesses with a social mission up and running. Conventional venture capital funding seeks to protect the rights of the private shareholder, while social venture funds elevate the welfare of all stakeholders.

Susan Davis, president of Capital Missions Company, helped found The Investors' Circle, one of the most effective networks of social venture capital investors. It has invested more than $80 million in over 100 start-up companies that use business to solve social problems. Davis said that she creates investor networks for a living because "I'm inspired by the principle that the earth is one living organism—Gaia—and that we are all one, all connected." She started Capital Missions Company "because I always believed that socially responsible companies are more profitable long-term than other companies."[4]

The Social Venture Network works with business and social leaders to build a just economy and sustainable planet. It offers information, conferences and training that share best practices and resources to help companies generate healthy profits and serve the common good.

Today there are new financial indexes that track the performance of socially responsible companies. The leading benchmark is the KLD Domini 400 Social Index for socially and environmentally responsible investing worldwide. The new Dow Jones Dharma Global Indexes track 3,400 companies aligned with principles such as good corporate governance, human rights, nonviolence and earth stewardship. Now there is also a South African Social Investment Exchange and a Social and Environmental Stock Exchange in Brazil.

Spiritual Approaches to Financial Crisis

In the midst of financial crisis, personal and/or collective, how can you change your consciousness and weather the storm? How can you attract or protect financial resources and be prepared for any future upheavals? Here are some spiritual approaches that are always important but especially needed in times of crisis.

Deepen your trust in a Higher Power and in your higher purpose. Putting God or Spirit first is the best insurance policy—the ultimate safety net. Prioritize what's essential in your life. You'll attract the resources you need to fulfill your soul's purpose and make your contribution to a better world. Meditate to calm your subconscious fears, invoke creative solutions, and make wiser financial decisions.

Stay present in the moment. Not even the best financial experts know what will happen to the economy in the future, so the best approach is to stay aware and awake in the present so that you can be flexible and respond as needed. When fears of the future arise, focus your intention in the present and allow your intuition to guide you.

Focus on emerging opportunities. Be alert to new doors opening as old ones close. Crisis can sometimes bring wonderful surprises and much needed changes that are blessings in disguise.

Be practical, and do your financial homework before investing in or buying anything of significant value. Don't believe everything you see or hear. If something sounds too good to be true, it probably is. Despite all the corruption and deceptions coming to light recently, there's still more corruption in the system that has not been exposed. So it's important to research everything as thoroughly as you can, using alternative as well as mainstream sources.

Invest some of your resources in the New World. Find quality companies that are ahead of the curve in honoring the triple bottom line—people, planet and profit—as they'll do better in the long run. Keep a very diversified portfolio so that all of your eggs aren't in one basket.

Welcome change, and embrace it. Explore where you may be stuck in old patterns—physically, emotionally, mentally—in relation to money, and release these patterns through conscious awareness and choice. Invoke your spiritual will to help release the old patterns and strengthen more positive patterns.

Practice detachment from personal comfort, and release the need to be in control at all times. Be flexible and flowing so that you can adapt to any personal or collective upheavals that might emerge. The world is undergoing rapid change right now. Let go of needing any particular outcomes for yourself personally.

Transform anger into forgiveness. Acknowledge any strong feelings catalyzed by recent crises, such as anger toward greedy or dishonest bankers, corrupt government regulators or anyone who contributed to your financial problems. Then work on releasing anger at your mistakes and the mistakes of others and embrace forgiveness. Uncover and explore the deeper fears behind your worries. Honestly face what you most fear—poverty, bankruptcy, etc.—and understand what fear can teach you. Is there any rational basis to your fear that you need to face squarely? Keep a larger perspective so that fear doesn't overwhelm you.

Appreciate the many wonderful things you already have. Avoid focusing on your impoverishment and what you lack, and give thanks for what you have—the many blessings in your life, such as family, friends and good health.

Simplify your lifestyle to reduce your spending. Do you really need all of that stuff? The planet could certainly use some lightening up and reduction of energy use. Go deeper and explore what quality or experience you are trying to satisfy with a material product, and discover a new way to draw this quality into your life.

Develop practical self-sufficiency. It's empowering to know how to grow food in your backyard garden, collect rainwater from roofs and create independent sources of water and heat. In this way, you know you can survive any problems without the systems you usually depend on.

Be a producer, rather than a consumer, of energy. Like the sun, your soul is a creative generator of energy. Your ego, on the other hand, often seems like an endless, hungry, black hole needing to be filled. Invoke your soul, and get juiced up so that you can give energy to others.

Create community and networks of mutual support. Good relationships help you get through all kinds of problems and bring you new, creative solutions. Overcome isolation through connection with others, which will help you attract what you need.

Be generous to others as an act of confidence in an abundant universe. There are always others in greater need than you, and what you give from your heart will return to you a hundred fold — it's true! When you help others, you experience a "helper's high" that is spiritually more satisfying than any material reward.

Although you might feel fearful about facing tough economic times, in reality the economy isn't a monolithic entity. It's a financial climate influenced by our collective consciousness, as Eric Butterworth noted in his brilliant *Spiritual Economics*. So work on transforming any negative attitudes about money and appreciate money as simply a flow of energy and life force. Donate and/or invest in the New World as a vote for a positive future for yourself and for humanity.

SPIRITUAL PRACTICES

Questions About Money for Reflection

- When you were growing up, what were some common attitudes and sayings about money that you heard from your family or friends?

- What are your deeper feelings about money? Do you experience ambivalence about having a lot of it or anxieties about not having enough?

- Are you confident that you will receive what you need from a loving God and an abundant universe?

- Do you sometimes pursue money as an end in itself or a way to keep score with others?

- Do you ever struggle with greed or desires that get out of control?

- Do you have any wasteful spending habits that you could change?

- Can you imagine yourself as wealthy? What would you do with your money?

- How do you feel about debt? Do you have any?

- In what ways might you be using money to try to buy happiness or meaning in your life? Is this fulfilling? How could these needs be met in nonmonetary ways?

- If you examined your credit card bills and your check stubs, what would they say about your values? What would your use of your discretionary income (available after paying necessities such as food, housing, health care , etc.) say about your values?

- How could money be more of a spiritual asset in your life?

- Do you currently make donations to charitable causes? What percentage of your yearly income or your assets do you give away?

- What more could you do financially to assist the spiritual development of humanity?

Meditation to Attract Financial Abundance

Begin by relaxing and taking a few deep breaths to breathe in peace and stillness and exhale tensions and worries. Let go of any place in your body where you are holding on, feeling fear or lack or trying to maintain control. Allow yourself to be fully present in this moment.

Visualize a star above your head connecting you with your higher self.

Feel yourself connected to the earth, as if you have roots growing into the earth. Feel supported and nurtured by the earth, the mother of all.

With each breath, connect more deeply to the earth, synchronizing with the rhythm of life itself, the tides, the seas, the movement of the stars. Feel the flow of unlimited life force. Align with this beauty and power. Feel yourself in harmony with all life.

Experience the presence of God within you, filling every cell in your body with love and light. Know that you are loved and supported by the benevolent heart of the universe.

Affirm your faith in God and the abundance of the universe to provide all that you need. Experience this abundance as a golden stream of energy being magnetically attracted to you to help you fulfill your life's purpose.

Allow a picture, an image or a symbol of abundance to arise in your mind. (Pause.) Feel it energize you and become a part of you.

See this abundance helping your spiritual growth, supporting your work and making your service more effective in the world.

See money as a spiritual asset, and embrace it as a useful tool, rather than an end in itself. See yourself using this wealth wisely to help others. Realize that to people who give, much will be given so that they can give again.

Visualize the money in the world as a great stream of flowing golden energy, passing out of the control of the forces of materialism and into the control of the spiritual forces.

See unlimited sums of money pouring into the hands of spiritual servers who are doing good work to aid humanity and all life on our planet.

Ask your soul what practical next steps you can take to ground this experience in your life.

Give thanks for the many wonderful things you already have in your life.

End by dedicating money you have saved from the previous week to spiritual work.

Slowly, return your awareness to the room, open your eyes, and write down the symbol of abundance you saw and any insights you've had as a way to remember this experience.

KEY INSIGHTS TO REFLECT ON

◆ Money is a neutral instrument for measuring exchange based on community agreement.

◆ Metaphysically, money is concretized energy or life force.

◆ Many spiritual people have money problems because they are too abstracted, living in the higher, spiritual worlds and not connecting to the earth and practical realities.

◆ It's important to release subconscious memories of vows of poverty from the past that may no longer be appropriate today.

◆ Need, love and magnetic power are three key things which must be present to attract money for spiritual work.

◆ You can do well by doing good; spirituality and financial abundance can work together.

◆ Socially screened investing, shareholder advocacy, community investing and socially responsible venture capital are powerful tools for change.

◆ Invest in the New World—support socially responsible businesses and nonprofits—as a vote for a positive future.

Key #8

Transform Duality and Conflict Into a Higher Synthesis

Find Common Ground Personally and Politically to Change the World

---

Again and again in history some special people wake up ...

And demand room for bold and audacious action.

The future speaks ruthlessly through them.

They change the world.

— Rainer Maria Wilke[1]

Changing the Adversarial Mindset

One of the most valuable resources in the tool kits of practical visionaries is transforming adversarial mindsets and conflicts by using a common-ground approach and tools such as mediation and multistakeholder dialogues. We have to learn to work collaboratively and harmoniously if we want to create authentic, lasting change. This approach is also the seed of new, transpartisan politics that is needed today.

I've seen many wonderful partnerships, businesses and movements dedicated to social change be undercut by polarized thinking, conflict and competition among members. So many people see others who have different views as enemies with whom they have to desperately battle in order to make their views prevail. Tools for transforming conflict are widely needed to create a useful synthesis from divergent perspectives.

Isn't it about time that we changed the adversarial metaphor that power and politics are like football—with two opposing teams charging at each other and trying to push past each other to reach their team's goal? Instead, can we see one team for humanity that honors individual differences but looks for mutual interests and works together for the same higher goals?

After being wounded by conflicts in idealistic groups and frustrated by adversarial approaches to social change, I had a life-changing experience in the early 1980s. I attended a live satellite broadcast of one of the early "Space Bridges"—a meeting between U.S. Congresspeople and their Soviet Politburo counterparts. It was fascinating to see adversaries actually dialoguing, getting to know one another as fellow human beings and honestly exploring differences and common ground. Skillful, professional facilitators experienced in conflict transformation were essential in making the process successful.

Adversaries meeting like this can create an alchemical reaction in which two opposite substances ignite and transform the whole field. A new energy is released, and anything seems possible. The many American and Russian "citizen exchanges" over the years were credited by President Gorbachev as a major contributor to the collapse of Soviet communism.

This experience of enemies coming to understand each other affected me deeply, and when I walked outside the meeting to join a nearby demonstration against government policies in Central America, as I had planned earlier, I just didn't have the heart for it. I couldn't get back into a polarized mindset, even though I fully supported the cause. I knew then that I was being called to a new way of creating social change and dealing with conflict—a New World approach.

Around the same time, I had another personal breakthrough about adversarial relationships. For many years as a social activist, I was politically polarized and angry at my opponents and I totally identified with only one side of the political spectrum. All of my friends saw the world pretty much as I did, and nearly everyone I talked to agreed with my views. I often joined righteous demonstrations against the war in Vietnam and demonstrations supporting women's rights or environmental protection, and there was always a long list of bad guys to blame—government, big corporations, etc.

My friends and I were always pointing fingers at our political opponents for being aggressive, greedy and obsessed with power. But then one day I participated in a political role-playing seminar, which I had helped create with colleagues in the New World Alliance, and it changed everything for me. We were asked to pair with another participant, imagine our partner as one of our political opponents and tell him or her how we felt. I imagined that my partner was the governor of my state, and I told him in no uncertain terms how aggressive and dogmatic he was. Then we exchanged roles, and I had to role-play the governor talking to my partner, who was pretending to be me.

What a revelation! The experience of standing in the governor's shoes and seeing the world from his perspective was transforming. I realized that as a radical activist, I had some of the same negative qualities, such as being aggressive and dogmatic, that I was accusing the governor of having. I realized that I had to stop pointing fingers at others and projecting my shadow on my adversaries and clean up my own act.

Once we recognize and transform our personal psychological issues, we won't project our negative qualities onto our opponents and accuse them of our faults. This transformation helps us see our opponents more clearly for who they really are and helps reduce conflicts.

Since these revelatory experiences, I've never been quite as adversarial or politically polarized. I continue to work on my psychological issues so that I don't project them onto my opponents, and I've participated in many dialogues between adversaries. I've hosted transpartisan dialogues with Democratic and Republican congresspeople and interfaith dialogues with Christians, Muslims, Jews and others. I've helped bring together opponents around environmental issues—people who wanted to protect jobs and people who wanted to protect the environment—to find common ground.

Michelle Sujai Harvey, a diversity trainer and former engineer, and I co-hosted a series of yearlong citizen dialogues on racial healing at our Center for Visionary Leadership. As a black-white team, the two of us were able to create a sense of trust and safety to explore difficult issues. We asked people to share their stories and their life experiences, which were often very painful and full of anger or fear. Each side learned a great deal from the other, and we all found that we actually had many needs in common—such as the need for love and understanding and the need to be treated fairly and respectfully.

I also learned about resolving deep-seated ethnic conflict worldwide through conflict transformation techniques while serving on the board of the Institute for Multi-Track Diplomacy for several years. When people hear the personal stories and suffering of those on the other side for the first time they often have powerful breakthroughs and are open to exploring common ground and finding solutions for mutual benefit.

I'm convinced that this common-ground approach is the wave of the future. Working to consciously resolve conflicts is the way to create more effective social organizations, solve problems and nurture a sense of unity on local, national and international levels.

To me, working together to find common ground is the seed of the politics of the New World. At its core is a recognition of the value of every human being. The keynote is *synthesis*—transcending polarized positions and bringing together the best of both sides of an issue. It all begins with a willingness to listen to people with whom you disagree and to find a grain of truth in their perspective.

Training in paradoxical thinking—holding two opposite ideas at the same time and seeing the truth in both ideas—was part of the preparation of initiates in ancient mystery schools. Many religions, such as Hindu nondualism, teach deep spiritual practices to transcend duality. Buddhists follow the Noble Middle Path between the pairs of opposites. Taoists teach about yin and yang, the polar opposites, that are held in a dynamic balance. Jews study the middle pillar in the Kabbalah, or Tree of Life, to understand the path of balance between the opposites.

Often in life we can best perceive one polarity by experiencing the contrast with its opposite. For example, the color red is more vibrant when seen next to the color blue. Artists know how to contrast light and shadow for dramatic effect. Great poets know the secret of polarity and often put two words with opposite meanings side by side, as Shakespeare did in his sonnets. The alternation between opposites is what creates consciousness or awareness on a higher level. On a material level, it's what creates electricity.

Just as each atom needs positive and negative particles to be complete, we need the best of both sides of a political issue to construct a clear picture of reality and make more effective policies.

Changing our inner consciousness and transcending duality starts impacting the outer world through the choices and actions we make, and collectively these choices and actions change the world. As the world transforms around us, this in turn, affects our inner state of consciousness and makes it easier to go beyond polarized thinking.

Transcending the Duality of Political Versus Spiritual

One of the polarizations I've worked on is politics and spirituality. For people caught in dualistic, either/or thinking, politics and spirituality seem worlds apart. They are two different arenas that should never be mixed because they produce deadly results, such as we see today when people try to impose their religious beliefs on others through public policies. Most people would say that you can be either a spiritual seeker — or a political activist — but never both because this makes you a fanatic who does crazy things.

As Jim Wallis wrote in *God's Politics*, we shouldn't ask if God is on our side, but rather we should ask if we are on God's side. Are we embodying our spiritual values and promoting compassion, justice and peace?

In our book *Spiritual Politics*, Gordon and I wrote at length about how to synthesize the seeming duality of spirituality and politics. In actual practice, true spirituality can ennoble politics and politics can ground spirituality. Spirituality can help people leave ego and power trips at the door and truly serve the good of others. Politics can provide a practical arena for applying spiritual principles, such as compassion, because instant feedback is given if someone doesn't "walk the talk" — if their words are more pious than their deeds. Bringing spiritual values, such as altruism and courage, into politics can offset the immense power of moneyed interests to influence policy. It can also offset the cynicism and apathy of much of the public.

Gandhi had no trouble bringing his spirituality and politics together. He said, "I could not lead a religious life unless I identified with the whole of mankind, and that I could not do unless I took part in politics."[2]

In Chinese, the word for *politician* is the same as their word for *healer*. A good politician should be a social healer — although Chinese politicians aren't great models of social healers themselves.

Many people today have been exploring the New World within themselves and transforming themselves spiritually, which naturally leads to greater engagement in our democracy and demands for a different type of politics.

People are yearning for politics guided by moral values, politics that don't appeal only to self-interest and pit one group against another. They are yearning for political discourse that speaks to their deepest values as human beings and provides a greater sense of community and a transcendent purpose as a nation. They want politics that offer a higher vision of public life and service to the common good. When the uprising cry of humanity for help invokes the downflow of spiritual ideas and vision, there is a powerful release of energy.

You'll find surprising success wherever you engage in this new approach to politics because this has an evolutionary thrust behind it. It gives me great hope for the future of our democracy. And I can guarantee that this way of working is more fun and fulfilling than the old style of power and politics you find on the evening news!

Finding Higher Common Ground Through Multistakeholder Dialogues

Across the country, more and more people are engaging in a new multistakeholder approach that goes beyond divisiveness and partisanship and focuses on solutions for the common good. Signs of this nonadversarial politics are emerging everywhere— from local conflict mediations between environmentalists and developers to national dialogues between Republicans and Democrats. Participants on either side of a conflict don't have to give up their deeply held values, but rather they have to find common interests to act on together.

As Albert Einstein famously remarked, you can't solve a problem from the same level of consciousness that created the problem. He said that two sides disagree because they're both wrong, and I would add, they're both also right. Or to be more accurate philosophically, you could say that two sides are both right and wrong and neither right nor wrong, as Buddhist teacher Nagarjuna wisely noted in his commentaries on *The Madhyamika* way back in the second century.

Let me be clear: transcending polarization doesn't mean that darkness, deceit and injustice are not brought to light and confronted when necessary. But nonadversarial approaches are what's needed most of the time because they can find solutions for mutual benefit.

This approach is called the "third side" by William Ury, author of *Getting to Yes* and *The Third Side*, because it builds bridges rather than walls and broadens and includes all points of view in a conflict, which then leads to finding new solutions. The impact of globalization is generating economic, environmental and ethnic problems that are too complex and interconnected to be solved on an adversarial basis. The most effective and long-lasting solutions to problems are based on a whole-systems, integral approach that includes the different values and different stages of development of all of the stakeholders in a conflict.

This approach reduces violence by helping people listen more deeply to the voices on all sides of an issue, even in the midst of ethnic strife. It helps people both recognize their common humanity and create a new synthesis based on identification with the whole.

One success story is the overcoming of deep-seated religious strife in Northern Ireland, where a peace settlement has held for several years. Despite an attempt by dissident IRA members to stir up violence by killing British police officers after the peace settlement had been in effect for years, thousands of former enemies, Catholics and Protestants, held silent vigils and mourned the deaths together, refusing to be drawn into conflict.

Multistakeholder dialogues are proving to be the most effective way to develop unity and reduce conflict on divisive issues, such as race, abortion and the environment. All parties who have a stake in the outcome are invited to a professionally facilitated dialogue to find what many in the field are calling "win-win-win" solutions. A triple win means that both sides in a conflict, as well as the larger community, benefit from the outcome.

In dialogues led by professionally trained facilitators, such as those with the Institute for Multi-Track Diplomacy, a safe space is created where opponents can hear each other's pain and understand their values, needs and points of view. An essential step is enabling people to communicate and have accurate information about each other. When there are many participants in a dialogue with diverse values and perspectives on an issue, each person can see more of the big picture and get closer to the full truth about the issue.

The listening process is powerful because it draws people out and creates opportunities for deeper reflection on an issue. Some people call this process creating a "sacred space." Each participant learns to respect the perspectives of others, even if they're totally different from his or her own. Others may have had different life experiences and different journeys that have led them to the opinions they hold.

Multistakeholder dialogues offer a means of navigating through conflict and identifying possibilities that are not apparent from an adversarial mindset. They draw upon the strengths of diversity and interconnectedness to find cooperative solutions.

"Understand the differences; act on the commonalities" is the way that Search for Common Ground (SFCG), the largest organization in the conflict-resolution field, describes this process. It was founded by my friend John Marks more than 25 years ago in

Washington, D.C. All parties to a conflict are invited to the table and guided in how to shift from an adversarial stance toward a cooperative, problem-solving one.

Finding common ground is not the same as having two sides meet in the middle or settle for the lowest common denominator. It's about participants generating a new "highest common denominator" and identifying something that they can work toward, such as the health of children if they're dialoguing in a war-torn country. When people who really care about an issue come together and bring their best thinking from their various perspectives, there is the potential for new options to be generated, which neither side might have thought of on their own.

Public Conversations Project in Boston discovered that a first step in finding common ground on an issue is to refrain from polarizing rhetoric, personal attacks and stereotypes of the other side. Toning down the rhetoric is critical and is also better politics, because it reaches more people. It is essential to distinguish between the problems and the people involved in a conflict. Helping people focus on common concerns rather than seeing each other as the problem is essential. Rather than facing each other on opposite sides of the table, both parties are invited to sit on the same side with the problem to address on the other side.

It is especially important to help people involved in a conflict distinguish between positions and interests. Underlying someone's position on an issue are usually broader interests, such as security, respect and/or the well-being of his or her family. Interests can be discovered by continuing to ask "why" and inviting people to go deeper. Interests relate to basic needs, while positions are opinions about how to achieve those needs. Positions may appear mutually exclusive, while interests tend to overlap, which is the key to having both (or all) sides work together to transform the conflict.

One fascinating example is the deeply divisive issue of abortion and the work pioneered more than 10 years ago by the Network for Life and Choice convened by Search for Common Ground and Public Conversations Project. The Network convened a series of professionally facilitated dialogues around the country with conservatives who advocated "right to life" and liberals who advocated "freedom of choice." They began by setting ground rules to create a safe space and by honoring the values on both sides—the sacredness of both the mother and the fetus.

Rather than continuing the emotionally devastating focus on abortion, arguing about exactly when the fetus in the womb becomes life and whether abortion is murder, they wisely reframed the debate and focused on the *causal* level (conception). Here they found common ground, because their interests overlapped and both sides wanted to prevent unwanted pregnancies.

So they agreed to work together on promoting "conscious conception" (that is, carefully choosing to become pregnant), and pregnancy prevention through the National Campaign to Prevent Teen Pregnancy. Both sides found a whole range of other options on which they could work together, such as promoting adoption, reducing infant mortality rates and preventing violence around abortion clinics.

Search for Common Ground has also convened people on the extreme right and the extreme left of the political spectrum in the United States to find common ground on issues such as national health care , same-sex marriage and faith-based social services (whether the government can fund religious-based homeless shelters, for example). SFGC came up with 29 consensus recommendations on this, many of which were incorporated into governmental initiatives.

A fascinating example of the power of multistakeholder dialogues is how citizens in Chattanooga, Tennessee, transformed their city from being the worst polluted urban center in America to a model of environmental sustainability through a series of community-wide multistakeholder dialogues facilitated by a professional team. All citizens were invited to a series of planning projects to envision what they wanted for the future. More than 5,000 ideas were generated, put into a computer and categorized. Everyone was invited back to discover the patterns and relationships between the ideas and to create a consensus on strategic goals.

This project eventually culminated in a Vision Fair, celebrating the goals and inviting citizens to sign up for working on the goals that matched their priorities. The excitement of creating a community-wide consensus inspired everyone, including government, business and philanthropic leaders, who helped make the visions a reality. Chattanooga attracted more than $800 million of investments in 223 projects, which created 1,500 new jobs and 7,000 temporary jobs, and it won an award from the President's Council on Sustainable Development.

The multistakeholder approach has also been used innovatively in finance by RSF Social Finance, which was started by the Rudolf Steiner Foundation to apply the spiritual principles of Steiner's teaching. Rather than the RSF bank announcing its loan rates, as most banks do, it created a participatory process. It invited investors, borrowers and lenders to meet to establish fair prices for borrowing. When lenders were asked how much they wanted to make, they came up with a rate that was good for them. When borrowers were asked what they wanted to pay   in interest, they came up with a rate that was best for them. Then, the RSF bank stated what rate they needed to keep the bank functioning. After they heard from one another, each side changed its demands and they worked together to come up with a rate that they could all live with and that seemed fair all around.[3]

Creating Transpartisan, Synthesis Solutions

Let's Talk America, a group that sponsors transpartisan dialogues, asks, "What if what unites us is more than we realize, and what divides us is less than we fear?" Debates on every issue have become polarized and stalemated, making it extremely difficult to find solutions that will serve the real needs of people. But some practical visionaries are now developing a transpartisan approach that goes beyond left and right adversarial politics and is distinct from the efforts of independent political parties.

This is not to say that fighting and partisanship is always wrong, that all polarities must be resolved, or that common ground (or even compromise) is always the highest path. Clearly there are times to advocate for one side of an issue or to fight against injustice. Most religions have a tradition of the spiritual warrior who defends the weak, for example. Although peaceful conditions can be fruitful for nurturing the spiritual development of a nation, for example, if peace is enforced and authoritarian and lacks justice, then forcefully challenging the status quo can be an act of spiritual power.

If the motive for transpartisanship is not genuine—like a power move disguised in idealistic language—it should be challenged, not embraced. Too often there are wolves in sheep's clothing, cloaking their nefarious goals in ideals such as transpartisanship. The motive needs to be serving the highest good.

Behind our two major parties today are key principles, even though they may not clearly embody these essential principles. The liberal or progressive party theoretically represents the future, the next evolutionary ideas and the need for government-initiated change and regulation. The conservative party theoretically preserves the best of the past, makes sure that change isn't too rapid and emphasizes personal values and personal change. There is wisdom in both of these parties' principles, and each is needed to balance the other.

A transpartisan approach works to create a higher synthesis of the best of both sides of an issue. Synthesis is very different from compromise. Compromise is not the most effective way to deal with polarities, because sometimes the deeper wisdom in each side is lost. Compromise usually includes half of each position and can be seen as the midway point between two polarities.

LIBERAL_____^_____CONSERVATIVE
COMPROMISE

Synthesis is found by using our intuition to take the best of both sides and raise them to a higher level. Synthesis can be visualized as the apex of a triangle with liberal and conservative at each side of the base.

SYNTHESIS

LIBERAL   Δ   CONSERVATIVE

A polarized political issue that seems to be a paradox on a lower level can actually resolve into a greater wisdom on a higher level. Georg Hegel described this more than a century ago

273

as "thesis, antithesis, synthesis." From a more-integrated, synthesized perspective, we can craft more-effective and creative public policies.

The philosophical dividing line between the liberal and conservative positions is a disagreement over whether social problems are caused by economic factors or by a breakdown in individual values, and thus whether government or individual solutions are best. Conservatives argue that the problem is with values and see little benefit, for example, in the government spending more on the poor. Liberals argue that having good values doesn't help if there is not equal economic opportunity with a supportive social environment. Liberals accuse conservatives of coercive moralism, and conservatives accuse liberals of moral relativism that allows evil to flourish.

The policy deadlock is based on trying to separate values and economies from each other, with neither conservatives nor liberals admitting any wisdom in the other's perspective. However, both perspectives are needed. Although the poor may suffer from some of their values and lifestyle choices, they also suffer from inadequate diet and a lack of access to health care, both of which can be helped by government spending.

Both liberals and conservatives promote important values. Liberals promote values of generosity, tolerance and inclusiveness. Conservatives promote values of self-help, hard work and taking initiative.

Liberals promote government regulation in the economic sphere but freedom in the personal sphere, such as the right to choose abortion Conservatives promote freedom in the economic sphere, but government regulation in the personal sphere. Conservatives promote states' rights in relation to federal regulation but not when it relates to key issues for them, such as gay marriage. Here are their opposing views on each side of some issues and a possible synthesis for each issue:

Liberal	Conservative	Synthesis
Government is the solution	Government is the problem	Smart, lean government to ensure fairness
Regulation of the economy	Freedom of the economy	Market-based approaches (e.g. emissions trading)
Protection of the environment	Protection of jobs	Environmental "green collar" jobs
Economic solutions for crime prevention	Law-and-order solutions for crime prevention	Training in positive behavior
Right to choose	Right to life	Preventing unwanted pregnancies and making adoptions easier

Theorists such as Mark Satin, Paul Ray, Ted Halstead, Ken Wilber, Drexel Sprecher, Lawrence Chickering, Jim Turner and Joseph McCormick have been outlining some key components of a new politics beyond left and right. Today there are several national political groups working along these lines, such as Radical Middle, the New America Foundation and the Transpartisan Alliance.

Many organizations, such as Tikkun, Sojourners, Praxis Peace Institute, State of the World Forum and Alliance for a New Humanity, are now working collaboratively to build a consensus around values needed for a more effective social change movement. In 2000 our Center for Visionary Leadership organized   a national conference called *Re-Igniting the Spirit of America: Values and Spirituality in Governance* with key values for a consensus created by many New World political groups.

To create a New World that transcends old adversarial approaches, new ways of thinking and acting are needed, both personally and organizationally. There are no complete road maps yet. An expansion in consciousness with a willingness to transcend polarities and enfold them into a higher synthesis, can help solve both personal and global problems. A spirit of goodwill toward people with opposing views, a win-win rather than win-lose approach and a compassionate, healing spirit are the keys to this new politics—and to a better personal life and more harmonious organizations.

SPIRITUAL PRACTICES

Techniques for Good Communication and Resolving Conflicts

Listen Attentively

- Strive for a deeper understanding of—but not necessarily agreement with—the views of others.

- Get inside the other's frame of reference.

- Listen with empathy, with an open mind and heart.

- Give the speaker your full attention while maintaining eye contact.

- Listen for feelings as much as for content.

- Honor what is true for the speaker in the moment.

- Don't invalidate another's experience because it is different from yours.

- Use active listening—rephrase the content of a statement and reflect the feeling.
- Listen carefully to constructive feedback.

Speak Carefully

- Ask problem-solving questions rather than judgmental ones.
- Use "I" messages, rather than "you" messages that blame.
- Criticize the action, not the person
- Make criticism clear and specific, and offer a solution.
- Avoid placating—resist pressure to agree or conform.
- Avoid passive resistance—be direct.
- Avoid preaching and "shoulds."
- Avoid monopolizing the conversation—ask questions of others.
- Build on previous ideas—avoid tangents.
- Give only constructive feedback.
- Express appreciation, and empower and affirm others.
- Use humor to break up tension and negativity.

Be Honest and Direct

- Make it safe for others to be honest by speaking the truth about your own experience.
- Be straightforward and don't make others guess your intentions.
- Don't assume their intentions from your fears—ask direct questions.
- Be aware of your cultural assumptions and prejudices.
- Don't make an agreement that you know you can't keep.

- Reflect on whether a problem you see in someone else is also in you.
- Match nonverbal communication—tone of voice, body language, etc.—with verbal.

Reframe How You View Conflict

- Conflict and differences are natural and not to be feared.
- Differing opinions have validity because they are based on different personal experiences.
- Different people may have important pieces that contribute to a better solution.
- Wiser decisions and better solutions can come from wider input.
- See your adversary as a messenger bringing new information.
- Look for the grain of truth, the value or the positive intent in your opponent's position.
- Restate an opposing view in your own words (active listening or mirroring).
- Take responsibility—avoid blaming others for how you feel.
- Share and acknowledge negative feelings and painful experiences.
- Surface what is hidden, and explore assumptions to re-evaluate if needed.
- Clarify perceptions, and explore deeper roots or patterns.
- Reflect on your own contribution to the problem and how you can change.

Explore Shared Interests and Common Ground

- Create a positive and open atmosphere to build trust.

- Separate the people from the problem or conflict.

- Define the problem in a way that is acceptable to both sides.

- Focus on interests, not entrenched positions and past history.

- Ask "why" to discover the interests behind the position.

- Distinguish between short-term and long-term interests.

- Acknowledge interests based in more deeply rooted needs or values.

- State agreements along the way to build confidence and momentum.

Brainstorm Win/Win Options for Mutual Benefit and Find Consensus

- Make proposals consistent with your opponent's values.

- Don't assume a fixed pie to divide up—be creative and explore additional resources.

- Dovetail differing interests—each side may want different things.

- Find a way for your opponent to save face so it will be acceptable.

- Base proposals on objective standards when possible—precedent, market value, efficiency, measurements, moral or equal treatment, etc.

Meditation on Finding a Higher Synthesis of Opposing Views

Relax your body and mind, getting into a deeper, more reflective state, and then visualize a horizontal line connecting the two opposing sides of the issue, like the bottom line in a triangle.

Focus on the left side of the line and imagine a picture or a symbol that represents the best aspects of this side of the issue. Move your awareness to the right, and imagine a picture or symbol that represents the best aspects of this opposite side of the issue.

Move your awareness back and forth between the two images. See a dance between the two evolving as you move your attention from one to the other.

Let go of these images, take a few deep breaths and imagine that you're becoming lighter and more expanded as you become one with your soul, or higher self.

Visualize a triangle with a bottom horizontal line connecting the two sides of the issue and with lines drawn from each end of the line up to a top point. Move your awareness to this top point of the triangle, the place of synthesis.

Ask your soul to create a picture or symbol that represents a higher synthesis of the best of both sides of the issue. Stay with that picture, and explore its deeper meaning. See if the image changes or transforms.

Ground your experience by applying this synthesis to a practical issue or a polarized policy debate, and see if any new insights emerge.

Meditation on the Soul of a Nation

This meditation uses an American symbol, but other national symbols can be used to meditate on the souls of other nations. Read through this meditation first. Then take yourself on an inner meditative journey using your own imagery.

Take a few deep breaths to relax, breathing in peace and stillness and exhaling any tensions or worries.

Focus in your heart, breathing in the quality of universal love.

Align with your higher self.

Imagine that you are standing at the foot of the Statue of Liberty in the New York harbor. See her holding aloft a torch of light, with a book of wisdom in her other arm, welcoming all of those who are "yearning to breathe free." See this inspirational statue as a symbol of the soul of America.

Now imagine yourself entering the statue and slowly climbing the spiral staircase that leads to her crown.

As you reach the crown of the statue (symbolic of the crown chakra), you stand on a platform and look at the beautiful view for miles around.

As you look out across the land from this expanded view, see events in the life of this nation in a larger context and in a longer time frame.

What lessons is America learning at this time? Take a few minutes, and see what you observe.

Now ask for new insights into the soul of America.

Give thanks for the many blessings showered upon our nation.

See America aligning with its higher purpose and truly serving the greatest good of all. See it transcending self-interest and expressing its full potential and spiritual destiny.

Visualize sending out rays of light and love to all of the people of America, seeing the nation healed and reunited in common purpose.

Now visualize light and love radiating out from America to all of the people of the world, affirming ourselves as one human family.

Slowly, as you are ready, leave the platform where you are standing, remembering all that you've experienced, and slowly begin to descend the stairs of the statue to the ground floor.

When you are ready, slowly open your eyes, and write down any insights you've received.

Prayer for Your Nation

This prayer can be adapted to the specific images and needs of any country.

May we as nation be guided by the Divine to rediscover the sacred flame of our national heritage, which so many have given their lives to safeguard.

May we let the wounds of separation and division be healed by opening our hearts to listen to the truth on all sides, allowing us to find a higher truth that includes us all.

May we learn to honor and enjoy our diversity and differences, even as we more deeply touch our fundamental unity.

May we, as a people, undergo a transformation that will draw forth leaders who embody courage, compassion and a higher vision.

May our leaders inspire us, and may we inspire each other so that a new spirit of forgiveness, caring and honesty can be born in our nation.

May we, as a united people, move with clear, directed purpose to take our place within the community of nations to help build a better future for humankind.

May we as a nation rededicate ourselves to truly living as one nation, under God, indivisible, with liberty and justice for all.

And may God's will be done for our nation, as we, the people, align with that will.

KEY INSIGHTS TO REFLECT ON

◆ We need to transform the adversarial mindset and conflict that undermines many good projects.

◆ Spirituality can ennoble politics, and politics can make spirituality more practical.

◆ The key to conflict resolution is learning to listen and understand differences, but to act on commonalities.

◆ There is a grain of truth on each side of a conflict that can be included in a higher synthesis.

◆ Multistakeholder dialogues to find higher common ground and mutual benefits are the seeds of the new politics.

◆ The evolutionary edge is transpartisan initiatives that embody the wisdom of both liberal and conservative principles.

The Practical Visionary

Conclusion

Become a Mapmaker for Our Journey Into the New World

A Call to Action and Co-Creation

"As rose petals are strewn the signs, for the time is near.

Think of the New World ..."

— The Agni Yoga Society[1]

Now is the moment—the cosmic tipping point we've been expecting for decades has arrived. The crises are mounting, but the evolutionary tide is turning. Humanity is awakening to a global awareness, and we're all needed to help our planet's transition into the New World.

Collaborative efforts are exponentially potent. This is the era of group consciousness and group work. If each of us makes a contribution from a dedicated soul level, together we can become the catalyst in a solution that transforms the planet. We can create the world our hearts yearn for. We can find noble work and steady companions. We can become mapmakers for our journey into a more expansive, joyful future.

We all need to become practical visionaries and apply our visions by using skill in action to meet real human needs. We can help steer the new energy that is flowing into our planet into effective, soul-based solutions to our problems. Humanity needs upliftment and a skillfully applied new vision, and together we can do it!

By invoking the help that is nearer than your heartbeat—your radiant soul (the same soul that is in all of us)—you'll find your unique mission in the higher evolutionary plan and attract the resources you'll need to fulfill it.

In the light of your soul, you can transcend duality—the seeming conflict between inner and outer, Spirit and matter, and self and society. You can change yourself and change the world at the same time. Synthesis is the keynote of the New World. It helps you see the world with new eyes and appreciate our current crises as blessings in disguise that bring essential, life-giving changes.

The choices that each of us makes every moment either contribute to the growth of the New World or hold it back. Our thoughts, words and actions are powerful, so we need to become careful guardians of what we are creating.

It's going to take all of us working together to turn things around. We need courageous politicians and whistle-blowers to speak truth to power and revitalize our democracy. We need insightful psychologists and educators to help us understand our innermost psyche and transform what ails us. We need savvy policy experts and administrators to create institutional support for innovative ideas. We need inspirational artists and writers to express our hopes and create visions of a better future. We need pioneering scientists to develop technologies for finding new sources of energy and improving our lives. We need authentic spiritual teachers and healers to remind us of the deeper purpose of life and restore our well-being. We need practical business people to develop products and services that meet our real needs, help us live fuller lives, and protect our environment.

It is both our challenge and our blessing to be gifted with the opportunity to create a New World from the decay of the old world. We are each prepared and worthy of this challenge. Indeed, it is ultimately the purpose for which we have been born.

So take heart, and seek out the forces of new life wherever you find them. Give them your love, time and financial support.

Discover your tested and true allies, and join the worldwide movement of inspired and dedicated souls who live in the consciousness of the One Life. Embody your values in daily life with great joy and anticipation, because we are at the dawn of a new era.

Let us together create oases of light and sanity, sacred places amidst the decay of the old world where people can find support and inspiration regardless of outer conditions. Let us build for the future and release what is passing away. Out of the current crisis and purification comes new birth, the New World. Together we can help guide this planetary birth and nurture the new life it carries for a radiant, enlightened civilization.

Keep your eyes on the horizon, your feet on the ground, and your heart on fire!

Endnotes

Introduction

[1]Jalal Al-Din Rumi, "The Breeze at Dawn" from *The Essential Rumi*, San Francisco: HarperOne, 1995, © Coleman Barks. Reprinted with permission.

Key 1

[1]David Spangler, from a talk by David Spangler at the Findhorn Foundation, Scotland, 1972.

[2]Mohandas K. Gandhi, quoted in the 1982 film *Gandhi*, produced and directed by Richard Attenborough.

Key 2

[1]Francis Thompson, "The Mistress of Vision," Nicholson and Lee, editors, *The Oxford Book of English Mystical Verse*, Oxford: Oxford University Press, 1917.

[2]Ken Wilber, "The Interdynamics of Culture and Consciousness," from an interview in *EnlightenNext* magazine, Dec.2008–Feb.2009 © 2009 EnlightenNext, Inc. All rights reserved. Reprinted with permission.

[3]Roberto Assagioli, "The Balancing and the Synthesis of the Opposites," *The Essentials of Psychosynthesis*, Psychosynthesis and Education Trust manual, London, England, quoted with permission of publisher.

Key 3

[1]Robert F. Kennedy, University of Capetown speech, South Africa, June 6, 1966.

[2]For more information on communities, see the Fellowship of Intentional Communities at *www.fic.org.*

[3]See *www.WiserEarth.org,* an open-source community reporting on thousands of groups and activities and Sustainable World Sourcebook (*www.swcoalition.org*).

[4]Curtis Verschoor, "Principles Build Profits," *Management Accounting,* October 1997, p. 42.

[5]United Nations Global Compact press release, *Corporate Social Responsibility (CRS) Newswire,* July 5, 2007.

Key 4

[1]Henry David Thoreau, *Walden,* New Haven, CT: Yale University Press, 2004.

[2]Plato, *The Republic,* New York: Penguin Classics, 2007.

[3]Ken Wilber, *The Integral Vision,* Boston: Shambhala Publications © 2007 Ken Wilber. Reprinted by arrangement with Shambhala Pulications Inc., Boston, MA. *www.shambhala.com.*

[4]Charles Fillmore, *Dynamics for Living,* Unity Village, MO: Unity House, 1967.

[5]Agni Yoga Society, *Leaves of Morya's Garden I: The Call,* New York: Agni Yoga Society Publishing, 1953, quoted with permission.

Key 5

[1]The Dalai Lama, from a talk in Dharamsala, India, 1998.

[2]Alice Bailey, *Esoteric Psychology II,* New York: Lucis Publishing, 1971. Permission granted by Lucis Trust, which holds the copyright.

Key 6
[1]Mahatma Gandhi quote, *The Way to God: Selected Writings From Mahatma Gandhi*, North Atlantic Books, 2009.

Key 7
[1]Sir Winston Churchill, The Churchill Trust Web site: *www.churchilltrust.com.au*

[2]For further information, go to *www.socialinvest.org.*

[3]For further information, go to *www.greenamericatoday.org /go/2009ShareholderAction, www.asyousow.org,* or *www.Proxy Democracy.org.*

[4]Interview with Susan Davis in *Hope Magazine* (January/ February 2003).

Key 8
[1]Rainer Maria Rilke, quoted by Desmond Tutu at prayer breakfast with the Dalai Lama at the Seeds of Compassion Conference, Seattle, Washington, April 15, 2008.

[2]Mahatama Gandhi, *A Letter: Mahadevbhaini Diary*, Vol 1, May 30, 1932.

[3]For more information on organizations, books and resources promoting multistakeholder dialogues and deliberative, consensus-based democracy, go to *www.democracyinnovations.org, www.sfcg.org or www.imtd.org.*

Conclusion
[1]The Agni Yoga Society, *Leaves of Morya's Garden II: Illumination*, New York: Agni Yoga Society Publishers, 1952, quoted with permission.

Index

P

shadow(s): confronting and reowning parts of, 157; dealing
with, 223; responsibility for, 92;
for spiritual mystics and political activists, 104; transforming,
156
shareholder advocacy, as an SRI
strategy, 249
Sheldrake, Rupert, 157
ShoreBank of Chicago, 249
silence, during group meditation,
187
Simons, Nina, 37
simplicity networks, 243
Singularity University, 75
Sirius Community: building,
110–112; current state of, 112;
decision to purchase land for,
189; purchasing land for,
238–239; startup of, 56
sixth ray: dangerous effects of,
66–67; of devotion and idealism, 65; effects of, 65–67; primary influence for the past
2,000 years, 65
SMART, but flexible goals, 217
Social and Environmental Stock
Exchange, 250
social benefit companies. See
social entrepreneurs
social change: keys to spiritual
growth and, 13; meditation for
invoking, 183–185; practical
approaches to, 16–20; synergiz-
ing and mutually supporting,
102; values needed for more
effective, 275
social entrepreneurs, 30, 44–45
social healer, good politician as,
265
social innovator, creating alternative institutions, 110–115

Social Investment Forum, 38, 248
social networking sites, 40
social problems, causes of, 274
Social Venture Network, 250
social-benefit corporations, 71
socially responsible businesses,
investing in, 117, 248
socially responsible investment
(SRI), 248
socially responsible venture capital, 250
Sojourners, 108
solar conference center, building,
111
Solar Living Institute, 37
solar plexus center (pancreas
gland): energizing, 218–219;
energy expressed by, 160; lower
psychic guidance through, 193;
raising energies to the heart
center, 162
Solix Energy, 44
solutions, examples of New World,
41–47
soul: aligning with a great master,
182; aligning with during meditation, 181–182; anchored in
your body, 141; building rainbow bridge to, 158–159; clearest
guidance from, 193; clothed in
denseness of matter, 25–26; as
compass, 138; dealing with
world of causes, 143; download-
ing reliable guidance from,
194–195; as essence and true
identity, 136–141; experiences
of, 137; experiencing sense of
connection, 153; identifying
with, 243; invoking help of, 286;
as link between Spirit and matter, 141–142; meditation for
invoking, 167; as nonlocal, 138;

ACKNOWLEDGEMENTS

We would like to thank our good friends Jacqueline and Bob Pogue, Olivia Hansen, Byron Belitsos, Ginger Young, Sharon Rose and Liz Williams for their support of this book on many levels. We would like to appreciate the insightful and skillful help of our marvelous editor Stephanie Oliver and editorial assistant Sharon Sartin, as well as Charlotte Shelton, Paula Coppel and Mary Earls, and all their wonderful team whom we were very fortunate to have! A special thank you is also due to all those in the spiritual dimensions who provided continual inspiration and opened many doors.

ABOUT THE AUTHORS

Corinne McLaughlin is co-author of *Spiritual Politics* and *Builders of the Dawn*. She is the executive director of the Center for Visionary Leadership, based in the San Francisco area, and a co-founder of Sirius, a spiritual and ecological community in Massachusetts. Corinne directed a national Task Force on Sustainable Communities for President Clinton's Council on Sustainable Development and served on the adjunct faculty of the American University and the University of Massachusetts. A Fellow of the World Business Academy and the Findhorn Foundation, and a member of The Transformational Leadership Council, she has taught courses on spiritual development and social change with her husband, Gordon Asher Davidson, for more than 30 years in the United States and Europe. They have been interviewed for more than 130 newspapers, magazines and radio and television shows, including *The New York Times*, *The Washington Post*, *The Wall Street Journal*, *USA Today*, *The Boston Globe*, *NBC TV*, and *Fox News*. They live in the San Francisco area and appreciate silence in quiet, beautiful places in nature.

Gordon Asher Davidson is the president of the Center for Visionary Leadership and a co-founder of Sirius Community, and has served as the founding director of the Social Investment Forum and the Coalition for Environmentally Responsible Economies (Ceres). Through Joyful Evolution Consulting, he serves as a consultant and personal coach in spiritual growth, leadership, conflict resolution and group decision-making, and has worked closely with many corporate, government and nonprofit leaders and groups. He is co-author of *Spiritual Politics* and *Builders of the Dawn,* author of *The Transfiguration of Our World,* and is a Fellow of the World Business Academy and the Findhorn Foundation, and a member of the Transformational Leadership Council. He has taught courses on meditation, leadership and spiritual development for more than 30 years in the United States and Europe. He expresses his creative nature through gardening, photography, and painting and his well-developed sense of cosmic humor.

TO CONTACT THE AUTHORS

For information on Corinne McLaughlin and Gordon Asher Davidson's seminars, teleconferences and books, visit their websites:www.livethefuturenow.com; www.thepracticalvisionary.org and www.visionarylead.org, or e-mail cvldc@visionarylead.org. To invite Corinne and/or Gordon to speak at your conference or event, you can email corinnemc@visionarylead.org. or call 415-472-2540.

Gordon offers counseling and coaching services through Joyful Evolution Consulting, helping people connect more deeply with their inner spiritual wisdom and transform old subconscious patterns and blockages to become successful practical visionaries and leaders. For information, visit www.joyfulevolutionconsulting.com or e-mail worldtransfiguration@gmail.com.

B0090

Made in the USA
Coppell, TX
03 November 2019

10925592R00184